Don't
Stop
the
Music

Don't Stop the Music

A Year of Pop History One Day at a Time

Justin Lewis

Elliott&Thompson

First published 2023 by
Elliott and Thompson Limited
2 John Street
London WC1N 2ES
www.eandtbooks.com

ISBN: 978-1-78396-716-2

9 8 7 6 5 4 3 2 1

A catalogue record for this book is available from the
British Library.

Typesetting: Marie Doherty
Printed by CPI Group (UK) Ltd, Croydon, CR0 4YY

For my mother Jennette and my nephew Harry,
with love, and for those we have lost along the way,
especially Viv, Jonathan, Enid and Ruben.

CONTENTS

INTRODUCTION

Don't Stop the Music is a history of pop, but arranged a little differently. It could have been a linear trip through history, beginning in 1950 or so, and winding up in the 2020s. Instead, we're going to begin on 1 January and end on 31 December, while sampling the years seemingly at random.

So, for each day of the calendar year, yes including the unsung 29 February, we've selected some events from pop's annals: births and deaths, record releases and live shows, TV and radio, introductions and departures, encounters and coincidences. Consider it a kaleidoscopic sampling exercise, pinballing across the decades in, hopefully, a genre-defying fashion.

When I started researching and selecting the material for this book, it occurred to me that events in any kind of history fall into two main categories: the planned (Live Aid is a good example here) and (much more commonly) the unexpected.

I was especially drawn to the early days of a song or an artist. How far back can you trace the origin of something, the eureka of inspiration? Especially when I found examples by artists whose careers have not already been presented as literal day-by-day itineraries.

One of the things that forever interests me about history in general is the way events happen simultaneously, but independently of each other. I love the word 'meanwhile' – one event takes place somewhere, while another one is unfolding thousands of miles away. Especially fascinating back in the pre-digital age, before most of the globe was connected.

I don't know why I have a penchant for dates and anniversaries. I have for as long as I can remember. I enjoy that they are both random and accidental. Who knows what events get remembered, and why, while others are discarded and forgotten and should be reappraised?

And the randomness comes to mean something in itself. Why are we interested in who or what shares our birthday?

Before we get to business, a few disclaimers.

We decided in the end not to include an index. There was a specific reason for this, and it wasn't just so that we didn't have to have the 'why is my favourite group not included?' discussion. Honest. We have included about 900 artists or so, so there's a fair chance at least *some* of your favourites have made it to publication.

No, the reason for no index is a creative one. We wanted the book to be a little more than a dipping-in exercise. Sure, we understand that you'll look up your own birthday first, you're only human. But once that's out of the way, the book is constructed to tell a story through hundreds of fragments. The story of music, of trends, of technology, from the songs that immediately made an impact to the ones that were almost completely ignored at the time, but have since had seismic effects on the direction of popular music and entertainment. Nobody can guarantee what will break through, or predict what will be recalled.

We hope to have mixed up the memorable and the underrated in what follows. And we hope you enjoy the ride.

Justin Lewis
March 2023

A few additional notes before we begin:

I have used several abbreviations throughout the book:

- BOTD – born on this day
- DOTD – died on this day
- ROTD – released on this day

Where release dates vary in different territories, I have usually opted for the earliest, or in the artist's or group's country of origin. Often, especially between the mid-1980s and 2015 (after which just about everything came out on a Friday), new releases came out on Mondays in the UK, and Tuesdays in the US, even by US acts. In these cases, I have gone with the Monday date, which is often not what Wikipedia says.

Still there? Ah. Anyway, I am on Twitter and Threads at @WhenIsBirths, should you (politely please – cheers!) wish for further explanations that are too niche even for these pages.

Unless stated, highest chart positions for the US refer to those compiled by *Billboard* magazine. Chart positions for the UK refer to a succession of sources, all now owned under one archive by current compilers Official Charts.

JANUARY

1 JANUARY

1958 Johnny Cash plays the first of many concerts at San Quentin State Prison, California. He and his band are touring the west coast of the US when they are asked at short notice to take part in the traditional New Year's Day extravaganza staged by the San Francisco Musician's Union for the prison's 4,000 inmates. Accepting the invitation, Cash appears on the bill alongside dancers and a 17-piece jazz ensemble, although his bass guitarist Marshall Grant is forbidden from bringing in a toy pistol (a standard prop in their stage act).

In the captive audience is 20-year-old **Merle Haggard**, serving a 15-year sentence for petty crimes. '[Cash] had the right attitude,' Haggard later recalls. 'He chewed gum, looked arrogant and flipped the bird to the guards. When he walked away, everyone in that place had become a Johnny Cash fan.'

Granted early parole in 1960, Haggard later embarks on his own career as a country-and-western singer. In 1969, the same year that Cash's *At San Quentin* live album is released, he guests on Cash's national TV show, where the pair duet on 'Sing Me Back Home'. Three years later, Haggard is pardoned for his past teenage crimes by the governor of California, and future US president, Ronald Reagan.

1962 The Beatles record five songs as an audition for Decca Records but will be turned down by the label in favour of the Dagenham group Brian Poole and the Tremeloes.

1964 The BBC relaxes its 'artists don't mime' rule on its pop music shows as the first edition of *Top of the Pops* is broadcast at 6.35 p.m. from a converted Methodist chapel in Manchester. Appearing are

Dusty Springfield, The Rolling Stones and The Hollies. 'I Want to Hold Your Hand' by The Beatles is at #1. Meanwhile, in a Hollywood studio, **The Beach Boys** are recording 'Fun, Fun, Fun'.

1990 Florida rock radio station WKRL begins a two-week marathon as a **Led Zeppelin**-only station by playing 'Stairway to Heaven' non-stop for 24 hours.

2 JANUARY

1926 Songwriter Horatio Nicholls adorns the front cover of *Melody Maker*, his own new music newspaper. Across its 74-year run, it will champion jazz, popular music and eventually indie-rock.

1986 ROTD: **The Bangles'** *Different Light* album, which opens with their breakthrough 'Manic Monday' single (written by Prince under the name 'Christopher').

1994 Who's the only artist to have a UK #1 with 'Twist and Shout'? The Isley Brothers? The Beatles? No – it's Jamaican duo **Chaka Demus & Pliers**.

1995 ROTD: 'Glory Box' by **Portishead**. Based around a string sample from 'Ike's Rap 2' by Isaac Hayes, the track will peak at UK #13.

3 JANUARY

1926 BOTD: **George Martin**, record producer for not just The Beatles but also Cilla Black, Elton John, Ultravox and Celine Dion. Martin also worked on three #1 singles for Gerry and the Pacemakers in 1963, whose frontman **Gerry Marsden** DOTD in 2021.

1976 Scottish teen idols the **Bay City Rollers** briefly make a splash Stateside when their single 'Saturday Night' reaches US #1. A flop in the UK on its previous release in 1973, the track's chanting style is credited by Tommy Ramone as a sizeable influence on the Ramones' debut single 'Blitzkrieg Bop'.

1987 Queen of Soul **Aretha Franklin** is inducted into the Rock & Roll Hall of Fame, just as her 'I Knew You Were Waiting (for Me)' duet with George Michael is about to hit UK #1 and US #2.

4 JANUARY

1967 ROTD: For their debut LP, **The Doors** become the first major rock band to be advertised on billboard hoardings, which bear the slogan, 'Break on through with this electrifying album!'

1969 On Lulu's BBC TV Saturday night variety show, *Happening for Lulu*, closing guest act **The Jimi Hendrix Experience** halt their live rendition of 'Hey Joe' ('We're gonna stop playing this rubbish') in favour of a freewheeling, impromptu take on 'Sunshine of Your Love', as a tribute to Cream, who have recently announced their dissolution.

As a result, the group is banned by BBC Television, but thanks to the efforts of canny archivists — mindful of how easily footage could be wiped in those days — the clip has survived. Watching at home, at least one teenage viewer, Declan MacManus, will keep it in mind; eight years later, as **Elvis Costello**, he disrupts the flow of NBC's *Saturday Night Live* when he and the **Attractions** suddenly abandon their agreed performance of 'Less Than Zero' in favour of their raucous new protest song 'Radio, Radio'. 'They've run that clip forever,' Costello later says. 'But I was copying Jimi Hendrix.'

Incidentally, at the time of the Lulu appearance, Hendrix is recovering from a leg injury he suffered in New York over the Christmas period, and is preparing for a live concert at London's Royal Albert Hall, although his preferred choice of MC (Spike Milligan) will be unavailable.

1971 Controversial film *Performance*, starring **Mick Jagger**, premieres in London, over two years after it was made. Its dialogue will later be sampled for tracks by Happy Mondays and in Big Audio Dynamite's 1986 chart hit, 'E=MC^2'.

2010 ROTD: New York singer-songwriter Lizzy Grant uses her new stage name, inspired by the actor **Lana** Turner and the Ford **del Rey** sedan, for her first album: *Lana del Ray*. Soon after, she changes the spelling to 'del Rey'. All eight of her subsequent albums to date have reached the top 10 around the world with major label Universal, but this initial one languishes in obscurity.

5 JANUARY

1965 **The Supremes** begin recording 'Stop! In the Name of Love' at Motown's Hitsville USA Studio A. The single will become their fourth consecutive US #1.

1973 ROTD: Two enduring rock acts unveil debut albums. From Boston comes **Aerosmith**, with their self-titled album, while *Greetings from Asbury Park, N.J.* introduces 23-year-old **Bruce Springsteen**.

1975 *The Wiz*, the multi-Tony winning African American remake of *The Wizard of Oz* co-written by **Luther Vandross**, opens on Broadway. Portraying Dorothy is future soul hitmaker **Stephanie Mills**.

1984 At UK #35 and heading for #1, **Frankie Goes to Hollywood** perform 'Relax' on *Top of the Pops* for the only time in the record's original chart run; a week later it is banned by BBC radio and TV when Radio 1 DJ Mike Read sees the explicit artwork and content of the single sleeve, despite it having been played over 70 times on Radio 1 already (including once on Christmas morning 1983). Though the suggestive lyrics also presented a problem, Read claims it was the sleeve that made up his mind.

6 JANUARY

1964 With **The Ronettes** as opening act, **The Rolling Stones** begin their first full tour of the UK in Harrow, Middlesex.

1976 ROTD: **Peter Frampton**'s double album *Frampton Comes Alive!*, which will become the best-selling live album of the 1970s in the US.

1977 EMI Records terminates the **Sex Pistols'** recording contract. The group go on to sign, briefly, with A&M, before a longer association with Richard Branson's Virgin label, where they will record a withering take-down of their former record company in their track 'E.M.I.'.

1981 **John Lennon**'s 'Imagine' single posthumously reaches UK #1, 10 years after it was recorded and almost a month after he was murdered in New York.

7 JANUARY

1954 In Chicago, **Muddy Waters** records Willie Dixon's 'Hoochie Coochie Man', which will become Waters' biggest hit, inspiring a future generation of rock'n'roll pioneers.

1962 DJ Alan Freeman's BBC Radio chart show *Pick of the Pops* moves from Saturday night to Sunday afternoons, establishing the slot for decades thereafter as the new home of the British top 20.

1986 A revamped version of their 1984 single 'West End Girls' becomes the first of four UK #1 singles for **Pet Shop Boys**. Inspiration for its lyric came partly from Grandmaster Flash's 'The Message', T. S. Eliot's *The Waste Land*, and an old Jimmy Cagney film that singer Neil Tennant once caught on late-night television.

8 JANUARY

1937 BOTD: **Shirley Bassey**, the only singer to record two James Bond film themes, namely 'Goldfinger' (1964) and 'Diamonds Are Forever' (1971), is born in Tiger Bay, Cardiff, to a Nigerian father and a mother from Teesside.

1968 ROTD: A month after his death in a plane crash comes **Otis Redding**'s '(Sittin' On) The Dock of the Bay' (US #1, UK #3), a paean to isolation that he had begun writing on a houseboat in California in August 1967.

2013 ROTD: On his 66th birthday, with no advance warning, **David Bowie** breaks a near 10-year recording silence with 'Where Are We Now?', a reflection on his time in Berlin, where he lived during the late 1970s. For his comeback, he is reunited with his regular collaborative producer, Tony Visconti.

2016 Exactly three years later, **Bowie** and Visconti's *Blackstar* is unveiled. The artist had always been inspired by new music, and his 26th studio album, recorded over four months in early 2015, is no exception, with influences including Kendrick Lamar, Boards of Canada and D'Angelo. Many of the personnel on the record have a jazz background, with Visconti later explaining to *Mojo*: 'Having jazz guys play rock music turns it upside down.'

For the first time, a David Bowie album has no picture of the artist on its sleeve. It proves to be his final album: the following Monday morning, it is announced on the world's media that he has died of liver cancer.

2016 Several artists have been simultaneously #1 and #2 in the UK singles chart – The Beatles, Madonna and Frankie Goes to Hollywood among them – but with 'Love Yourself', 'Sorry' and 'What Do You Mean?' **Justin Bieber** becomes the first to monopolise #1, #2 and #3.

9 JANUARY

1943 BOTD: **Scott Walker** in Hamilton, Ohio, as Noel Scott Engel. In 1964, he will join forces with the unrelated John Maus and Gary Leeds to form The Walker Brothers trio. Incidentally, the final ever Walker Brothers single, 'The Electrician' (1978) substantially influences **Ultravox**'s 'Vienna', ROTD in 1981.

1963 Graphic designer and drummer with Blues Incorporated, **Charlie Watts**, joins **The Rolling Stones**.

1981 ROTD: 'In the Air Tonight', with its memorable gated reverb drum sound, marks **Phil Collins'** debut as a solo performer.

1995 ROTD: **Massive Attack**'s 'Protection', with fragments of James Brown's 'The Payback', is enhanced by the vocals of Tracey Thorn, who the group approached as big fans of her 1982 song 'Plain Sailing'.

10 JANUARY

1917 BOTD: **Jerry Wexler**, later to become one of the top soul record producers, responsible for classic hits such as Ray Charles' 'What I'd Say', Aretha's 'Respect' and Wilson Pickett's 'Mustang Sally'.

1949 Nine years in development, RCA Victor announces the **7-inch single 45 rpm record**, which can house up to eight minutes of sound on each side. Portable, cheap to produce and affordable for young consumers, it becomes a major factor in the subsequent rise of rock'n'roll.

1994 ROTD: 'Cornflake Girl' by **Tori Amos**. A 'cornflake girl' is what you would call a woman close to you who betrays you, explains Amos of her new single (UK #4), while raisin girls, who are open to new ideas, are harder to find. Possibly her cereal bowl metaphor was inspired by her appearance in a Kellogg's commercial in 1987. But further ideas for the song came after Amos read Alice Walker's novel on female genital mutilation, *Possessing the Secret of Joy*.

2007 ROTD: **Robyn's** 'With Every Heartbeat'. A collaboration with fellow Swede and producer Kleerup, and inspired by the unlikely dual influences of Giorgio Moroder and ZZ Top, the song peaks at #23 in Sweden, but #1 in the UK.

11 JANUARY

1895 BOTD: **Laurens Hammond** is born in Illinois. He will invent the Hammond organ, first manufactured in 1935, and three years later will also develop the first polyphonic synthesiser, the Novachord, a haunting counterpoint to Vera Lynn on her 1939 recording of 'We'll Meet Again'.

1971 BOTD: **Mary J. Blige** is born in the Bronx. After becoming a telephone operator on the 411 local directory line prior to her singing career, Blige will appropriately go on to call her first album *What's the 411?* It will spawn a pioneering remix album in which every track features a guest rapper.

1982 ROTD: 'Mickey' by **Toni Basil**. A flop on its first outing in 1981, 'Mickey' becomes an international smash for Basil, who has been chiefly known until this point as a choreographer (for the film *American Graffiti*, and Talking Heads' 'Once in a Lifetime' video). The song began life under the title 'Kitty' as a vehicle for the British group Racey in 1979, but Basil's masterstroke was to add a high-school chant to the retitled track. 'That's where I probably got all my choreography background,' she later explains, 'because I was always head cheerleader.'

1985 In Brazil, the first **Rock in Rio** festival opens with a bill of headliners including Queen, Iron Maiden, Whitesnake (a substitution for Def Leppard), and homegrown artists like Baby Consuelo e Pepeu Gomes, Erasmo Carlos and Ney Matogrosso. Over a million people will attend the 10 days of events.

12 JANUARY

1944 BOTD: **Cynthia Robinson** in Sacramento. Initially discouraged from pursuing her career as a trumpeter (the instrument was seen as 'unfeminine'), her potential will later be spotted by Sly Stone for his Family Stone group, in which she will also excel as a vocalist.

1955 ROTD: 'The Wallflower (Roll With Me, Henry)' by **Etta James** (a #1 on the US R&B chart) is intended to be about dancing, but many US radio stations have a different interpretation . . .

1959 In Detroit, **Berry Gordy** launches a new record company, Tamla, which boasts the slogan, 'The Sound That Makes the World Go 'Round'. Its first release, Marv Johnson's 'Come to Me', will eventually peak at US #30.

2004 ROTD: 'Toxic' by **Britney Spears**. Co-written by Cathy Dennis and reportedly turned down by Kylie Minogue, the song contains samples from 'Tere Mere Beech Mein' from the soundtrack to the 1981 Hindi film, *Ek Duuje Ke Liye*.

2018 ROTD: *Camila*, **Camila Cabello**'s first solo LP after breaking away from Fifth Harmony, includes the track 'Something's Gotta Give', which sums up 'the story of my journey from darkness into light'.

13 JANUARY

1963 Philip Saville's BBC TV play, *The Madhouse on Castle Street*, is broadcast, with **Bob Dylan** in the cast. Dylan performs four songs, notably 'Blowin' in the Wind', but unfortunately no telerecording survives.

1964 ROTD: *The Times They Are a-Changin'*, **Dylan**'s first entirely self-penned LP, whose title track is a conscious call for societal change.

1986 ROTD: **Janet Jackson**'s 'What Have You Done for Me Lately' (US #4, UK #3) is a Jimmy Jam and Terry Lewis song, the lyrics of which were rejigged by Jackson to reflect her reactions to a short-lived marriage and new-found sense of independence.

1997 ROTD: **White Town**'s irresistibly catchy 'Your Woman' combines Marxist lyrics with an early 1980s Casio keyboard setting, and a trumpet sample from Lew Stone's 1932 recording, 'My Woman'. White Town's sole member, Jyoti Mishra, who first heard the latter as a teenager when watching Dennis Potter's television series *Pennies from Heaven*, described it as 'really weird and twisted, like the best pop'.

And 'Your Woman' turns out to *be* the best pop. Within a week of release, it hits UK #1, and will chart all over the world.

When making the track in his Derby home, Mishra says he took great pains to make the ingredients 'slightly out of sync', explaining that 'the most interesting things in life are always those with imperfections'. As if to underline this, the single, when it was issued in 1996 on the tiny Illinois label Parasol, had an unwieldy but irreverent subtitle: '>Abort, Retry, Fail?_'. A copy made its way into the hands of DJ Mark Radcliffe, who gave the song its all-important first national play on BBC Radio 1. Simon Mayo, the station's mid-morning show presenter, also championed the song,

2017 'Shape of You' by **Ed Sheeran** enters the UK singles chart at #1. It was initially intended as a vehicle for Rihanna and Rudimental, but Sheeran soon realises that, with its references to Van Morrison, the song suits his own oeuvre more effectively. It will top the charts in 34 countries.

14 JANUARY

1970 At the Frontier Hotel, Las Vegas, **The Supremes** perform with Diana Ross for the last time, closing their set with 'Someday We'll Be Together' and introducing Ross's replacement: Jean Terrell.

1977 ROTD: **Heatwave**'s first hit, 'Boogie Nights'. Complete with harp contributions from Sheila Bromberg – the first woman to play on a Beatles recording ('She's Leaving Home') – the track is written by Cleethorpes' very own Rod Temperton, who will soon begin writing for Michael Jackson.

1978 'This is no fun.' So says Johnny Rotten at the Winterland Ballroom in San Francisco as he parts ways with the original **Sex Pistols**.

2008 ROTD: 'Chasing Pavements' is **Adele**'s second single release, a vow to move on after experiencing infidelity. It reaches UK #2 and US #21.

15 JANUARY

1941 BOTD: Don Glen Vliet, who in 1964 will become **Captain Beefheart**. Matt Groening, creator of *The Simpsons* and *Futurama*, becomes a fan after hearing Beefheart's *Trout Mask Replica* in 1969: 'a sloppy cacophony . . .' but even so '. . . the greatest album I'd ever heard.'

1965 ROTD: For 'Tired of Waiting for You', **The Kinks'** second UK #1 hit, Ray Davies revisited a melody from his time studying at Hornsey School of Art – but had to write new words as he had forgotten the original ones.

1967 **The Rolling Stones** reach some kind of compromise with US TV's *The Ed Sullivan Show*; Mick Jagger agrees to change the title of 'Let's Spend *the Night* Together' to '*some time*' but while doing so rolls his eyes, enraging the host. Their ensuing ban from the show lasts two years.

1974 Hit sitcom *Happy Days*, an idealisation of rock'n'roll adolescence in the 1950s and early 1960s, debuts on ABC. Initially adopting Bill Haley's 'Rock Around the Clock' as its signature tune, the show will run for 10 years.

16 JANUARY

1957 The **Cavern Club** opens in a former air-raid shelter 11 feet below Mathew Street in Liverpool. One of the men responsible for constructing the stage is Harry Harris – uncle to a certain Paul McCartney.

1981 ROTD: With some bonus airplay on BBC Radio 2, **Madness**'s lyrically sparse 'The Return of the Los Palmas 7', their sixth UK top 10 hit in just 15 months, sneaks in a reference to 'Tommy McGloin', who just happens to be the uncle of the band's Chas Smash.

1994 'Things Can Only Get Better' by **D:Ream** reaches UK #1. Borrowing its motivational title from a phrase overheard by lead singer Peter Cunnah during his office-job days, the song will be revived in 1997 as a Labour Party campaign anthem.

1998 ROTD: *Moon Safari* is the debut album from Versailles duo **Air**, whose name is an acronym for 'amour, imagination, rêve' (love, imagination, dream). Like many artists, Nicolas Godin and Jean-Benoît Dunckel are defined not just by what they are (in this case, trying to combine the past and the future), but what they aren't. 'French pop was synonymous with Sacha Distel. I hated it,' Godin will tell the *Guardian*. Instead, Air's influences come from a variety of sources: Ray Bradbury, Albert Einstein, astrophysics, and even *Charlie's Angels*, whose star Jaclyn Smith inspired their song title 'Kelly Watch the Stars'. 'Sexy Boy', their first hit, started as a joke, but 'it's important to have humour in a record'. The sound of a Hofner bass, just like Paul McCartney's, pervades the sound of the whole record, which is also characterised by the duo's use of analogue synthesisers from the 1970s – not least because that was all they could afford.

Joining the duo on two songs ('All I Need', 'You Make It Easy') is American singer Beth Hirsch, Godin's neighbour in Montmartre, who makes them sound like 'a space-age Carpenters'.

Moon Safari will reach #21 in the French album charts, but becomes bigger abroad, peaking at UK #6. And one smitten fan is the film director Sofia Coppola, who invites them to write the score for her next movie: *The Virgin Suicides*.

17 JANUARY

1933 BOTD: Cairo-born French/Italian singer **Dalida**. After relocating to Paris in 1954, she will have a 30-year international recording career, achieving 28 #1 hits in France. Her breakthrough single in 1956 is 'Bambino', which adds lyrics to Perez Prado's instrumental 'Guaglione' (from that Guinness advert in the 1990s), and she will go on to release cover versions of songs ranging from 'The Lambeth Walk' to Wham!'s 'Last Christmas'. In 1968, President Charles de Gaulle will award her the Medal of the President of the Republic.

1967 Today's *Daily Mail* becomes the focus for a new **Beatles** song, 'A Day in the Life'. Investigations are continuing into the death in London of Guinness heir Tara Browne, who was killed in a traffic accident after driving his car through a red light shortly before Christmas. John Lennon's eyes are also drawn to another short piece headlined 'The holes in our roads', in which – according to a council survey – there are '4,000 holes in the road in Blackburn, Lancashire'.

Moved to pen a few verses, Lennon needs a middle section and, fortunately, his songwriting partner has one. Paul McCartney recalls the morning ritual of his formative teenage years, of getting up and racing to catch the bus to school. Juxtaposing these elements of past and present, the pair compose 'A Day in the Life' and start recording it two days later at Abbey Road, ready for use as the final track of their forthcoming album *Sgt. Pepper's Lonely Hearts Club Band*.

'It was a good piece of work between Paul and me,' Lennon will tell *Rolling Stone* magazine in 1968. 'Now and then we really turn each other on with a bit of song.'

1972 ROTD: 'Mother and Child Reunion' (US #4, UK #5), recorded in Jamaica with Jimmy Cliff's backing band and singer Cissy Houston (mother of Whitney), is **Paul Simon**'s first solo single.

1974 In Hialeah, Florida, **George McCrae** records his vocal for the KC & the Sunshine Band song 'Rock Your Baby', which becomes a worldwide #1 in the summer. (McCrae's then wife Gwen will herself enjoy several hits, most notably 1975's US top-tenner, 'Rockin' Chair'.)

1978 Taking their name from the middle section of David Bowie's 'The Jean Genie', **Simple Minds** play their first concert at Satellite City, Glasgow.

18 JANUARY

1955 BOTD: Francis Nicholls Jr in New York. In 1977, as **Frankie Knuckles**, he becomes a resident DJ at Chicago's Warehouse club, where he and the club's name will together give rise to what becomes known as 'house' music.

1969 ROTD: Later considered by many to be her best LP, **Dusty Springfield**'s *Dusty in Memphis* will sell comparatively poorly on its release, despite the inclusion of 'Son of a Preacher Man'. During its making, Dusty suggests her label Atlantic should sign brand new band Led Zeppelin, purely because bass player John Paul Jones once backed her in concert.

1993 ROTD: 'No Limit' by the Dutch pop techno-techno-techno-techno duo **2 Unlimited** is the record that will finally put an end to the 10-week reign of Whitney Houston's 'I Will Always Love You' at the top of the UK charts.

2019 ROTD: **Ariana Grande**'s friendship anthem '7 Rings' contains an interpolation of 'My Favourite Things' from Rodgers and Hammerstein's *The Sound of Music*, content that will cost 90 per cent of the publishing rights.

19 JANUARY

1949 BOTD: **Robert Palmer** in the Yorkshire town of Batley. Making his name in the 70s rock band Vinegar Joe with Elkie Brooks, Palmer will go on to have solo hits like 'Addicted to Love' and 'She Makes My Day'.

1955 The prison drama movie *Unchained* is released, now forgotten but for its title song, first sung by Todd Duncan. '**Unchained Melody**' has now been UK #1 four times thanks to the efforts of Jimmy Young, The Righteous Brothers, Robson & Jerome and Gareth Gates.

1963 BOTD: **Caron Wheeler** in London. A teenage reggae chart topper in Brown Sugar with 1977's 'I'm in Love with A Dreadlocks', Wheeler will go on to co-found vocal group Afrodiziak, backing The Jam, Howard Jones and Elvis Costello. At the end of the 1980s, she will enjoy pop success with Soul II Soul.

1980 Spizzenergi's 'Where's Captain Kirk?' and **Adam and the Ants'** *Dirk Wears White Sox* become, respectively, the best-selling single and album in the first independent charts to be published in the UK.

20 JANUARY

1965 On the day that rock'n'roll and R&B-championing broadcaster **Alan Freed** dies in California, and M People's **Heather Small** is born in London, **The Byrds** record 'Mr Tambourine Man' in Hollywood – just five days after its composer Bob Dylan has laid down the original. The Byrds' cover, already approved by Dylan, differs significantly in length, tone and structure – only one of Dylan's original four verses appears, with greater emphasis given to the chorus. Roger McGuinn is the only Byrd to appear on the recording, and the session's producer is Terry Melcher, the son of Doris Day.

1967 In Muscle Shoals, Alabama, **Arthur Conley** records 'Sweet Soul Music', a homage to Sam Cooke's 'Yeah Man' (for which Cooke ultimately receives a composer credit). Whereas Cooke's song celebrates a succession of activities (dancing, sports, swimming), Conley's cites the giants of soul.

1972 At the Dome in Brighton, **Pink Floyd** debut a suite of new songs in their live set – later to feature on *The Dark Side of the Moon* – but experience technical difficulties during 'Money'.

1978 ROTD: 'Shot By Both Sides' is the first single by Manchester band **Magazine**. Fronted by Howard Devoto, late of Buzzcocks, the song just misses out on reaching the top 40, but on *Top of the Pops* Devoto spends the entire performance standing motionless. 'I decided I just wouldn't react.' The single starts to fall back down the charts.

1986 ROTD: **Public Image Ltd**'s new single has the word 'Single' on the sleeve. The A-side is in fact called 'Rise' and features none other than the great Ginger Baker on drums. Five years earlier, after the band had managed to run through six different drummers in two years, the *NME* had published an April Fool gag suggesting that Baker was about to become their latest and most unlikely new member. It seems both the band and Baker decided to play up to the joke.

21 JANUARY

1957 In New York, **Patsy Cline** wins CBS-TV's talent show *Arthur Godfrey's Talent Scouts*, with the song that will become her first hit: 'Walkin' After Midnight'.

1965 BOTD: Jason Mizell, aka Run-DMC's **Jam Master Jay**. Exactly 20 years later, on the group's *King of Rock* LP, 'Jam-Master Jammin'' will offer a supreme encapsulation of Mizell's imagination and skills as a turntablist.

1983 ROTD: **Eurythmics'** 'Sweet Dreams (Are Made of This)'. Reaching UK #2 and US #1, the track combines Annie Lennox's 'hopeless and nihilistic' feelings with a more motivational middle section suggested by Dave Stewart. Its memorable promotional video juxtaposes dreams of consumerism (like computers in boardrooms) with a cow in a field, 'who has none of these aims in life', says Stewart.

1991 ROTD: 'Motown Junk' by **Manic Street Preachers**. Complete with Skids and Public Enemy samples, the single marks the first national impact of the Welsh band after their formation in the town of Blackwood in 1986.

22 JANUARY

1931 BOTD: **Sam Cooke** in the Mississippi town of Clarksdale. In his brief 33-year life, Cooke will become a much-respected soul and gospel singer and civil rights campaigner. Starting out as frontman for the Soul Stirrers, his first solo single in 1957 is slated to be a cover of Gershwin's 'Summertime', before the flip side receives top billing: 'You Send Me'.

1963 While **The Drifters** are recording 'On Broadway' in New York, **Gerry and the Pacemakers** are in London laying down Mitch Murray's 'How Do You Do It?', which their producer George Martin had recorded with The Beatles the previous September.

1973 ROTD: **Roberta Flack's** interpretation of 'Killing Me Softly With His Song', credited officially to the writing team of Charles Fox and Norman Gimbel, will become an international hit but its origins are actually more complicated.

Many people are aware that the track was conceived as a response to a Don McLean concert, but perhaps fewer will know the full story. Folk singer-songwriter **Lori Lieberman** was in the audience at the Troubadour club in Los Angeles in mid-November 1971, where McLean was supporting Carly Simon. Lieberman had been initially reluctant to go, but was persuaded by her 44-year-old manager, Norman Gimbel, to attend. As McLean performed 'Empty Chairs', Lieberman began scribbling notes on a napkin.

'She told us about this strong experience she had listening to McLean,' Gimbel will later say in April 1973. 'I had a notion this might make a good song, so the three of us discussed it.' Unfortunately, only two of those three people ended up with a composer credit, even though Lieberman recorded the song herself in 1972, before it was brought to Flack's attention.

'I'm not looking for money,' Lieberman told the *Washington Post* years later. 'I just want the truth of how the song was written to come out.' Roberta Flack's response? 'I hope Lori knows I am forever grateful for her part in the writing of the song.'

1996 ROTD: **Garbage**'s 'Stupid Girl' is 'really about squandering potential,' says Shirley Manson, likening it to Madonna's 'Express Yourself', 'but a little more subversive.' That drum sample, by the way, is Topper Headon on The Clash's 'Train in Vain (Stand by Me)'.

23 JANUARY

1910 BOTD: Guitarist **Django Reinhardt** in Liberchies, Belgium. A major influence on a generation of rock guitarists including Jeff Beck, Jimmy Page and Willie Nelson, Reinhardt will also inspire Jerry Garcia and Tony Iommi, both of whom, like Reinhardt, will lose fingers in accidents and have to adapt their style of playing accordingly.

1964 ROTD: 'The Way You Do the Things You Do', which becomes the first **Temptations** single to significantly chart, reaching US #11. The song is the work of two members of the Miracles: Robert Rogers and William 'Smokey' Robinson.

1981 ROTD: 'Reward' by **The Teardrop Explodes**. Destined to reach UK #6, the single is the result of the band's typically grand ideas. Lead singer Julian Cope describes how he wanted it to be a Northern soul classic, 'like we were playing in an ice rink', while keyboard player David Balfe (later to establish Food Records, home of Blur) wanted the horn solo 'to sound like wild elephants'.

1988 Producer Jack Endino at Reciprocal Studios in Seattle welcomes Kurt Cobain, Krist Novoselic and Melvins drummer Dale Crover, who, as **Nirvana**, record and mix 10 songs in six hours. Endino is impressed by Cobain's voice at their first-ever session: 'I thought he had a good scream.'

24 JANUARY

1944 BOTD: **Klaus Nomi** in Bavaria. In the 1960s, while working as an usher at West Berlin's Deutsche Oper, Nomi will wow fellow staff with his extraordinary singing voice, before finding his niche in 1970s New York, notably on rock operatic reworkings of 'Lightning Strikes', 'You Don't Own Me' and a doomy version of 'The Twist'.

1970 Moog's **Minimoog** synthesiser hits the stores. Its portability, especially for live performances, will make it an attractive purchase for many musicians, including Stevie Wonder, Kraftwerk, Giorgio Moroder, Gary Numan and ABBA.

2018 DOTD: **Mark E. Smith**, at the age of 60. 'If it's me and your granny on bongos, it's a Fall gig,' **Smith** had said in 1998. Now there will be no more Fall gigs.

25 JANUARY

1915 BOTD: **Ewan MacColl** as James Miller, in Salford. Father of Kirsty MacColl, and composer of 'The First Time Ever I Saw Your Face' and 'Dirty Old Town', the singer-songwriter will also originate the arrangement of 'Scarborough Fair' later popularised by Simon and Garfunkel.

1980 ROTD: 'Games Without Frontiers' by **Peter Gabriel**. The anthemic anti-war song's title is a translation of 'Jeux Sans Frontières', the title of a long-running pan-European TV gameshow (the original French name is sung by Kate Bush for the track's backing vocals).

1980 Meanwhile, **Black Entertainment Television (BET)** launches on US cable TV. Initially a two-hour Friday night block of classic Black films, plus R&B and jazz music, it will expand to become the only place to exclusively screen music videos by Black artists.

26 JANUARY

1937 BOTD: **Alison Steele** in Brooklyn. Later known as 'The Nightbird', she benefits from the decision of WNEW-FM in 1966 to appoint an all-female team of radio DJs. From 1968 to 1979 she becomes the station's regular night-time presenter, playing rock of the progressive and countercultural variety. She apparently inspires Jimi Hendrix to write the song 'Night Bird Flying', a single released in 1971 a few months after the guitarist's death.

1970 ROTD: *Bridge Over Troubled Water*, **Simon and Garfunkel**'s final studio LP, will become the biggest-selling album of the 1970s. Its title track is also out today, as a single.

1975 BBC1's arts strand *Omnibus* premieres 'Cracked Actor: A Film About **David Bowie**', narrated and directed by Alan Yentob, and filmed during Bowie's Diamond Dogs tour the previous summer.

1982 **Shakin' Stevens** has been reliant on cover versions for his hit songs, but 'Oh Julie', which hits UK #1, is one of his own compositions. In the US, it is itself covered by, of all people, Barry Manilow.

1997 At UK #1 is 'Beetlebum', reminiscent of The Beatles' 'White Album', and **Blur**'s first new material since *The Great Escape* in 1995, representing a radical shift away from the Britpop movement.

27 JANUARY

1956 ROTD: 'Heartbreak Hotel' by **Elvis Presley**. The song that will make Presley a national and worldwide star was written 'in just 22 minutes' the previous September by steel guitar player Tommy Durden and high school teacher and part-time DJ Mae Boren Axton. It was inspired by a Miami newspaper report about a man's suicide note, which included the phrase, 'I walk a lonely street'.

Soon after completing the song, Mullen and Axton approached Elvis in Nashville. Taking advantage of the fact that Axton had already met and interviewed the singer at a Jacksonville concert, the pair played him the demo and agreed to give him one-third of the publishing royalties on condition that he make it his next single.

Presley's first release after signing to the RCA Victor label, the song will reach the top of the country and pop charts in the US. In Britain it will reach the #2 spot, although an unimpressed BBC Radio confines it to restricted play.

By summer 1957, there will be much debate about Presley's suitability as a role model for teenagers (thanks to his gyrations during performances and the often frenzied audience reactions at concerts, among other things), but Axton – teaching in a Jacksonville high school – tells *Billboard* magazine that she rewards her pupils' efforts at studying by allowing them to discuss their idol or play some of his records in class: 'You'd be surprised how enthusiastic they become.'

1973 **Marc Bolan** appears on Cilla Black's BBC variety show *Cilla*, where they perform a duet of T. Rex's 'Life's a Gas', and Bolan previews a song that will not be released for another year: 'Mad Donna'.

1992 ROTD: 'Movin' On Up' by **Primal Scream**. The lead track on the band's new EP gets the airplay, but the record also includes the bonus 10-minute epic 'Screamadelica' sung by Denise Johnson, which confusingly is not included on the group's LP of the same name.

28 JANUARY

1975 In the nick of time, 'January' by Scottish foursome **Pilot** becomes a UK #1.

1984 ROTD: Pioneering hip hop record label **Def Jam**'s first-ever single: 'It's Yours' by T La Rock and Jazzy Jay.

1990 Sinéad O'Connor's 'Nothing Compares 2 U', written by Prince, reaches UK #1. It is perhaps equally well-remembered for its stark, captivating video. In the final verse, two tears roll down her cheeks, a reaction – she later says – to suddenly remembering her late mother.

29 JANUARY

1969 Peggy Lee records Jerry Leiber and Mike Stoller's 'Is That All There Is?', inspired by an 1896 story by Thomas Mann called 'Disillusionment'. The arranger on the session is one Randy Newman.

1977 ROTD: *Spiral Scratch* by **Buzzcocks**. The release of the Manchester band's debut four-track EP is a defining moment in British music: it doesn't come from one of the major record companies (EMI, CBS, Pye) nor from one of the newer labels (Island, Virgin, Stiff) that pride themselves on seeking out adventurous acts. Instead, it comes out on the New Hormones label, founded by the group itself and financed by a £250 loan from singer Pete Shelley's dad. Within a week of its release, the first 1,000 pressings will sell out and the record will be awarded a rave review by the *NME*'s Paul Morley.

Buzzcocks began in 1976, when founder members Howard Trafford and Peter McNeish saw Johnny Rotten in the *NME* saying, 'We're not into music, we're into chaos!' They formed a band, taking their name from a *Time Out* review of TV drama *Rock Follies* – 'getting a buzz, cocks!' – and went to watch the Sex Pistols at several venues, including Manchester's Free Trade Hall. Six weeks later, when the Pistols played there again, Buzzcocks were the support group, and

Trafford had become Howard Devoto while Peter McNeish was now Pete Shelley.

Spiral Scratch was recorded with producer Martin Hannett (under the pseudonym 'Martin Zero') just after Christmas 1976. 'Boredom', the lead track, is a glorious slab of wild apathy, and will later be covered by glove puppet Sweep on local television, while its one-note guitar solo will be consciously echoed in Orange Juice's 'Rip It Up' (1983).

Yet despite immediate acclaim for Buzzcocks, Howard Devoto soon wants out. 'I don't like movements,' he will say of the burgeoning fashion for punk rock. 'What was once unhealthily fresh is now a clean old hat.' Instead, he goes on to form the hitless but magnificent Magazine, while Shelley and the rest of Buzzcocks build on their 15,000 sales of *Spiral Scratch* by signing to United Artists and releasing a remarkable string of snappy, witty and charming singles between 1977 and 1980: 'Orgasm Addict', 'What Do I Get', 'Ever Fallen in Love . . . (With Someone You Shouldn't've?)' and 'Everybody's Happy Nowadays'.

1982 ROTD: All released on this day alone: 'Say Hello Wave Goodbye' by Soft Cell; 'Town Called Malice'/'Precious' by The Jam; 'See You' by Depeche Mode; and 'Party Fears Two' by **Associates**. The last of these four, with an expressive, agile lead vocal by Billy Mackenzie, will peak at UK #9, and from May, its sprightly piano intro will be adopted for the next 11 years as the opening theme for BBC Radio 4's satirical comedy show *Week Ending*.

30 JANUARY

1968 ROTD: *White Light/White Heat* by **The Velvet Underground**. Described by the band's John Cale as 'consciously anti-beauty', its 17-minute-long finale 'Sister Ray' is summed up by Lou Reed as 'a scene of total debauchery and decay'. Recorded in one take, the engineer reportedly left the session saying: 'When you're done, come get me.'

1969 The Beatles present a 40-minute set on the roof of Apple Records in London, accompanied by keyboard player Billy Preston. It will be their final public live performance.

1995 ROTD: **Leftfield's** *Leftism*. A debut album for the electronic music duo, it is already more like a greatest hits collection including singles – 'Song of Life', 'Release the Pressure', 'Open Up' – released over the previous three years.

2000 R.E.M. reach their highest ever UK singles chart placing (#3) with 'The Great Beyond', taken from the soundtrack of the Jim Carrey movie *Man on the Moon*.

31 JANUARY

1962 BOTD: **Sophie Muller** in London. The filmmaker comes to prominence and acclaim when she directs several videos for Eurythmics' 1987 album *Savage*. She will also collaborate with Annie Lennox on her solo career, and with Garbage, Sparks, PJ Harvey and Kylie Minogue.

1969 DOTD: Spiritual figure **Meher Baba**, a devotee of the value of observed silence. Pete Townshend will dedicate *Tommy* – the next album by The Who – to him, and compose 1971's 'Baba O'Riley' in his memory.

2005 ROTD: *I Am a Bird Now* (UK #16) is the Mercury Prize-winning debut from Antony and the Johnsons, a showcase for the talent of singer-songwriter **Anohni**, whose potential was recognised early on by Lou Reed. 'He advocated for me very intensely,' she will later say of Reed, who guests on the track 'Fistful of Love'. 'He convinced people it was worth listening to me.'

FEBRUARY

1 FEBRUARY

1965 Unable to record for a year due to contractual disputes, **James Brown** and his band are on their way to a show when they stop off at a North Carolina studio to record 'Papa's Got a Brand New Bag'.

According to Arthur Smith, who owns the studio, Brown 'had the run of the house. He'd play the piano the way he wanted it played and ask, "You got that?" Then he'd go to the person on the guitar and play it and say, "You got it?" He did that with the horn section – all the instruments. He could play everything.'

On the full unedited seven-minute recording of 'Bag', just before guitarist Jimmy Nolen kicks proceedings off with the now-familiar riff, Brown shouts, 'This is a hit!' And it will be a hit. Nine years after breaking the R&B charts with 'Please, Please, Please', 'Bag' will become Brown's first top 10 pop hit in the US. It also becomes his first UK hit, and wins a Grammy Award for the year's best R&B recording.

'Bag' also marks Brown's break away from the soul market, of which he was known as the Godfather, and a move into funk. Its urgency is enhanced when the track is edited and sped up, to help it with radio play. It will transform Brown's career.

1972 ROTD: **Neil Young**'s *Harvest* features the London Symphony Orchestra, and backing vocals from James Taylor and Linda Ronstadt on the single 'Heart of Gold', but Young later says of the latter that it 'put me in the middle of the road. Travelling there soon became a bore, so I headed for the ditch.'

1995 Richey Edwards checks out of the Embassy Hotel on Bayswater Road in London, and drives to Cardiff. It marks the last confirmed sighting of **Manic Street Preachers'** guitarist.

2004 ROTD: **Scissor Sisters'** debut of the same name – with songs about friendship, cruising, coming out to one's parents, and the effects of crystal meth on America's gay community – will become the year's best-selling album in the UK.

2 FEBRUARY

1968 The band previously known as Candy Coloured Rain, Navy Blue and Ian Henderson's Bag o'Nails perform for the first time under their new name of **Jethro Tull**, opening for Savoy Brown at London's Marquee Club.

1980 **Bob Dylan** has never had a #1 single in the UK or US, but today he begins five weeks at the top of the Spanish charts with the reggae-tinged kids' favourite 'Man Gave Names to the All the Animals'.

1982 Overtaking the likes of The Human League, Soft Cell and OMD – all of whom cite them as inspirational – German electronic heroes **Kraftwerk** belatedly reach #1 in the UK with a reissue of 1978's 'The Model'. On the flip side is a newer track, 'Computer Love', which will form the basis in 2005 for Coldplay's 'Talk'.

1988 ROTD: **Leonard Cohen's** *I'm Your Man* tackles the state of the world ('Everybody Knows'), 'psychic terrorism' ('First We Take Manhattan') and the craft of songwriting itself ('Tower of Song').

3 FEBRUARY

1959 Just before 1 a.m., and only a few minutes after its take-off from Mason City, Iowa, a four-seater Beechcraft Bonanza crashes into a cornfield at Albert Juhl farm. All four people on board – pilot Roger Peterson, J. P. Richardson (aka **The Big Bopper**, 28 years old), **Ritchie Valens** (17) and **Buddy Holly** (22) – are killed.

The three musicians had just played a concert at Clear Lake's Surf Ballroom and were heading to Moorhead, Minnesota. Their travelling manager, Sam Geller, later explains their reasons for wanting to fly rather than share a rigorous bus journey with the other performers: 'Buddy wanted to get a suit cleaned, Valens wanted a haircut, and Richardson just wanted to get some sleep.' Because there are only four seats on the plane, Valens is said to have agreed to flip a coin with a fellow musician and, on calling correctly, exclaimed: 'That's the first time I've ever won anything in my life.'

In the wake of the tragedy, 'It Doesn't Matter Anymore' becomes Holly's biggest hit, and the event will inspire many tribute songs, most famously Don McLean's 'American Pie' in 1971, and The Clash's 'If Music Could Talk' (1980).

1972 Supported by Slade and Billy Preston, **Chuck Berry** headlines the Lanchester Arts Festival in Coventry, from which an eleven-and-a-half-minute live version of Dave Bartholomew's 1952 novelty song 'My Ding-a-Ling' is whittled down to four minutes. It will become Berry's only #1 in the UK and (surprisingly) in the US.

1978 ROTD: 'Denis', a cover of Randy and the Rainbows' 'Denise' (US #10 in 1963), will provide new wave group **Blondie** with their breakthrough British hit, eventually peaking at #2.

1992 ROTD: 'Leave Them All Behind' by **Ride**. The Oxford band's eight-minute epic will become the first UK top 10 single for Alan McGee's Creation label.

2017 ROTD: **Sampha**'s debut album, *Process*, which explores his experience of bereavement and sudden success, will go on to win the year's Mercury Prize.

4 FEBRUARY

1948 BOTD: Vincent Furnier in Detroit. Beginning his career in high-school band The Earwigs (parodying songs by The Beatles), Furnier later finds fame as pantomimic shock-rocker **Alice Cooper**.

1977 ROTD: *Rumours* by **Fleetwood Mac**. Recorded under the working title 'Yesterday's Gone', the album, which is heavily influenced by the fractured personal relationships within the group, will sell 10 million copies in its first year.

1980 After its owners are convicted of tax evasion, New York's **Studio 54** club closes, with Diana Ross and Liza Minnelli performing there on its swansong night.

1991 ROTD: *Innuendo*, **Queen**'s final album within Freddie Mercury's lifetime, and **My Bloody Valentine**'s queasy, hypnotic EP, *Tremolo*.

2014 ROTD: **Future Islands**' 'Seasons (Waiting On You)'. A clip of lead singer Samuel T. Herring beating his chest while performing the song on David Letterman's talk show later goes viral. 'Lots of people said, "This guy dances like nobody's watching",' says Herring. 'But no. I knew everyone was watching.'

5 FEBRUARY

1929 BOTD: **Hal Blaine** in Massachusetts. As part of the Wrecking Crew pool of session musicians, he will play drums on 39 US #1 hits including 'Be My Baby', 'Good Vibrations' and 'Bridge Over Troubled Water'.

1941 BOTD: Mississippi songwriter **Barrett Strong**. The first artist to score a US hit single for the Motown label with 1959's 'Money (That's What I Want)', Strong will also co-write some of the label's finest songs including 'I Heard It Through the Grapevine', 'War' and 'Papa Was a Rollin' Stone'.

1986 ROTD: As a song, 'Kiss' was originally given by **Prince** to the Minneapolis funk band Mazarati, but their background vocals end up on his own version, with the Revolution, which will become his third US #1.

1996 ROTD: *Murder Ballads* by **Nick Cave and the Bad Seeds**. Described by the *NME* as 'grotesque, horrifying, and vaudevillian all at once', the album features vocal cameos from Kylie Minogue, PJ Harvey, Shane McGowan and Blixa Bargeld.

2023 A year after winning a Lifetime Achievement Grammy Award, Californian singer-songwriter and guitarist **Bonnie Raitt** (whose first album was released in 1971) wins a further three Grammy Awards bringing her career tally to 15. One of the accolades comes in the Song of the Year category, where her composition 'Just Like That' beats off rival artists Taylor Swift, Lizzo, Beyoncé, Steve Lacy and Adele.

6 FEBRUARY

1967 As **The Monkees'** 'I'm a Believer' continues its UK #1 run, drummer-singer Micky Dolenz arrives in London for a five-day visit, having just completed the filming of the group's first television series. He meets Paul McCartney, who treats him to a spin of The Beatles' imminent single, 'Penny Lane'/'Strawberry Fields Forever', before the pair head to a party at the Speakeasy nightclub attended by, among others, Mama Cass Elliot from The Mamas and the Papas.

The events of that night will find their way into the lyrics and spirit of a new, darker Monkees song, which will take its name from a phrase Dolenz overhears earlier that evening while watching the BBC sitcom *Till Death Us Do Part*.

'The father figure calls the young son a "randy scouse git",' Dolenz later recalls. 'I didn't know what it meant, but I just thought, "Whoa, that's really cool."'

'Randy Scouse Git' will become the closing track on The Monkees' third LP, *Headquarters*, the first on which the group will adopt greater creative control, but it is initially referred to as 'Randy S' in the press, and when released as a UK single (reaching #2), it is under the even coyer name of 'Alternate Title'.

1967 Meanwhile, the **Bee Gees** complete a five-week voyage from Australia back to England, arriving at Southampton on *The Fair Sky*. The Gibbs had emigrated to Queensland in August 1958, and in late 1966 had reached the Australian top 10 with 'Spicks and Specks'.

1974 ROTD: Although featuring sporadic vocals from **The Three Degrees**, 'TSOP (The Sound of Philadelphia)' by **MFSB** (Mother Father Sister Brother) is predominantly instrumental. The work of writer-producers Leon Huff and Kenny Gamble, by April it becomes the first-ever TV theme to top the US charts, following its use on *Soul Train*.

1989 ROTD: *Spike*, **Elvis Costello**'s first album without the Attractions since 1977, is not a reference to comedian Spike Milligan but to musical humorist Spike Jones. Two of its songs are co-written with Paul McCartney, including the hit 'Veronica'.

7 FEBRUARY

1934 BOTD: Curtis Montgomery in Fort Worth, Texas. Later taking the name **King Curtis**, Montgomery will become a tenor saxophonist in the Lionel Hampton Band, before naturally gravitating towards R&B. He will go on to back The Coasters, LaVern Baker and Aretha Franklin (not least on 'Respect'), but will also have hits of his own in his all-too-short life: 'Soul Twist' in 1962, and 1967's 'Memphis Soul Stew'.

1964 The Beatles arrive in the US for the first time, flying from London to the newly renamed John F. Kennedy International Airport. Over 2 million copies of 'I Want to Hold Your Hand' have been sold in America in just six weeks, and so to deal with the waiting crowds, over 50 extra police officers are drafted in.

1975 A wide range of pop is broadcast on British television: **Carpenters** perform 'Please Mr Postman' on BBC1's kids variety show *Crackerjack*; **The Sensational Alex Harvey Band** cover Jacques Brel's 'Next' on BBC2's *The Old Grey Whistle Test*; while over on ITV **Slade** unveil new single 'How Does it Feel' (from their new film *Flame*) on Russell Harty's chat show.

2000 ROTD: *Nixon* by Nashville rock band **Lambchop**. The country- and soul-infused album proves to be the band's commercial and critical apex. One song, 'The Book I Haven't Read', credits the late Curtis Mayfield, as it borrows a line from his song 'Baby It's You'.

8 FEBRUARY

1963 ROTD: What better time for **Cliff Richard and the Shadows'** new single, 'Summer Holiday' (UK #1), to arrive in the shops than during the coldest British winter since 1740?

1977 ROTD: **Television**'s *Marquee Moon* album fails to chart in the US, but will reach #28 in the UK, partly due to Nick Kent's rave review of a preview copy in the *NME*.

1988 ROTD: 'Beat Dis' by **Bomb the Bass** and 'Doctorin' the House' by **Coldcut** (introducing Yazz). Both singles sample Afrika Bambaataa as well as Gerry Anderson's *Thunderbirds*, and both will reach the UK top 10.

2015 Ellie Goulding climbs to UK #1 with 'Love Me Like You Do', featured in the film adaptation of the international bestseller *Fifty Shades of Grey*.

9 FEBRUARY

1942 BOTD: Carol Klein in Manhattan. As **Carole King** her catalogue of songs for others (often written with Gerry Goffin) will include 'Will You Still Love Me Tomorrow?', 'The Loco-Motion', 'One Fine Day' and '(You Make Me Feel Like) A Natural Woman'. For herself, there will be 'It Might as Well Rain Until September' and a series of solo albums, most famously 1971's *Tapestry*.

1968 ROTD: **Dave Dee, Dozy, Beaky, Mick & Tich's** 'Legend of Xanadu'. It is their only single to reach #1 in the UK.

1972 Paul McCartney's new band **Wings** play their first-ever concert, as part of a spontaneous tour of college venues. Around 800 people at Nottingham University pay 40p to see them play oldies, current material and the group's future smash, 'My Love'.

1979 UB40's live debut forms part of a private party at the Hare and Hounds pub in Kings Heath, Birmingham.

1996 Providing the music on the first *TFI Friday* on Channel 4: Shed Seven, Skunk Anansie and Ocean Colour Scene.

10 FEBRUARY

1956 **Little Richard** and his backing group arrive at J&M Studios, New Orleans, fresh from seeing a watered-down Pat Boone version of their song 'Tutti Frutti' make it into the pop charts. They are determined to record something so frantic and intense, both in content and delivery, that it will be impossible for Boone to cover. 'Okay, Pat,' says co-writer Robert Blackwell. 'Get your mouth together to cover this "Long Tall Sally"!'

Regardless, Boone will record it anyway, before shuffling away into the ballads market. Fortunately, though, so will The Beatles, who include it in their live act, and The Kinks, who will release it as their debut single in 1963.

Meanwhile, Earl Palmer, the drummer on Little Richard's original version, will go on to have an incredible session career, playing on the definitive versions of 'You Send Me', 'Summertime Blues', 'La Bamba', 'You've Lost That Lovin' Feelin'', 'River Deep Mountain High' . . . and the theme to *The Flintstones*.

1966 During a break in recording, **The Beach Boys** visit San Diego Zoo, where their feeding of seven goats becomes the incongruous cover shot for *Pet Sounds*.

1978 ROTD: A stand-out track on **Van Halen**'s debut album is the brief but blazing 'Eruption', a showcase for Eddie Van Halen's guitar virtuosity, and a prelude to the hard-rock quartet's cover of 'You Really Got Me'.

1987 ROTD: 'The government's responsible,' declares the sleeve of **Public Enemy**'s first LP, *Yo! Bum Rush the Show*. A powerful mix of wit and fury, the record is marginalised even by many Black radio stations in the US but will still sell half a million copies within the year.

11 FEBRUARY

1963 At 10 p.m., **The Beatles** are at EMI (now Abbey Road) Studios needing to record one more song for their debut album, *Please Please Me*. A cover of the Isley Brothers' 'Twist and Shout' is suggested – it's regularly in their live act – and they nail it in the first take. (A second recording is made but considered unusable because John Lennon's voice has gone.)

1977 ROTD: **David Bowie**'s 'Sound and Vision'. Extracted from his *Low* album, it has an unusual structure for a three-minute pop song: its first half is vocal-free, save for backing singer Mary Hopkin. Yet it reaches UK #3, partly due to exposure on BBC TV programme trails.

1983 ROTD: 'Total Eclipse of the Heart' by **Bonnie Tyler**. Written by Meat Loaf associate Jim Steinman, the single will go on to reach #1 in the UK, USA, Australia and Canada.

2008 ROTD: Exactly 25 years later, another Welsh-born singer, **Duffy**, emerges with 'Mercy', which reaches #1 in Britain and across Europe. She first rose to prominence in Wales on the Welsh-language TV talent show *Wawffactor*.

2010 ROTD: **Janelle Monáe**'s 'Tightrope', with rap contributions by OutKast's Big Boi, is all about keeping one's balance in life, and keeping any praise and criticism in perspective.

12 FEBRUARY

1982 ROTD: *English Settlement*, with its sleeve depicting the Uffington White Horse in Oxfordshire, marks **XTC**'s move into more studio-based work, less suited to live performance. It proves to be their sole UK top 10 album, following their only top 10 single: 'Senses Working Overtime'.

1992 **The KLF** perform '3 a.m. Eternal' at the Brit Awards with thrash metal band Extreme Noise Terror. At the end of their arresting performance, during which Bill Drummond fires blanks at the audience with a machine gun, it is announced that 'The KLF have left the music business.'

2012 UK #1 'Somebody That I Used to Know' by **Gotye featuring Kimbra** is based around a sample of Brazilian Luiz Bonfá's 'Seville', and a xylophone part inspired by 'Baa Baa Black Sheep'.

13 FEBRUARY

1967 ROTD: 'Strawberry Fields Forever' and 'Penny Lane', the first new **Beatles** material since they gave up live performance to become a studio entity, will be blocked from reaching UK #1 by Engelbert Humperdinck's more middle-of-the-road offering 'Release Me'.

1989 ROTD: Two of the many **Stock Aitken Waterman** singles. 'This Time I Know It's for Real' will return Donna Summer to the British top three, while 'I'd Rather Jack', a dig at the conservative and middle-aged values of pop radio and the music industry, becomes a one-hit wonder for Liverpudlian sisters The Reynolds Girls.

1996 ROTD: *The Score* by the **Fugees**. 'It's almost like a hip hop version of *Tommy*,' says Lauryn Hill of their new album, which combines samples, DJ'ing and live instrumentation. To date it has sold 22 million copies.

Meanwhile, on former member Robbie Williams' 22nd birthday, **Take That** hold a press conference to announce they are splitting. But is it really the end? 'Our dream,' says Gary Barlow, 'is that after five or ten years we'll come back and do it all again.' In late 2005, they keep their word.

14 FEBRUARY

1967 **Aretha Franklin** records 'Respect' in New York, transforming Otis Redding's song into an anthem for civil rights and women's rights, and kick-starting her career as a pop artist. It will peak at US #1 and UK #10.

1970 **David Mancuso** holds a private party at his loft apartment in New York, christening the event 'Love Saves the Day'. The first of many underground dance parties to be held at 'The Loft', it turns out to be an idealistic but influential precursor to communal disco club culture, where sexual and racial equality is celebrated. Mancuso chooses a wide variety of music, and does not cut or mix between tracks.

1970 Meanwhile, **The Who** record *Live at Leeds* at the city's university, including an expanded 15-minute take on 'My Generation'.

1977 **The B-52's** play their first-ever concert at a Valentine's Day house party in their hometown of Athens, Georgia.

1985 ROTD: 21-year-old **Whitney Houston**'s eponymous debut album contains three worldwide hits: 'Saving All My Love for You', 'How Will I Know' and 'Greatest Love of All'.

15 FEBRUARY

1977 Sid Vicious replaces Glen Matlock as bass guitarist with the **Sex Pistols**. Manager Malcolm McLaren claims, 'If Johnny Rotten is the voice of punk, then Sid Vicious is the attitude.'

1995 BOTD: Megan Pete in Texas. As **Megan Thee Stallion**, she will rise to fame in the late 2010s with a style of strident and sexually frank rap.

2010 ROTD: Almost exactly a year after her debut single, 'Obsessions', **Marina and the Diamonds** unveils her first album, *The Family Jewels*.

16 FEBRUARY

1955 **Elvis Presley** plays the Odessa Senior High School Field House in Texas. 'His energy was incredible, his instinct was just amazing,' is how 18-year-old **Roy Orbison**, in the audience, will remember it.

1957 As British television ends its practice of showing nothing between six and seven in the evening (so that parents can put children to bed), at 6.05 p.m. BBC TV plugs the gap and establishes a new form of Saturday-night music entertainment: *Six-Five Special*. Created by the Canadian producer Jack Good, the hosts are Josephine Douglas and DJ Pete Murray, who narrowly wins the job over a young Scottish actor and model named Sean Connery.

A wide variety of British musical guests will appear over its run, among them Tommy Steele, Chris Barber, Humphrey Lyttelton and Lonnie Donegan. The first edition showcases singer Michael Holliday, the jazz trumpeter Kenny Baker, the Ukrainian-born concert pianist Lev Pouishnoff and pop trio The King Brothers, whose leader Denis King would later write the themes to TV's *Black Beauty* and *Lovejoy*. There was comedy in the mix too: one performer, Trevor Peacock, would show up decades later in *The Vicar of Dibley*.

What *is* missing from the programme is the rock'n'roll wave from the USA — American performers tend not to appear due to musicians' union disagreements. In addition, the entire show has a budget of £1,000, and so expensive sets are eschewed in favour of bare studio space and an audience in shot.

1992 Shakespears Sister — comprising the former Bananarama singer Siobhan Fahey and the American singer and guitarist Marcella Detroit — begin an eight-week run at UK #1 with 'Stay'.

1998 At 10.30 a.m., BBC Radio 2's **Ken Bruce** introduces a daily music phone-in quiz to his morning show: 'Popmaster'. Twenty-five years later, both Bruce and his quiz move to the commercial station Greatest Hits Radio and to a TV spin-off on More4.

17 FEBRUARY

1940 BOTD: **Gene Pitney** in Connecticut. He will make the grade not only as a singer — 'Town Without Pity', 'Twenty Four Hours from Tulsa', 'Something's Gotten Hold of My Heart' — but as a successful songwriter in the 1960s with credits including 'He's a Rebel' for The Crystals, 'Rubber Ball' by Bobby Vee and 'Hello Mary Lou' by Ricky Nelson.

1960 **The Everly Brothers**, Don and Phil, sign a ten-year contract with the Warner Bros label. After enjoying previous hits on the Cadence label, their first single for Warners will be the US and UK #1 'Cathy's Clown'.

1986 ROTD: 'Love Missile F1-11' by **Sigue Sigue Sputnik**. After reportedly signing to the EMI label for £4 million (£350,000 is a bit more like it), the British technopunks' debut single is produced by Giorgio Moroder and incorporates samples from *Scarface* and *The Terminator*.

1997 Mark Radcliffe and Marc Riley (**Mark and Lard**) step in as hosts of the BBC Radio 1 breakfast show following the sudden departure of Chris Evans, but will last just eight months in the job.

2001 **Manic Street Preachers** play at Havana's Karl Marx Theatre, the first Western rock act to perform in Cuba. Among the 5,000-strong audience is President Fidel Castro.

18 FEBRUARY

1959 **Ray Charles** records 'What'd I Say' at Atlantic Studios, New York. Produced by Jerry Wexler with Tom Dowd as engineer, it will become his first pop hit and also, some claim, create the genre of soul music.

1972 ROTD: 'Mouldy Old Dough' by **Lieutenant Pigeon**, the only UK #1 to feature a mother and son. Meanwhile also ROTD: **Gilbert O'Sullivan**'s 'Alone Again (Naturally)', will top the US charts for six weeks.

1977 ROTD: On lead singer Brian James' 22nd birthday, **The Damned**'s *Damned Damned Damned*, produced by Nick Lowe, is the first British punk rock album.

2008 ROTD: *Seventh Tree*, **Goldfrapp**'s fourth album, abandons the electropop of their previous two records in favour of haunting tributes to psychedelia, sci-fi and surreal poetry.

19 FEBRUARY

1951 BOTD: Horace Hinds in Jamaica. As **Horace Andy** (a homage to songwriter Bob Andy), the reggae singer will work in the US and, from the mid-1980s, in Britain, with the likes of Massive Attack, Adrian Sherwood and Mad Professor.

1958 ROTD: On his 18th birthday, **Smokey Robinson**'s first single emerges on End Records in Detroit. 'Got a Job', recorded with his group the Miracles, is a response to The Silhouettes' 'Get a Job', and details the disappointment and drab reality of working for an awful boss. The record is produced by Berry Gordy.

1972 The BBC bans **Wings**' new single 'Give Ireland Back to the Irish', recorded in response to the Bloody Sunday massacre in Derry on 30 January, refusing to even announce the title on air. But the single becomes a surprise hit in Spain, where it tops the charts.

1991 ROTD: **R.E.M.**'s first single for two years, 'Losing My Religion', is more about 'losing one's temper or civility', according to Michael Stipe. The musical content of the song is the result of Peter Buck's efforts to learn the mandolin.

1996 At the Brit Awards in London, **Michael Jackson** turns up to accept the specially created Artist of a Generation Award, but his live stage performance of 'Earth Song', in which he appears to adopt the role of a healing messiah surrounded by 'sick children', is interrupted by a protest dance conducted by Pulp frontman **Jarvis Cocker**. Cocker is arrested and questioned by police – with solicitor-turned-comedian Bob Mortimer representing him – but is swiftly released.

Several artists including Everything but the Girl, Pete Waterman and Brian Eno support Cocker's stance. Cocker himself will refute the allegations from Jackson's record company that he might have attacked children: 'I just ran on and showed off. I did not make any physical contact with anyone. I just could not go along with it . . . the way Michael Jackson sees himself as some Christ-like figure with the power of healing.'

20 FEBRUARY

1950 BOTD: **Anthony H.** (or Tony) **Wilson** will have two simultaneous but very different careers: one for the ITV company Granada as a news presenter/reporter in Manchester; the other as founder of the city's Factory record label, which will discover acts such as Joy Division, New Order and Happy Mondays.

1981 ROTD: Basildon quartet **Depeche Mode**'s debut single, 'Dreaming of Me', written by founder member Vince Clarke.

1995 ROTD: Formerly part of Bristol hip hop collective The Wild Bunch, **Tricky**'s first album, *Maxinquaye*, is a gritty, hypnotic study of bereavement, addiction and survival.

2001 ROTD: 'Get Ur Freak On' is the result of being one song short for **Missy Elliott**'s third LP, whereupon producer Timbaland finds a six-note bhangra-style riff sampled from a single-stringed Punjabi instrument called a tumbi and lays it over a rhythm pounded out by a pair of Indian hand drums known as a tabla.

21 FEBRUARY

1961 BOTD: Roger Charlery, as **Ranking Roger**, will become resident toaster with The Beat on hits like 'Ranking Full Stop' and 'Stand Down Margaret', before co-founding offshoot group General Public.

1975 ROTD: **David Bowie**'s 'Young Americans' single – recorded two days after Richard Nixon's resignation as US president in August 1974 – with a young Luther Vandross on backing vocals.

1994 ROTD: 'I Want You' becomes the final UK top 20 hit for **Inspiral Carpets**, and the first-ever top 20 hit for the record's guest vocalist: Mark E. Smith of The Fall.

1995 **Blur** win four awards at the Brits: Best British Group, Best British Album (for *Parklife*), Best British Single (for 'Parklife'), and Best British Video (for, erm, 'Parklife').

2012 Five members of the feminist protest and performance art group **Pussy Riot** perform inside Moscow's Cathedral of Christ the Saviour. Their aim is to protest against the support shown by the leaders of the Orthodox Church for Vladimir Putin in his election campaign to become president of Russia. It is just one of Pussy Riot's notorious 'unsanctioned concerts' – impromptu performances deliberately held in forbidden places as, they argue, making their point illegally is the most effective way to garner media attention. The members of the group, which often samples British punk rock recordings by groups like Angelic Upstarts and Cockney Rejects, wear colourful balaclavas and hide behind aliases in interviews to protect their identities.

Scarcely one minute into a song entitled 'Punk Prayer (Mother of God Drive Putin Away)', a plea for the Virgin Mary to reject Putin and embrace feminism, the group are removed from the almost deserted cathedral. Three of them will be arrested and given prison sentences, attracting support from human rights groups including Amnesty International. One is granted a suspended sentence, while the other two are finally released in December 2013.

22 FEBRUARY

1989 Two new awards are introduced at the Grammys. Taking the prize for Best Rap Performance (over Salt-N-Pepa's 'Push It') are **DJ Jazzy Jeff and The Fresh Prince** for 'Parents Just Don't Understand'. More controversially, the winners of the inaugural Hard Rock/Metal Performance award are not favourites Metallica, nominated for . . . *And Justice for All*, but **Jethro Tull** with *Crest of a Wave*. Some members of the audience respond with audible laughter and booing after the result is announced by Alice Cooper, who accepts the award on behalf of the absent Tull. Ian Anderson later expresses his relief that his group weren't there to collect their first-ever Grammy, telling *Kerrang!*: 'There's no way I could have accepted it under those circumstances.'

1993 ROTD: **Radiohead** take the title of their debut album, *Pablo Honey*, from a sketch by phone pranksters The Jerky Boys, sampled on the track 'How Do You'. Also included is the song that will become the best-selling of their singles to date, 'Creep' (UK #7, US #34).

2021 Eight years after releasing *Random Access Memories* and 'Get Lucky', **Daft Punk** announce they are splitting up.

23 FEBRUARY

1967 Made in 1964, 'Al Capone' by **Prince Buster** – who describes himself as 'The Voice of the People' – belatedly enters the UK charts, eventually peaking at #18. It kick-starts a wave of Jamaican pop in the late 1960s and early 1970s, and inspires the 2-Tone scene at the end of the decade: the song's screeching tyres will be sampled by The Specials for their adaptation, 'Gangsters', while Madness will release a cover of another Prince Buster song (also called 'Madness') and pay tribute to him on their debut single, 'The Prince'. Perhaps more surprisingly, 'Al Capone' will also form the basis for the 1975 debut single 'Baby Do You Wanna Bump' by German-based studio group Boney M.

1999 ROTD: *FanMail*, containing the hits 'No Scrubs' and 'Unpretty', is the final **TLC** album released within Lisa 'Left Eye' Lopes's lifetime. Also ROTD: **The Roots'** *Things Fall Apart*, which is named after Nigerian author Chinua Achebe's novel of 1958.

2015 ROTD: London quartet **Public Service Broadcasting's** new album *The Race for Space* traces the history of the American and Soviet space race from 1957 to 1972, and makes use of a famous John F. Kennedy speech from 1962.

24 FEBRUARY

1976 Howard Schuman's incisive and imaginative music business serial ***Rock Follies***, with original songs by Roxy Music's Andy Mackay, premieres on ITV. Starring as fictional singing trio The Little Ladies are Charlotte Cornwell, Julie Covington and Rula Lenska.

2004 Grey Tuesday – a day of protest against the decision of EMI, who own The Beatles' catalogue. The record label has been trying to put a stop to hip hop producer **Danger Mouse's** inspired idea to combine vocal elements of Jay-Z's *The Black Album* with fragments of 1968's *The Beatles* (aka the 'White Album'). *The Grey Album* had taken shape over two weeks in December 2003, with Danger Mouse (aka Brian Burton) describing it as an art project and a deconstruction. For instance, he combines Jay-Z's original 'Change Clothes' song with the guitar riff from 'Piggies' (White, side two) and the bassline from 'Dear Prudence' (White, side one) to form a 'grey' incarnation of 'Change Clothes'.

If EMI aren't impressed, Paul McCartney doesn't sound too upset. 'Take it easy, guys, it's a tribute. It's exactly what we did in the beginning – introducing black soul music to a mass white audience.' Jay-Z, meanwhile, is 'honored to be on, quote-unquote, the same song with The Beatles.'

As for Danger Mouse, it is suggested maybe he should make 'The Turquoise Album' incorporating elements from Joni Mitchell's *Blue* and R.E.M.'s *Green*: 'While that's funny to say, it could be interesting if I sat down to do it.'

2017 ROTD: *Drunk* is bassist **Thundercat's** woozy, escapist and whimsical new album, with cameos from Kendrick Lamar, Michael McDonald and Kenny Loggins. Meanwhile, South Norwood's Michael Omari – **Stormzy**, no less, who describes grime as 'the sound of the UK' – arrives with *Gang, Signs and Prayer*.

25 FEBRUARY

1966 ROTD: A memorable feature of **The Yardbirds'** 'Shapes of Things' (UK #3, US #1) is guitarist Jeff Beck's innovative use of feedback.

1977 Polydor Records announce they have signed Woking trio **The Jam** for £6,000 to record a single and album, both called 'In the City'.

1985 ROTD: *Songs from the Big Chair* by **Tears for Fears**, so titled after Roland Orzabal saw the 1976 film *Sybil*, about a woman with a multiple personality disorder whose safe space is the big chair in her analyst's therapy room.

2002 ROTD: Clocking in at under two minutes, 'Fell in Love with a Girl' by **The White Stripes** also attracts considerable attention for its Lego animation video, directed by Michel Gondry.

26 FEBRUARY

1965 ROTD: Based on the same traditional gospel song that inspired The Staple Singers' 'This Could Be the Last Time' in 1954, 'The Last Time' is the first A-side by **The Rolling Stones** to be written by Mick Jagger and Keith Richards.

1971 BOTD: Karl Martin Sandberg in Stockholm. As **Max Martin** he will begin his career fronting rock band It's Alive, before finding international success as a writer-producer for Backstreet Boys, Britney Spears, Katy Perry, Taylor Swift and Ariana Grande.

1980 ROTD: **Blondie**'s 'spaghetti-Western disco tune' 'Atomic' becomes the first of three UK #1s for the band this year, the others being 'Call Me' and 'The Tide is High'.

27 FEBRUARY

1983 Manchester foursome **The Smiths** spend one day at Strawberry Studios, Stockport, recording their self-produced first single, 'Hand in Glove'. They will soon sign to Geoff Travis's Rough Trade label.

1995 ROTD: *To Bring You My Love* is the first of **PJ Harvey**'s many collaborations with John Parish. Meanwhile, Creation band **The Boo Radleys** unleash their future top 10 single, 'Wake Up Boo!'

2006 ROTD: The title of 'Hips Don't Lie' by **Shakira** came into being when the Colombian singer instructed her band in the studio to watch the movement of her hips to see if a song was working.

28 FEBRUARY

1964 ROTD: 'A World Without Love', credited to Lennon–McCartney (although it was composed solely by McCartney some six years earlier), is released as a cover by **Peter** Asher and **Gordon** Waller – the former being the brother of McCartney's actor girlfriend Jane.

1976 Accepting his Grammy Award for Record of the Year, for *50 Ways to Leave Your Lover*, **Paul Simon** thanks **Stevie Wonder** (winner of Record of the Year in 1973, 1974 and 1975) for not making an album in the past 12 months.

1983 DOTD: **Winifred Atwell** in Sydney, Australia. Born in Trinidad, she remains the only woman to have topped the UK charts with an instrumental track, a feat she achieved twice – once in 1954 (with 'Let's Have Another Party') and again two years later (with 'The Poor People of Paris'). She was also the first Black artist ever to reach #1 in the UK charts.

Atwell initially pursued a career in medicine, but arrived in Britain in 1945 to study at the Royal Academy of Music. Bookings in theatres and spots on radio followed, with her repertoire extending from classical music (performed on a grand piano) into ragtime, honky-tonk and jazz (on an upright piano). A fierce campaigner against racism and bigotry who notably stood up for the rights of Aborigines in Australia, she mentored the singer Matt Monro, and influenced several later keyboard wizards including Keith Emerson and Rick Wakeman. Elton John – another Royal Academy of Music student – was an Atwell fan. 'My first pianist hero,' he told BBC 6 Music in 2016. 'She played the piano so joyously and she smiled.'

1994 ROTD: **The Beautiful South**'s 'Good as Gold (Stupid as Mud)' is their first single with their new singer, Jacqueline Abbott.

2010 ROTD: The debut single from British rapper Patrick Okogwu, alias **Tinie Tempah**, is 'Pass Out', which will hit UK #1, and win awards at the Brits and the Ivor Novellos.

29 FEBRUARY

1968 At London's Royal Albert Hall, **Yoko Ono** performs as a vocalist in the premiere of Ornette Coleman's new work, *Emotion Modulations*.

1968 Meanwhile, at the Grammy Awards, **The Beatles'** *Sgt. Pepper's Lonely Hearts Club Band* is the first rock LP to win the Best Album category (after two consecutive wins for Frank Sinatra), while the introduction of the Female R&B Vocal Performance category sees **Aretha Franklin** triumph for 'Respect', the first of her eight consecutive wins.

1988 ROTD: Having played bass guitar in The Housemartins for three years, **Norman Cook** (as Double Trouble) officially debuts as DJ and producer, incorporating a sample of The Jackson 5's 'I Want You Back' into his remix of Eric B & Rakim's 'I Know You Got Soul'.

1996 **Status Quo**, at #24 in the UK singles chart with a cover of 'Fun, Fun, Fun' (recorded with some of The Beach Boys), announce they intend to sue BBC Radio 1 for not putting the record on their playlist. After the station had radically changed its brand in 1993, it had decided to focus on mostly playing new music by younger artists.

MARCH

1 MARCH

1958 **Buddy Holly and the Crickets** begin their only tour of the UK at the Elephant and Castle Trocadero in south London.

1974 With 'Seven Seas of Rhye' about to give them their debut UK hit (#10), **Queen** embark on their first headlining UK tour at the Blackpool Winter Gardens. They have previously supported Sparks and Mott the Hoople.

1974 ROTD: Written by two former members of the Pete Best Four for a never-made 'rock'n'roll musical', and showcasing Paul da Vinci's distinctive falsetto, 'Sugar Baby Love' by **The Rubettes** will take two months to enter the charts, but once there, will rocket to UK #1.

1984 **Prince** records 'When Doves Cry' in Hollywood, without his group the Revolution. It is the final track to be recorded for the *Purple Rain* album.

2 MARCH

1960 **Elvis Presley** is discharged from the US Army in Germany and flies back to his homeland – stopping off for two hours at Prestwick Airport, Scotland, the only time he ever steps onto British soil. 'Where am I?' he asks the crowd who have gathered.

1963 **The Beatles'** 'Please Please Me' overtakes Frank Ifield's 'Wayward Wind' on the *NME* singles chart, giving them their first UK #1 hit, although on most of the rival published charts (and so most subsequent books and websites on UK chart history) they do not rise above #2.

1976 Tina Charles' 'I Love to Love', produced by Bangalore-born Biddu Appaiah, reaches UK #1. Charles first came to prominence in 1971 as the regular singer on the first series of *The Two Ronnies*.

1984 *This is Spinal Tap* opens in US cinemas. 'The whole idea was to do a send-up of rock, but by people who loved it,' says director and co-writer Rob Reiner of the mock-rockumentary.

Spinal Tap began life in a Reiner TV special called *The TV Show* in July 1979 in which they performed a song called 'Rock and Roll Nightmare', but the model for the character of guitarist Nigel Tufnel dates back to 1974, when alter ego Christopher Guest happened upon an unnamed British heavy metal band and their road manager in an LA hotel foyer. The band's bass player had lost his instrument at the airport and, rather than go back there and find it, chose to sulk at the hotel manager. 'This went on for a good 20 minutes,' marvelled Guest.

Michael McKean, aka Tap singer David St Hubbins, told a *Rolling Stone* reporter of a press interview with another band: 'The guy is saying things like, "Well, we like to view ourselves like we're troubadours, you know. From the ancient days of song. Wandering around the countryside . . ."'

Getting a studio to agree to an improvised film was tricky, but Embassy finally gave the green light, and an estimated 50 hours of footage was amassed, before it was edited down to the final 80 minutes. Once each scene was agreed, nearly all the dialogue was created on the spot. The band also played two club dates in front of real audiences, one as opening act for Iron Butterfly.

'They sound longer than they are,' Harry Shearer (bassist Derek Smalls) tells *Village Voice* of Tap songs like 'Sex Farm' and 'Stonehenge'. 'We've been able to capture a feeling of 15 minutes of boredom in a nice two-and-a-half-minute package.'

1989 Just before its release as a single, **Madonna**'s 'Like a Prayer' premieres on a TV commercial for Pepsi subtitled 'Make a Wish' – but the company hastily pulls the ad due to its combination of sexual and religious imagery.

3 MARCH

1986 ROTD: **Metallica**'s third album, *Master of Puppets*, rapidly expands the band's fanbase when they tour US arenas for nearly six months supporting Ozzy Osbourne. The album's title track, as a single, will reach US #35.

1989 ROTD: **De La Soul**'s *3 Feet High and Rising*. Colourful, humorous and sharp, the short-lived movement called the Daisy Age dawns when Dave Jolicoeur (Trugoy the Dove), Vincent Mason (Mace) and Kelvin Mercer (Posdnuos) join forces with Stetsasonic DJ and producer Paul Huston (Prince Paul) to make this stunningly original 23-track debut LP.

The trio had rifled through not only their own record collections but those of their parents to find interesting sample material, and the resulting sonic patchwork quilt quotes everyone from Hall & Oates and Steely Dan to George Clinton and Liberace – producing a record that one critic will describe as 'Fear of No Music' and another as 'The *Sgt. Pepper* of hip hop'.

The album will spin off several hits – 'Me Myself and I', 'The Magic Number', 'Buddy', 'Eye Know' and 'Say No Go' – but one single sample will land them in trouble: an uncleared loop from 'You Showed Me' by The Turtles mashed up with material from a French instruction tape.

On 3 March 2023, with nearly all samples intact after reclearing, *3 Feet High* is finally reissued and debuts on streaming services, just three weeks after Jolicoeur's untimely death at the age of 53.

2017 ROTD: ÷ (*Divide*) by **Ed Sheeran** sells 672,000 copies in its first week, and sees nine of its tracks place in the UK top 10 singles chart.

4 MARCH

1966 The *Evening Standard* publishes its reporter Maureen Cleave's interview with The Beatles' **John Lennon**. 'Christianity will go,' Lennon believes. 'We're more popular than Jesus now; I don't know which will go first – rock'n'roll or Christianity.'

1976 **ABBA** arrive in Sydney, Australia, where 'Mamma Mia' has just been #1 for 10 weeks, and 'Fernando' will soon top the charts for another 14 weeks. During their nine-day promotional visit, they will record a special for Channel 9 and a string of other TV spots, including the game show *Celebrity Squares*.

1994 Victoria Adams, Melanie Brown, Melanie Chisholm and Michelle Stephenson attend an audition in London for a new all-female vocal group – initially called Touch. Later, with Emma Bunton added to the line-up as a replacement for Stephenson, they will find fame as the **Spice Girls**.

5 MARCH

1951 By playing through an amplifier that had been damaged after falling out of the group's vehicle, Willie Kizart accidentally invents guitar distortion during a recording session for Ike Turner's Kings of Rhythm's 'Rocket 88' (released under the name **Jackie Brenston & his Delta Cats**). It is also considered as a contender for the first-ever rock'n'roll recording.

1971 ROTD: **Nick Drake**'s second LP, *Bryter Layter*, is issued by Island Records. Meanwhile, at Belfast's Ulster Hall, **Led Zeppelin** unveil four yet-to-be-recorded songs in their live set, one of which is 'Stairway to Heaven'.

1985 **Dead or Alive**'s 'You Spin Me Round (Like a Record)' becomes the first of 13 UK #1 singles to be produced by Stock Aitken Waterman.

6 MARCH

1947 BOTD: Pauline Matthews from Bradford, who in 1970 as **Kiki Dee** will become the first white British artist to sign to Tamla Motown, before achieving several hits on Elton John's Rocket label.

1961 Fifteen-year-old Mancunian actor **Davy Jones** makes a single appearance in ITV's *Coronation Street*, playing Ena Sharples' grandson Colin Lomax. Five years later, he will become one-quarter of The Monkees.

1971 Exactly 14 years after gaining independence from British colonial rule (the first country on the continent of Africa to do so), Ghana stages an all-night 14-hour Independence Day concert in Accra. Part of an eight-day celebration, the concert is intended to encourage residents and visitors to unite and share musical traditions and humanitarian values.

Despite the dress rehearsal being disrupted by a typhoon, the *Soul to Soul* show goes ahead, with 100,000 spectators watching homegrown acts such as The Divine Drummer Guy Warren, Charlotte Dada and Kwa Mensah, plus visiting American ones, among them Wilson Pickett, Ike & Tina Turner, Roberta Flack, the Voices of East Harlem, and Santana, whose mix of Latin and rock music is said to have been a major influence on the rise of Afrobeat.

A subsequent film, *Soul to Soul*, directed by Denis Sanders, will document the concert itself and also show footage of the film-makers visiting Ghana's countryside, communities, churches, and even the slave fortresses, which were once debarkation points for slaves being transferred to the US.

1981 ROTD: Though it receives limited radio play and peaks at UK #45, '(We Don't Need This) Fascist Groove Thang' is the critically acclaimed first single from Sheffield's **Heaven 17**, two-thirds of whom have just broken away from The Human League.

7 MARCH

1969 ROTD: *From Genesis to Revelation*, the first album by **Genesis**: Peter Gabriel, Tony Banks, Anthony Phillips, Mike Rutherford and John Silver. On the same day comes **The Who**'s 'Pinball Wizard' single, the first fruits of their *Tommy* concept album.

1983 ROTD: The seven-minute 'Blue Monday' by **New Order**, packaged as a die-cut sleeve to look like a floppy disk, will reach only UK #9, but sells over 700,000 copies, exclusively on 12-inch vinyl.

2011 ROTD: **R.E.M.**'s *Collapse into Now*, with a sleeve depicting Michael Stipe bidding farewell, turns out to be the group's final album.

8 MARCH

1965 The BBC2 live show *Gadzooks! It's All Happening* welcomes guests including comedian Peter Cook and the **Manish Boys**, promoting their new single 'I Pity the Fool' (with 18-year-old proto-Bowie David Jones in the line-up). In America, new singles ROTD include 'Subterranean Homesick Blues' by **Bob Dylan** and 'Help Me, Rhonda' by **The Beach Boys**.

1968 In Manhattan, Bill Graham opens the **Filmore East** venue. Over the course of its short three-year life, it will act as the backdrop to many live albums by acts such as The Allman Brothers Band, Miles Davis, Grateful Dead and Derek & the Dominos.

2019 ROTD: *Psychodrama* by **Dave**. A debut for the Streatham rapper, the future #1 album is split into three sections ('Environment', 'Relationships' and 'Social Compass') chronicling his south London upbringing and circumstances.

9 MARCH

1970 On the day of a gig in Columbus, Georgia, most of **James Brown's** existing band – feeling underpaid and undervalued – threaten to quit. Brown calls their bluff, and hires Cincinnati group The Pacemakers, who will back him (as The J.B.'s) on such future hits as 'Sex Machine' and 'Talking Loud and Saying Nothing'.

1986 In New York, Steven Tyler and Joe Perry record their contributions to **Run-DMC's** remake of Aerosmith's 'Walk This Way'.

1987 ROTD: While **U2's** *The Joshua Tree* is the day's big new album, Bill Drummond and Jimmy Cauty issue their rough but satirical 'All You Need is Love' (with samples of Samantha Fox, The Beatles and John Hurt), their first single as **The Justified Ancients of Mu Mu.**

2018 The final print edition of the *NME* is issued, some 66 years after its original publication.

10 MARCH

1964 Two landmark recording sessions take place. In Nashville, **Roy Orbison's** 'It's Over'. In New York, the first (acoustic) recording of **Simon and Garfunkel's** 'The Sound of Silence'.

1981 **Roxy Music's** tribute to the late John Lennon, a dramatic six-minute reworking of his song 'Jealous Guy', becomes their only UK #1 hit.

1998 The Saehan **MPMan**, the first portable MP3 player, is launched at the CeBIT trade fair in Hanover, Germany. The device's eight-hour battery life, sound quality and portability are impressive; less so, perhaps, is its storage capacity, housing barely half-an-hour of music.

2003 Nine days before US forces begin air strikes on Iraq, Texan-born country music trio **The Chicks** (then known as Dixie Chicks) take the stage at London's Shepherd's Bush Empire venue. Lead singer Natalie Maines introduces their song 'Travelin' Soldier' with the words: 'We do not want this war, this violence, and we're ashamed that the President of the United States [George W. Bush] is from Texas.'

The words are reported in a review of the gig in the *Guardian*, and the traditionally right-of-centre country industry in the US acts swiftly: Clear Channel, owner of 1,200 radio stations, bans the group's records from broadcast. The trio receive support from artists including Bruce Springsteen and Madonna, but backing from within the country music fraternity is rather more limited. Though Maines initially apologises for her statement, she soon retracts her apology and will require round-the-clock armed protection.

Yet she and the other Chicks remain unrepentant. 'That night it felt just too strange not to say anything,' Maines would later reflect. 'It would have been trite to not acknowledge it.' On the trio's return to the same London venue in 2006, their merchandise will be emblazoned with 'The Only Bush I Trust is Shepherd's Bush'. A year later, a song about their experience, 'Not Ready to Make Nice' will win a Grammy for Song of the Year.

11 MARCH

1974 ROTD: **Dolly Parton**'s second single from her *Jolene* LP, 'I Will Always Love You' is said to be a tribute to Porter Wagoner with whom the singer has duetted for seven years on his TV show. It will become a #1 country hit for her twice (1974, 1982), before, of course, being covered by Whitney Houston and featuring in a TV advert for Birds Eye beef burgers.

1977 At the Coliseum in Harlesden, north London, **The Slits** break the monopoly of all-male British punk rock line-ups. Supporting The Clash, alongside Buzzcocks and Subway Sect, Ari Up (vocals), Palmolive (drums), Kate Corris (guitar) and Tessa Pollitt (bass) perform four songs, which demonstrate that they're as interested in the spaciousness of reggae as the traditions of rock'n'roll. DJ and filmmaker Don Letts films their set on Super8.

'For a first-ever gig, it was outstanding,' Vivien Goldman writes in *Sounds* the following week. 'See them AS SOON AS YOU CAN.' 'No-one expects perfection,' writes *Melody Maker*'s Caroline Coon, 'and the Slits, confounding chauvinist scepticism, win on guts alone.'

Viv Albertine, watching in the audience, soon becomes the group's guitarist. 'Every decision we made, made it difficult for us,' she later says. 'People had never seen a group like us,' Tessa Pollitt will remember in 2018. 'It's like we were aliens that had just landed.'

1983 ROTD: 'Speak Like a Child' by **The Style Council**. It is the first single released by Paul Weller after the break-up of his previous band The Jam. It reaches UK #4.

2002 At 7 a.m., BBC Radio digital station **6 Music**, devoted to alternative music, goes on air for the first time. Its opening record, played by breakfast host Phill Jupitus, is 'Burn Baby Burn' by Ash.

12 MARCH

1958 Although France win the third Eurovision Song Contest in the Dutch city of Hilversum, the Italian contender, 'Nel blu, dipinto di blu', which finishes third, will become its break-out hit. Released as **'Volare'** by Domenico Modugno, it will top the *Billboard* Hot 100, and be covered by, among others, Dean Martin and Gipsy Kings.

1969 **Paul McCartney** marries American photographer Linda Eastman at Marylebone Town Hall, London.

1982 ROTD: Few hits this year are as low-key as **Japan**'s suitably haunting 'Ghosts', which will climb as high as UK #5.

2011 ROTD: Although not actually a hit, **Metronomy**'s 'The Look' will become perhaps their best-known song, appearing on soundtracks for screen work by both Pedro Almodóvar (*I'm So Excited!*, 2013) and Julia Davis (the end theme for *Sally4Ever*, 2018). 'It's this song that becomes bigger the more it stays around,' says the band's Joe Mount on its tenth anniversary.

13 MARCH

1964 ROTD: Composed by Smokey Robinson, 'My Guy' will become the biggest hit of Motown's first female solo star, **Mary Wells**, reaching US #1 and giving the label its first UK top 10 single.

1968 ROTD: *Eli and the Thirteenth Confession* is New York singer-songwriter **Laura Nyro**'s second album. Its stand-out track, 'Stoned Soul Picnic' will shortly be covered – as will several of her songs – by The Fifth Dimension.

1979 'I Will Survive' by **Gloria Gaynor** reaches UK #1. A withering putdown of an ex, and penned after co-writer Dino Fekaris was fired as a songsmith by Motown, the single has already hit #1 in the US. On the flip side (which was the original A-side) is Gaynor's cover of 'Substitute', previously a hit for the all-female South African group, Clout.

1995 ROTD: Fronted by Justine Frischmann, **Elastica**'s self-titled debut LP features the singles 'Line Up', 'Connection' and 'Waking Up'. It will become a UK #1 album.

14 MARCH

1960 On his first tour of the West Indies, **Sam Cooke** plays a concert at Montego Bay in Jamaica.

1975 ROTD: 10cc's *The Original Soundtrack* is their most ambitious record to date, featuring tracks such as 'Une Nuit a Paris' and worldwide hit 'I'm Not in Love' (UK #1, US #2).

1981 Californian punk band **Black Flag** play their first New York concert at the Peppermint Lounge in Times Square. In the audience: three members of the future Beastie Boys; Thurston Moore (shortly to co-found **Sonic Youth**); and Henry Rollins, soon to become Flag's new frontman.

1996 Appearing on *Top of the Pops*, alongside Robert Miles, Take That, Gabrielle and Mark Morrison, are Glasgow indie trio **Bis**. Playing their single 'Kandy Pop', they are the first 'unsigned' act to perform on the show.

15 MARCH

1955 For the first time, **Fats Domino** records outside his hometown of New Orleans. 'Ain't That a Shame' is made in Hollywood, while Domino is on tour. The first song that the teenage John Lennon teaches himself to play on the guitar, it will also be covered in typically polite style by Pat Boone who almost decides to retitle it 'Isn't That a Shame?'

1968 ROTD: A pair of imminent UK #1 hits: 'Lady Madonna' by **The Beatles**, and 'Congratulations' by **Cliff Richard**.

1982 ROTD: 'Only You' introduces **Yazoo**: the bluesy voice of Alison Moyet and ex-Depeche Mode songwriter Vince Clarke. It will climb to #2 in the UK, with its B-side, 'Situation', becoming a cult club hit.

1998 'It's Like That' by **Run-DMC**, a remix of their 1983 track by house DJ Jason Nevins, begins a six-week run as UK #1.

16 MARCH

1970 DOTD: Succumbing to cancer at the age of just 24, the Motown singer **Tammi Terrell** also suffered physical abuse in relationships with James Brown and The Temptations' David Ruffin. She is best remembered for her duets with Marvin Gaye (including 'Ain't No Mountain High Enough' and 'You're All I Need to Get By').

1976 ROTD: The next hits to roll off the Motown production line: **Marvin Gaye**'s *I Want You* album, and **Diana Ross**'s 'Love Hangover' single.

1979 ROTD: *Live at the Witch Trials*, not actually live but recorded in a single day, is the first album released by **The Fall**, with tirades on drugs, dead-end jobs and the music industry.

2009 ROTD: **La Roux**'s 'In for the Kill'. Partly inspired musically by the Japanese-American 80s cartoon series *Pole Position*, the song will provide the English duo with a UK #2 hit.

17 MARCH

1958 ROTD: Beating *Elvis' Golden Records* by only four days to become the world's first 'greatest hits' collection, the 12-track *Johnny's Greatest Hits* is a stop-gap release by Columbia while **Johnny Mathis** is abroad on tour. It will stay on the *Billboard* album charts for nearly 10 years.

1978 In Limerick, teenage Dublin quartet The Hype enter the heats of the Harp Lager Contest under their new name of **U2**. They progress to the finals the following day where they win £500 and a recording contract with CBS Ireland.

1992 ROTD: **k.d. lang**'s *Ingénue*, 10 songs about a failed romance, sees her shifting away from her country roots towards a blend of pop, folk, jazz and samba. Closing track 'Constant Craving' (US #38, UK #15) will win her a Grammy Award.

18 MARCH

1967 Still just about part of The Spencer Davis Group for two more weeks, 18-year-old singer and organist **Steve Winwood** announces a new musical project with Dave Mason, Chris Wood and Jim Capaldi. 'I wanted to explore music a bit more . . . bring in folk, classical music and even elements of ethnic music.' The group will be called **Traffic**.

1977 ROTD: **The Clash**'s 'White Riot'/'1977'. The group's first single for CBS will peak at UK #38. Its A-side was written after Joe Strummer and Paul Simonon were involved in the Notting Hill riots the previous August. 'We participated in the riot,' Strummer later recalls, 'but I was aware all of the time that it was a Black people's riot. They had an axe to grind and they had the guts to do something about it.' The 'clash' between the community and the police also gave the group their name.

1996 ROTD: With samples from The Breeders, Art of Noise and house group Ten City, 'Firestarter' by **The Prodigy** is on its way to UK #1.

19 MARCH

1971 ROTD: **Leonard Cohen**'s third LP, *Songs of Love and Hate*, contains several of his most enduring songs: 'Joan of Arc', 'Avalanche' and perhaps above all, 'Famous Blue Raincoat'.

1990 ROTD: 'We called it *Violator* as a joke,' says **Depeche Mode**'s Martin Gore. 'We wanted to come up with the most extreme, ridiculously heavy metal title that we could.' A UK #2 album, it peaks at #7 in the US.

2021 One of the year's most unexpected chart hits is the remix of the sea shanty 'Wellerman' by **Nathan Evans**, which hits the UK #1 spot with the help of TikTok and TV exposure.

20 MARCH

1955 Richard Brooks' screen adaptation of Evan Hunter's novel *Blackboard Jungle*, exploring tensions in an inner-city school, opens in New York. It makes a star of the 27-year-old Bahamian-American actor Sidney Poitier, while the film's opening credits bring Bill Haley's 'Rock Around the Clock' to a mass audience, thanks to leading actor Glenn Ford's son Peter, who already owned a copy of the single.

1965 In Naples, the Eurovision Song Contest is won by the Luxembourg entry: 'Poupée de Cire, Poupée de Son' (Wax Doll, Rag Doll) sung by **France Gall** and written by Serge Gainsbourg. For the first time, contemporary pop has been embraced by the voting juries in the competition, and it is undeniably catchy and clever, if verging on the cynical; it's a sly and self-reflexive exploration of manipulation and control where the songwriter is baiting the performer. Gall will later feel she had been exploited by its tone and will be reluctant to perform it again.

The single will reach #1 in France, and the top 10 in most of Europe although not in the UK, where the song did not receive a vote. Two years later, though, the UK writing team of Bill Martin and Phil Coulter will create their own song about control, 'Puppet on a String', which, sung by Sandie Shaw, will go on to win the competition.

1969 John Lennon and Yoko Ono marry at the British Consulate Office in Gibraltar. The tale of their journey there is detailed in the lyrics of The Beatles' final UK #1 single, 'The Ballad of John and Yoko'.

1988 Albert Hammond and Diane Warren's song 'Don't Turn Around' becomes a UK #1, two years after it was first recorded by Tina Turner as a B-side. During the 12-inch version of reggae trio **Aswad**'s successful remake, the group add the middle section of the song 'You've Lost That Lovin' Feelin'.

21 MARCH

1952 Cleveland, Ohio, is the setting for **The Moondog Coronation Ball**, generally regarded as the first rock concert. Organised by the Moondog Radio Show host and DJ Alan Freed, the advertised bill comprises Paul Williams and the Hucklebuckers, Tiny Grimes and the Rocking Highlanders, plus Varetta Dillard, and Billy Ward and His Dominoes (featuring Jackie Wilson and Clyde McPhatter).

The Friday night extravaganza is held at the 10,000-capacity Cleveland Arena, the home of the city's Barons Hockey team, and also a prime venue for boxing matches, but the arena rapidly becomes over-crowded and the concert spirals out of control. Concerns are raised about crowd safety, and the doors are broken down. After the event, the press in Cleveland mounts a campaign against Freed, and he ultimately leaves for New York.

1955 Over two years before Jerry Lee Lewis, **Big Maybelle** (born Mabel Smith, and professionally named after her big voice) records the original version of 'Whole Lotta Shakin' Goin' On'. The arranger and conductor on the session is a 22-year-old jazz trumpeter named Quincy Jones.

1977 ROTD: The first solo single by **Peter Gabriel**, 'Solsbury Hill', a song about 'letting go', was recorded in Toronto. Guitarist Robert Fripp was in the studio, but in his magnanimous words in 2010, 'I had nothing to add to the track after Steve [Hunter]'s superb and fitting contribution, although I would love to be on it.'

1988 ROTD: Boston quartet **Pixies'** defining debut LP *Surfer Rosa*, produced by Big Black's Steve Albini, will spend over a year on the UK indie chart, peaking at #2. One track, 'Gigantic', is re-recorded for single release.

22 MARCH

1975 Entering the Dutch singles chart at #21, eventually peaking at #13, is **Donna Summer**'s risqué 'Love to Love You', written with Giorgio Moroder and Pete Bellotte. Later that year, the song is remade and extended (to 17 minutes in its fullest version) as 'Love to Love You Baby' (US #2, UK #4), whereupon Summer becomes an international star.

1983 After seven top 40 hits, four of them top 10, **Duran Duran** crash into the UK singles charts at #1 with the standalone single, 'Is There Something I Should Know?'

1999 ROTD: 'Flat Beat' by **Mr Oizo**. A slice of insistent electro created under an alias by filmmaker and musician Quentin Dupieux, the track is unarguably the most unorthodox accompaniment to a Levi jeans TV commercial so far, but the presence of the yellow puppet Flat Eric helps it go to #1 all over Europe, if not in Dupieux's native France (#5).

2010 ROTD: **Laura Marling**'s *I Speak Because I Can*. Backed by Mumford & Sons and featuring lyrical homages to Homer's *Odyssey* and Margaret Atwood's *The Penelopiad*, the album sees the British singer-songwriter reach UK #4.

23 MARCH

1978 After one independent single as a quartet ('Fall Out'), Anglo-American trio **The Police** — made up of Sting, Andy Summers and Stewart Copeland — sign to A&M Records.

1979 ROTD: **Sparks'** 'The Number One Song in Heaven' (UK #14) is the American duo's European disco collaboration with Giorgio Moroder, who they wanted to work with after hearing Donna Summer's 'I Feel Love'.

1983 ROTD: *Eliminator* by **ZZ Top** mixes the group's well-established boogie rock with drum programming and synthesisers, plus several memorable videos embraced by MTV. It sells 11 million copies in the US alone.

2004 ROTD: Californian harpist, keyboardist, singer and songwriter **Joanna Newsom** issues her debut album, *The Milk-Eyed Mender*.

24 MARCH

1935 BOTD: Carol Smith in Everett, Washington. As **Carol Kaye,** she will play bass and guitar on almost countless recordings. Not just in pop – 'La Bamba', 'You've Lost That Lovin' Feelin'', *Pet Sounds*, 'Wichita Lineman', 'Raindrops Keep Falling on My Head', 'Across 110th Street' – but on TV and film soundtracks too: the themes to *The Addams Family*, *Batman*, *Hawaii Five-O* and *Dirty Harry*.

1987 Hackney sisters **Mel and Kim** Appleby reach UK #1 with the single 'Respectable', written and produced by Stock Aitken Waterman.

1992 ROTD: Two of the year's defining LPs: vocal quartet **En Vogue's** *Funky Divas* – a collision of R&B, hip hop, new jack swing and rock; and Southern hip hop collective **Arrested Development**, whose debut LP is named after the length of time it took them to get a recording contract: *3 Years, 5 Months and 2 Days in the Life Of . . .*

25 MARCH

1986 **Cliff Richard** becomes the first artist to reach #1 in the UK with two different versions of the same song: 'Living Doll' in 1959, and now, with the help of TV's *The Young Ones* (starring Adrian Edmondson, Rik Mayall, Nigel Planer and Christopher Ryan), via the first Comic Relief charity single.

2002 ROTD: *Original Pirate Material* is the first album by Mike Skinner's **The Streets**, combining garage and hip hop as an expression of working-class Britain.

2015 **Zayn Malik** becomes the first member to leave **One Direction**, and exactly one year later the first to release a solo album.

26 MARCH

1985 **Stevie Wonder** wins an Academy Award for Best Song, for 'I Just Called to Say I Love You'. During his acceptance speech, he dedicates his Oscar to imprisoned African National Congress (ANC) leader, Nelson Mandela, whereupon the South African Broadcasting Corporation announces they will no longer play Wonder's music.

'Any reference to Mandela is considered outlaw in South Africa,' says David Ndaba, the ANC's spokesman in New York. 'You can't quote him in public or publish his picture.' Indeed, a year earlier, two members of a South African reggae group have been sentenced to four years in prison for singing the Special AKA's 'Free Nelson Mandela'.

Wonder insists he is 'not out to hurt anybody, yet I feel we have to say what we feel'. A few months later, he will shrug at the SABC ban: 'I really don't mind. As a matter of fact, you should hear this next song coming out.' It is called 'It's Wrong (Apartheid)'. (In September 1985, the SABC lifts the ban anyway, claiming it had made its point.)

1990 ROTD: A pair of superlative singles both heading for UK #1: **Madonna**'s 'Vogue', and 'Killer' by **Adamski**, which heralds the voice of **Seal**, albeit in uncredited form.

2021 ROTD: 'MONTERO (Call Me By Your Name)' by **Lil Nas X**. Inspired by the André Aciman coming-of-age novel *Call Me By Your Name* and specifically its 2017 film adaptation by Luca Guadagnino, the song explores Montero's identity (that is indeed Lil Nas X's real first name) and the pressures of his status as a spokesperson on LGBT issues.

27 MARCH

1972 Appearing on an all-winners' edition of ITV's talent-spotting show *Opportunity Knocks* are two acts who will finally make their mark on the music scene four years later: Merseyside vocal group **The Real Thing** ('You To Me Are Everything') and The **John Miles** Set (whose leader would record 'Music').

1976 **Elton John** records his half of 'Don't Go Breaking My Heart', with **Kiki Dee** adding her part of the duet later. Unusually for the John/ Taupin writing partnership, the music is written first, with Taupin adding lyrics second. In July, it will become the first Elton John single to reach #1 in his native UK.

1995 ROTD: 'Not Over Yet' by **Grace**. The track, created by DJ/producers Paul Oakenfold and Steve Osborne, will chart twice (1995, 1999), and be covered in 2007 by The Klaxons.

28 MARCH

1958 **Eddie Cochran** records 'Summertime Blues' in Hollywood. There can't be many rock'n'roll songs that include a plea to the singer's congressman and the United Nations to overrule his boss's ban on time off.

1964 At 12 noon: 'This is **Radio Caroline** on 199, your all-day music station,' announces Simon Dee before introducing the station's first record, 'Not Fade Away' by The Rolling Stones. Named after the daughter of late US president John F. Kennedy, Radio Caroline is designed for two primary purposes: to meet a need for committed pop coverage that isn't being filled by BBC Radio, save for a few weekend programmes like *Saturday Club* and *Pick of the Pops* (Radio 1 is still three years away); and to provide a platform for music released by smaller music labels (Caroline creator Ronan O'Rahilly has been trying and failing to get airtime for musician Georgie Fame on both the BBC and Radio Luxembourg).

Having chosen to devise his own radio station, O'Rahilly decides the only way to circumvent the laws of the land in 1964 is to broadcast from a ship in international waters, in this case off the coast of Felixstowe. Among the DJs who will become presenters on the station are Tony Blackburn, Tommy Vance, Johnnie Walker and even future Tory MP Roger Gale.

1980 ROTD: Two post-punk musical landmarks: 'A Forest' by **The Cure** and 'Treason' by **The Teardrop Explodes** (which finally becomes a hit a year later).

1996 Sixteen years to the day after the release of the band's *Duke* LP, singer and drummer **Phil Collins** announces his departure from **Genesis**.

29 MARCH

1980 Following the death of Bon Scott in February, Brian Johnson (previously of the group Geordie) is announced as the new lead singer of **AC/DC**.

1993 ROTD: 'Ain't No Love (Ain't No Use)' by **Sub Sub**. Featuring Melanie Williams on vocals, and containing an irresistible sample of 1979's 'Good Morning Starshine' by Disco Spectacular, the track becomes the biggest hit for the dance act, who will later rebrand themselves as **Doves**.

2007 ROTD: Previously turned down by Britney Spears and Mary J. Blige, 'Umbrella' by **Rihanna**, featuring **Jay-Z**, will be UK #1 for 10 weeks, becoming the soundtrack to one of the wettest British summers on record.

2019 ROTD: 'Bad Guy' by 17-year-old singer-songwriter **Billie Eilish** delivers the distinctive sound of the street – literally: it features a sample of the sound of the 'walk' signal played to assist visually impaired pedestrians at road crossings in the Australian city of Sydney. Eilish's acclaimed debut album *When We All Fall Asleep, Where Do We Go?* is also released today.

30 MARCH

1974 Around 30 people show up on East 20th Street in Manhattan to see the first live show by the **Ramones**. In the audience is Tommy Erdelyi, soon to be the band's drummer.

1992 ROTD: **Bruce Springsteen**'s *Human Touch* and the more stripped-down *Lucky Town*, two albums from 'The Boss' on the same day.

1997 **The Chemical Brothers** land their second UK #1 with 'Block Rockin' Beats', its title taken from its sample of rapper Schoolly D's 1989 track 'Gucci Again'.

31 MARCH

1958 ROTD: 'Rumble' by **Link Wray**. Shunned by radio due to the affiliation of its title to gang fights, the instrumental track still reaches US #16.

1985 BBC Radio 1 begins its first series dedicated to the genres of reggae and lovers' rock, hosted by Margaret Anderson (a sibling of Rita Marley) under the name **The Ranking Miss P**.

2014 ROTD: 'My Silver Lining' by **First Aid Kit**. The folk-pop song, which will become a live and airplay favourite, is the work of Swedish sisters Klara and Johanna Söderberg.

APRIL

1 APRIL

1958 The BBC Radiophonic Workshop is set up at Maida Vale Studios to develop electronic music and effects across the whole of the corporation's output, from current affairs and education to drama and sci-fi, notably from 1963, in *Doctor Who*. The work of musicians and composers like Daphne Oram, Delia Derbyshire and Desmond Briscoe will influence – sometimes unwittingly – generations of artists.

1969 Barry Beckett, Roger Hawkins, David Hood and Jimmy Johnson (aka The Muscle Shoals Rhythm Section) rent a building in Sheffield, Alabama, and name it the Muscle Shoals Sound recording studio. Cher's 1969 album is named after its address: 3614 Jackson Highway.

2006 *Spin* magazine reviews the endlessly delayed Guns N' Roses album *Chinese Democracy* – an April Fool's joke as the album still hasn't materialised. (It is ultimately released in 2008.)

2 APRIL

1973 ROTD: Three years after their official break-up, highlights from The Beatles' recording career are celebrated across two double compilation albums covering *1962–1966* ('The Red Album') and *1967–1970* ('The Blue Album'). Alan Partridge will be thrilled.

1982 ROTD: 'Promised You a Miracle' by Simple Minds. Peaking at #13, and the first of 24 consecutive top 40 singles for the band, the song marks their commercial breakthrough in the UK.

1991 ROTD: **The Orb**'s *Adventures Beyond the Ultraworld*, their debut double album, clocking in at nearly two hours, and a defining moment in the development of what becomes known as 'ambient house'.

2006 Gnarls Barkley's 'Crazy' — a collaboration between producer Danger Mouse and singer CeeLo Green — becomes the first single to reach UK #1 based entirely on download sales. (A physical CD single format is released the next day.)

3 APRIL

1968 ROTD: **Simon and Garfunkel**'s *Bookends*, a concept album about ageing, and with many of the duo's best-loved songs: 'America', 'Hazy Shade of Winter' and 'Old Friends', plus 'Mrs Robinson' from the just-released comedy film *The Graduate*.

1973 **Lynyrd Skynyrd** record the nine-minute 'Free Bird' in Doraville, Georgia.

1986 Today, and for the next five and a half years, the theme tune of BBC1's *Top of the Pops* is 'The Wizard' by **Paul Hardcastle** (which itself will reach UK #15 as a single in the autumn).

1995 RealNetworks' **RealAudio Player**, able to stream media over the internet, is introduced.

4 APRIL

1964 The *Billboard* Hot 100's top five singles: #1 'Can't Buy Me Love' by **The Beatles**; #2 'Twist and Shout' by The Beatles; #3 'She Loves You' by The Beatles; #4 'I Want to Hold Your Hand' by The Beatles; #5 'Please Please Me' by The Beatles.

1968 Martin Luther King Jr is fatally shot in Memphis, Tennessee, a tragedy commemorated in several future hit songs, among them 'People Got to be Free' by The Rascals, Dion's 'Abraham, Martin and John' (covered by Marvin Gaye) and U2's 'Pride (in the Name of Love)'.

1991 BBC Radio 1 begins transmitting Pete Tong's *Rap Selection*, the station's first regular programme on rap.

2008 Jay-Z and Beyoncé marry in New York, with only 40 guests in on the secret. (The significance of the wedding date is that both were born on the fourth day of a month, respectively December and September.)

5 APRIL

1968 ROTD: New singles released in the UK today include 'Lazy Sunday' by Small Faces and Brian Auger & the Trinity and Julie Driscoll's cover version of Bob Dylan's 'This Wheel's on Fire'.

1980 Under the name Twisted Kites, R.E.M. play their first-ever public gig, providing birthday party entertainment at St Mary's Episcopal Church, Athens, Georgia. In their two-hour set are cover versions of Jonathan Richman's 'Roadrunner' and the Sex Pistols' 'God Save the Queen'.

1984 At Marvin Gaye's funeral in Los Angeles, Stevie Wonder sings a new song, 'Lighting Up the Candles', which he had planned to record with Gaye as a duet. (He eventually records it for his *Jungle Fever* soundtrack album in 1991.) Later the same day, Wonder records his harmonica part for Chaka Khan's 'I Feel for You'.

1988 ROTD: DJ Mark Moore makes his recording debut with club anthem and crossover #1 pop hit 'Theme from S-Express', built around a sample of Rose Royce's 1979 hit 'Is it Love You're After'.

2019 ROTD: US singer-songwriter **Weyes Blood**'s widely acclaimed fourth LP is *Titanic Rising*, about surviving the pressures of modern life and climate change.

6 APRIL

1963 **The Kingsmen** record perhaps the most famous version of 'Louie Louie' (US #2) in Portland, Oregon. The song was first recorded in 1956 by songwriter Richard Berry and his group The Pharaohs.

1974 At just after 10 p.m., at the Brighton Dome, Sven-Olof Walldoff takes to the platform dressed as Napoleon Bonaparte to conduct the Swedish entry in the Eurovision Song Contest. 'Waterloo' is performed by **ABBA** – Agnetha, Björn, Benny and Anni-Frid – who were already firmly established as cornerstones of the Swedish music scene even before their official formation in 1972, and had entered Eurovision with 'Ring Ring' in 1973, finishing in third place (the single flopped in Britain, despite having had its lyrics translated into English by Neil Sedaka).

Prior to 1974, the Eurovision rules stipulated that songs had to be sung in the respective country's home language, but this rule is relaxed just in time for 'Waterloo' to be sung in English. Winning the competition, the song soon becomes the first of ABBA's nine UK #1 singles, although it's worth noting that the United Kingdom jury did not award it a single point in the voting.

It is an unusually strong year for Eurovision in the UK singles charts: the second- and third-placed songs (Gigliola Cinquetti's 'Go (Before You Break My Heart)' for Italy, and Mouth & MacNeal's 'I See a Star' for the Netherlands) also reach the top 10, with the UK's own entry (Olivia Newton-John's 'Long Live Love') peaking at #11.

1998 DOTD: **Tammy Wynette** at the age of 55. By quite some coincidence, today also sees the death of 39-year-old **Wendy O. Williams**

(lead singer of New York punks the Plasmatics), who happened to cover Wynette's 'Stand By Your Man' with Lemmy in 1982.

2016 DOTD: **Merle Haggard** at the age of precisely 79. The country music singer joins a select band of public figures – among them Ingrid Bergman, Betty Friedan and Sidney Bechet – who have died on their own birthday.

7 APRIL

1975 In Paris, guitarist **Ritchie Blackmore** plays his final gig with **Deep Purple**, before quitting to concentrate on his own new group, Rainbow.

1985 After 18 months of their management negotiating with the Chinese government, **Wham!** become the first Western band to play in the country when they perform at Beijing's Workers' Gymnasium. Footage from their visit forms part of the video for their belated American release of 'Freedom'.

2003 ROTD: 'Bring Me to Life' by Arkansas rock band **Evanescence** will become a worldwide hit, spending four weeks at UK #1.

8 APRIL

1929 BOTD: **Jacques Brel** in Brussels. As a singer, composer and chanson giant, Brel's songs and melodies will make a considerable impact on the worldwide pop scene, notably through Scott Walker ('Jackie'), David Bowie ('Amsterdam'), Alex Harvey ('Next'), Terry Jacks ('Seasons in the Sun') and over 1,400 recordings of 'Ne Me Quitte Pas' (known in English under the title 'If You Go Away').

1968 **The Crazy World of Arthur Brown** record a session version of forthcoming single (indeed, forthcoming #1 hit) 'Fire!' for BBC Radio 1's *Top Gear*.

1991 ROTD: 'Dance music for the head, rather than the feet' is how **Massive Attack**'s Daddy G perceives *Blue Lines*, the Bristolians' debut blend of hip hop, reggae, soul and electronic music. Shara Nelson and Horace Andy are among the featured vocalists.

2022 ROTD: Two very different, but much discussed records this year: the debut album from Isle of Wight duo **Wet Leg**, and 'As It Was' by **Harry Styles**. Both will win Grammy and Brit Awards in February 2023.

9 APRIL

1969 **King Crimson** make their live debut at London's Speakeasy Club, where their five-song set includes '21st Century Schizoid Man' and 'In the Court of the Crimson King'.

1984 **Alphaville**'s 'Big in Japan' is West Germany's new #1 single, replacing 'Relax' by **Frankie Goes to Hollywood** (whose frontman Holly Johnson spent much of 1978 in another Liverpool band, Big in Japan).

2000 **Craig David**, vocalist on Artful Dodger's 'Re-Rewind', enters the UK chart at #1 with his solo debut, 'Fill Me In'.

2021 ROTD: *Fearless (Taylor's Version)* by **Taylor Swift**. The first version of the album, which was recorded in 2008 when Swift was 18 years old, topped the US album chart for 11 weeks, and was America's best-selling album of 2009.

Ten years later, when Swift's contract with the Big Machine record label has ended and she signs a new deal with Republic Records, her former manager Scooter Braun holds the copyright for Big Machine's back catalogue, which includes the recordings of her first six albums. What Big Machine does not own, though, is the *publishing* rights to those six albums. And so, Swift sets about re-recording them, with the assistance of most of the same musicians and producers from first time around. The lyrical content of the album remains almost entirely intact for the re-recording but, as Swift explains, 'if there was any way we could improve upon the sonic quality, we did'.

The effort and commitment pays off – 'Taylor's Version' of *Fearless* replicates the original's chart-topping placing in America, and goes to #1 all over the world. 'I do want my music to live on,' Swift tells *Billboard*. 'I do want it to be in movies, I do want it to be in commercials. But I only want that if I own it.'

10 APRIL

1970 One week before releasing *McCartney*, his first solo record, **Paul McCartney** publicly announces in a press statement that he is leaving **The Beatles**.

1985 **Madonna**'s first concert tour, the Virgin Tour, opens in Seattle. Her 13-song set is mostly taken from her two albums, with two brand-new songs, both from feature films: 'Gambler' turns up in *Vision Quest*, while 'Into the Groove' appears in the just-released *Desperately Seeking Susan*. 'Groove' is an international hit, her first #1 single in the UK, although in the US it is available only as a bonus track on the 12-inch version of 'Angel'.

For a support act on the tour, the Fat Boys and Run-DMC are briefly considered, but finally, the Beastie Boys are chosen, with their DJ Rick Rubin. 'It's not like any of us knew Madonna that much,' the group's Ad-Rock later recalls, 'but we all used to hang out at [New York nightclub] Danceteria. It was great for her because we were so awful that by the time she came onstage, the audience had to be happy.'

'The audience always booed them,' Madonna tells *Spin* in 1998, 'and they always told everyone to fuck off. I just loved that.'

1990 ROTD: A double celebration for landmark hip hop albums: **Public Enemy**'s *Fear of a Black Planet* and, making their debut, **A Tribe Called Quest** with *People's Instinctive Travels and the Paths of Rhythm*.

2000 ROTD: *Things to Make and Do* (UK #3) has been preceded by two big hit singles for **Moloko**: a remix of 'Sing it Back' by Hamburg DJ Boris Dlugosch (#4) and 'The Time is Now' (#2).

11 APRIL

1966 In Hollywood, **Frank Sinatra** records 'Strangers in the Night' (a song he hated) as the theme for a James Garner movie called *A Man Could Get Killed*. Sinatra's ad-libbing on the fade-out of the song will inspire TV executive Fred Silverman to call an animated Great Dane 'Scooby-Doo' in 1968.

1986 Channel 4 begins televising *The Chart Show*, a weekly compilation of current promo videos with no linking presenter but with relevant information provided by a series of computerised captions. The programme will move to ITV in January 1989, where it will air until August 1998.

1992 The trio **Seo Taiji and Boys** finish last on a South Korean TV talent show, performing 'Nan Arayo' ('I Know'), but their mix of dance, pop and rap – relatively new to South Korean audiences – will become immensely popular, acting as the catalyst for a wave of 'K-pop' in the 21st century.

1994 ROTD: In Britain, Creation Records releases the first Oasis single, 'Supersonic'. Meanwhile in Paris, Guy-Manuel de Homem-Christo and Thomas Bangalter issue 'The New Wave', their first release as **Daft Punk**.

The French duo have previously been part of a guitar band called Darlin', named after The Beach Boys hit (and which they covered, in instrumental form). The band released a handful of tracks on Stereolab's record label Duophonic, but a desultory notice in *Melody Maker* ('a daft punky thrash') caused de Homem-Christo and Bangalter not only to reconsider their name but their musical direction.

As Daft Punk they began their move into techno via a demo tape that they handed to the Scottish-based label Soma Quality Recordings. Aside from one or two early shoots, the pair decide not to show their own faces in photographs or on stage. 'We're into art, not information,' Bangalter later tells the *Guardian* in 2001. 'To present our faces would just be information data. [With masks] we can transform any promotional activity into creative activity.'

Bangalter's father Daniel Vangarde, incidentally, has considerable credentials as a pop songwriter himself, with successes including 'Cuba' by the Gibson Brothers (1979) and 'D.I.S.C.O.' by Ottawan (1980).

12 APRIL

1954 **Bill Haley and His Comets** record '(We're Gonna) Rock Around the Clock' at the Pythian Temple Studios, New York. They are not the first act to record the song – that honour went to Sonny Dae and His Knights just a few weeks before. But there's no question which version will be better remembered.

Haley is already nearly 30 years old, although positively youthful next to the song's co-writer Max C. Freedman, who is nearly 60, and the recording of 'Rock Around the Clock' is almost an afterthought, laid down at the end of the session in two takes. The main reason for the session is to capture on tape the quasi-novelty song 'Thirteen Women (And Only One Man in Town)', about impending nuclear destruction, and written in the aftermath of the explosion of the thermonuclear device Castle Bravo, at Bikini Atoll, on 1 March. The session's producer is Milt Gabler, uncle of comedian and actor Billy Crystal, and behind many of Louis Jordan's 1940s recordings, as well as the first person to put Louis Armstrong and Ella Fitzgerald together on record.

To begin with, 'Thirteen Women' will be the single's A-side, but 'Rock Around the Clock' soon becomes the more popular side, even if it takes another year to reach #1 in America. Sadly, Comets guitarist Danny Cedrone doesn't live to see that success; he dies in a fall in June 1954, aged just 33.

1973 Stevie Wonder appears on *Sesame Street* with his band to perform a special seven-minute version of 'Superstition'.

1988 Sonny Bono is elected the Mayor of Palm Springs in California, a post he will hold for the next four years.

1994 ROTD: Only days after the death of her husband Kurt Cobain, Courtney Love's band Hole releases their second album, *Live Through This*. Two of the songs on the album feature Cobain on backing vocals.

13 APRIL

1965 The Beatles win their first Grammy Award, for Best New Artist. (The other nominees are Petula Clark, Astrud Gilberto, Antônio Carlos Jobim and Morgana King.)

1973 ROTD: Bob Marley and the Wailers' first album for Chris Blackwell's Island Records, *Catch a Fire*, hits the shops, as does David Bowie's reflection on his first experiences of stardom: *Aladdin Sane*.

1982 One year and nine days after winning the Eurovision Song Contest, vocal quartet Bucks Fizz have their third UK #1 single, 'My Camera Never Lies'.

1987 ROTD: 'Sheila Take a Bow' by The Smiths – the second single by the band to reach the UK top 10. Also ROTD: *Tango in the Night* by Fleetwood Mac. The album contains three UK top 10 singles: 'Big Love', 'Little Lies' and 'Everywhere'.

14 APRIL

1969 ROTD: 'In the Ghetto' by Elvis Presley. Coming hot on the heels of his recent *Elvis* TV special, the single, written by Mac Davis, is commonly regarded as spearheading Presley's recording comeback.

It will return him to the top three for the first time since 1964 in the US and 1965 in the UK.

1980 ROTD: Two key albums of the new wave of British heavy metal – **Iron Maiden's** eponymous debut, and **Judas Priest's** *British Steel*.

1986 ROTD: 'Lessons in Love' will become the biggest (UK #3) of 20 top 40 hits by jazz-funk-pop band **Level 42**, fronted by bassist and singer Mark King. Meanwhile, **Peter Gabriel's** 'Sledgehammer' is accompanied by an ingenious animated promo video made by Aardman in Bristol.

2017 ROTD: If **Kendrick Lamar's** preceding album, *To Pimp a Butterfly* (2015), was all about changing the world – one fan of the song 'How Much a Dollar Cost' was President Barack Obama, no less – his new one, *DAMN.* has an attitude of 'I can't change the world until I change myself'. While 'DNA.' is a dismissal of Fox News pundits and Obama's successor Donald Trump (inaugurated in January), the tone of the rest of the album oscillates between bravado and insecurity: 'FEAR.', for example, is a verse-by-verse survey of Lamar's previous struggles, at ten-year intervals, while the album as a whole compels the listener to evaluate if his behaviour is wicked or simply weak.

In 2018, *DAMN.* becomes the first album from any pop genre to win a Pulitzer Prize for Music, with the panel feeling that it perfectly captures 'the complexity of modern African American life'. 'We listened to it,' said one Pulitzer judge, the music critic David Hajdu, 'and there was zero dissent.'

15 APRIL

1894 BOTD: **Bessie Smith** in Chattanooga. From 1923 through to her untimely death following a car accident in 1937, Smith will become a prolific blues recording artist and magnetic live performer. An influence on numerous subsequent artists, she will have a song named after her by The Band, and she will be played by Queen Latifah in a 2015 film for HBO.

1975 A three-year-old album track enters the UK singles chart, heading for #7. Beginning life on **Frankie Valli and the Four Seasons'** *Chameleon* (the group's only LP for Motown), 'The Night' builds up support through Northern soul circles in the UK and becomes Johnnie Walker's record of the week on BBC Radio 1.

1983 ROTD: Rough Trade releases *High Land, Hard Rain*, the debut LP by **Aztec Camera**, fronted by 19-year-old singer and guitarist Roddy Frame. On the same day, the Chrysalis label issues **Spandau Ballet's** 'True', songwriter Gary Kemp's composition about his relationship with Altered Images singer Clare Grogan. It will become a UK #1 single for four weeks.

1997 ROTD: 'MMMBop' by brothers Isaac (16), Taylor (14) and Zac (11) **Hanson**, which will hit #1 in the US and UK later in the spring.

16 APRIL

1956 In Chicago, **Chuck Berry** records four of his own compositions, two of which are 'Brown Eyed Handsome Man' and the classical-music-baiting 'Roll Over Beethoven'.

1972 **Electric Light Orchestra**, co-founded by Roy Wood and Jeff Lynne in an attempt to fuse classical and rock music (and who are themselves about to cover 'Roll Over Beethoven'), make their live debut in Croydon.

1984 ROTD: **Duran Duran's** 'The Reflex', remixed by Nile Rodgers, will become the first song to reach UK #1 in remixed form. Meanwhile, independent label 4AD issues 'Pearly Dewdrops' Drops', the first **Cocteau Twins** record to cross over to the top 40.

17 APRIL

1960 DOTD: At 4.10 p.m., on what is Easter Sunday, 21-year-old **Eddie Cochran** succumbs to the injuries he sustained in a road accident the previous night, just after he and Gene Vincent had performed at the Bristol Hippodrome, the final scheduled date on their British tour.

1971 All four ex-**Beatles** have solo singles in the UK top 40 this week: John's 'Power to the People' is at #10; Paul is one place below with 'Another Day'; George is at #25 with 'My Sweet Lord'; and Ringo's 'It Don't Come Easy' is at #29. All four songs remain together in the top 40 for two further weeks.

1982 ROTD: Although not a big pop hit as such (US #48, UK #53), the influence of the electro-funk classic single 'Planet Rock' by **Afrika Bambaataa and the Soulsonic Force** will be seismic. A version of the track first appeared in 1981 under the name 'Jazzy Sensation' before Bambaataa and producer Arthur Baker decided to join forces with keyboard player John Robie to give it a more electronic sound.

Over the course of three nights, 'Planet Rock' gradually took shape. At its heart is the beat from 'Numbers', a track from Kraftwerk's *Computer World* album. Baker later explains that at the Music Factory club in Brooklyn, he had seen 'Black guys in their twenties and thirties asking, "What's that beat?" So I knew if we used that beat and added an element of the street, it was going to work.' The melody of Kraftwerk's 'Trans-Europe Express' was also added to the mix, as was Captain Sky's 'Super Sporm'.

On the second night, the Soulsonic Force came in to rap over the backing track, although they disliked it so much that they would rap only off the beat. (According to Baker, one member, 'Mr Biggs', stayed completely silent in protest.)

Kraftwerk were initially miffed that their permission had not been sought, but an agreement was reached: they were offered a dollar for each sale of 'Planet Rock', and the retail price was duly increased by the same amount.

1994 Prince begins his one and only spell at #1 in the UK singles chart as a performer, with 'The Most Beautiful Girl in the World'.

18 APRIL

1967 BOTD: **Todd Terry** in Brooklyn. As a DJ and producer, he will first come to prominence in 1988 as part of Royal House and their floor-filler 'Can You Party' (UK #14). Perhaps his most enduring remix remains his transformation of Everything but the Girl's 'Missing' in 1995.

1988 ROTD: **Prefab Sprout**'s 'The King of Rock'n'Roll' is a song about an artist trapped by his one hit. Even though the group's albums always sell well, this is their only single to reach the top 10 (UK #7).

1994 ROTD: Eleven years after their first album, *It*, **Pulp** from Sheffield reach the mainstream with *His 'N' Hers*, which will enter the UK charts at #9.

19 APRIL

1971 ROTD: **The Doors**' final album in Jim Morrison's lifetime, *LA Woman*. Meanwhile, in New York, **Gil Scott-Heron** re-records his poem 'The Revolution Will Not Be Televised' with a full band for the B-side of his forthcoming single, 'Home is Where the Hatred Is'.

1974 ROTD: The **Bay City Rollers**' 'Shang-A-Lang' is an attempt by songwriters Bill Martin and Phil Coulter not only to evoke the Brill Building song tradition of the early 60s but also to echo the sound of Glasgow's shipyards. But using the lyric 'clang clang' is out of the question because it has already featured in 'The Trolley Song' by Judy Garland.

2019 ROTD: *Cuz I Love You*, trailed by her single 'Juice', is **Lizzo**'s first album for a major label, Atlantic, and will be reissued twice to accommodate two more smash hits: 'Truth Hurts' and 'Good as Hell' (with Ariana Grande). In 2020 it will win a Grammy Award for Best Urban Contemporary Album.

20 APRIL

1939 In a Fifth Avenue studio in New York, 24-year-old **Billie Holiday** records Abel Meeropol's 'Strange Fruit' for the Commodore label. Meeropol first wrote the song as a protest against the lynching of Black Americans, but Holiday's interpretation is further infused with the memory of her father Clarence, who died in 1937 in part due to the racist medical-care policies pursued by the authorities in Texas.

1959 ROTD: Goldband Records issues 'Puppy Love', the first single release by 13-year-old **Dolly Parton**. She wrote the song two years earlier with her uncle, Bill Owens. Although it took scarcely longer than 90 seconds to sing, the journey (on which she was accompanied by her grandmother Rena) from East Tennessee to the recording studio in Lake Charles, Louisiana, took 30 hours. 'I don't think I'll ever forget the way the inside of that bus smelled,' Parton later recalled. 'It was a combination of diesel fuel, Naugahyde, and people who were going places.'

'Puppy Love' proves to be a local success, leading in July 1959 to Dolly's debut at the Grand Ole Opry in Nashville, where her rendition of 'You Gotta Be My Baby' by George Jones will be introduced on stage by Johnny Cash. Still in the business more than 60 years later, in 2022 Parton will launch a new fashion line for canines: Doggy Parton.

1992 **Queen**'s Freddie Mercury Tribute Concert for AIDS Awareness is staged at Wembley Stadium, five months after Mercury's untimely death. As well as a host of special guest acts, like Metallica, Def Leppard and Guns N' Roses, Queen's three surviving members – Brian May, John Deacon and Roger Taylor – are joined in the second half by Elton John, David Bowie, George Michael, Annie Lennox and Lisa

Stansfield, plus many many more. It is John Deacon's final full concert with the band.

1998 ROTD: *Music Has the Right to Children* by **Boards of Canada**. The haunting first full-length album from siblings Michael Sandison and Marcus Eoin revolves around lost memories of gone-forever experiences.

21 APRIL

1970 As part of the Pop Proms week at the Roundhouse in London, the Tuesday bill of Tyrannosaurus Rex, Pretty Things and Heavy Jelly is augmented by the appearance of **Elton John** – his live debut as a solo act.

1972 ROTD: 'I was sitting there just running my fingers up and down the piano,' recalls Bill Withers of the creation of 'Lean on Me'. Withers is based in Los Angeles, but the lyrical content of the song is based on reminiscences of his childhood in the close community of Slab Fork, West Virginia.

2003 Just 10 days after the premiere of their film *Seeing Double*, S Club (reduced from S Club 7 after the departure of Paul Cattermole the previous year) announce from the stage of the O2 in London that they will be splitting up as a group. In 2023, all seven original members will reform for a reunion tour, but sadly, shortly after the announcement, Cattermole dies suddenly at the age of 46, in turn leading to the departure of Hannah Spearritt. The remaining five members will decide that the upcoming shows should be a tribute to Cattermole's memory.

22 APRIL

1966 ROTD: 'Wild Thing' by **The Troggs**. Not many worldwide hits have an ocarina solo – and nor did the original demo of the song by

Chip Taylor, who reveals, 'That was the engineer messing about putting his thumbs together and blowing through them.'

1985 ROTD: 'Duel' by German pop quartet **Propaganda** is released by ZTT, and will have the unique and perhaps unenviable honour of spending three weeks locked at #21 in the UK.

2002 ROTD: A loop of 'Are "Friends" Electric' by Tubeway Army has an unexpected afterlife on one of the year's biggest hits: the UK #1 'Freak Like Me' by **Sugababes**.

2011 DOTD: 84-year-old **Hazel Dickens**. Writing and performing pro-union and feminist songs in a duo with Alice Gerrard, Dickens was among the first women in bluegrass to make an album – 1965's *Who's That Knocking?* – which epitomised the genre's 'high lonesome sound'.

23 APRIL

1965 **The Four Tops** record 'I Can't Help Myself' at Hitsville's Studio A in Detroit.

1976 ROTD: *Ramones* by the **Ramones**, a frantic 29-minute album of 14 songs including 'Blitzkrieg Bop', 'I Wanna Be Your Boyfriend' and a cover of Chris Montez's 'Let's Dance'.

2016 ROTD: Made over nearly a year, the starting point of **Beyoncé**'s critically and commercially successful *Lemonade* was discovering her husband Jay-Z's infidelity, and tracing similar patterns through her family and through Black ancestry, with references ranging from Sister Rosetta Tharpe to Alice Walker and from Octavia Butler to Dionne Warwick.

24 APRIL

1954 After the rising popularity of rhythm and blues sees record companies make $15 million in 1953, *Billboard* magazine concludes in a front-page headline that 'Teen-Agers Demand Music With a Beat'.

1989 ROTD: Halfway through the CD version of his first solo album *Full Moon Fever*, **Tom Petty** announces a short pause, as a mark of respect to everyone who at this point would have to turn the record or tape over, before resuming with: 'Thank you. Here's side two.'

1995 ROTD: 'Some Might Say', the final **Oasis** single with drummer Tony McCarroll, will become their first UK #1. Meanwhile, **Björk's** 'Army of Me', created with 808 State's Graham Massey, and about taking responsibility for oneself, will become her first UK top 10 single.

25 APRIL

1958 A mini kwela boom is kick-started in Britain when 'Tom Hark' by South Africa's **Elias and His Zig-Zag Jive Flutes** reaches the UK top 30, on its way to #2. Its popularity has been boosted by its use as the theme to an ITV diamond-smuggling drama called *The Killing Stones*, featuring Donald Pleasence and Geoffrey Palmer.

Series writer Wolf Mankowitz came across the song while sifting through a selection of tapes from Johannesburg, where Elias and Co. had started out as street performers in the township of Alexandra. Their sound was dominated by the penny whistles of Elias and Jack Lerole, and it was Lerole who wrote 'Tom Hark' (a mutation of 'Tomahawk') for the band to record for EMI in August 1956.

Although the record will go on to sell 3 million copies worldwide, the group (who will subsequently become known as Alexandra Black Mambazo) will only ever receive a one-off payment, and the composer credit will go to the producer Rupert Bopape.

In 1980, 'Tom Hark', with additional world-weary words, will return to the top 10 courtesy of a Brighton two-hit wonder ('The

Piranhas play KWELA!' announces the sleeve), but Elias's version will make an unexpected comeback in 2009 when it once again becomes a TV theme – this time for BBC2's *Stewart Lee's Comedy Vehicle*.

1978 'Night Fever' becomes the **Bee Gees'** first UK #1 since 'I Gotta Get a Message to You' in 1968. The song's string intro, according to the session's keyboard player Blue Weaver, came as he was trying to arrange a disco version of the 1960 instrumental hit, 'Theme from a Summer Place' by Percy Faith.

1988 ROTD: 'Oh Patti (Don't Feel Sorry for Loverboy)' by **Scritti Politti**. The track features a trumpet solo by the great **Miles Davis**, who covered Scritti's 'Perfect Way' for his *Tutu* album in 1986. During a 40-year recording career, 'Oh Patti' marks the only time Davis reaches the UK top 20.

1994 ROTD: One of the high points of **Blur's** *Parklife* album is 'This is a Low', a celebration of the BBC Radio 4 shipping forecast.

26 APRIL

1964 ROTD: **Dionne Warwick's** 'Walk on By'. Written by Burt Bacharach and Hal David, the song will later be covered in a variety of styles: slowed down and extended by Isaac Hayes (1969) or sped up and extended by The Stranglers (1978).

1978 *The Last Waltz*, Martin Scorsese's documentary of the last concert performance of **The Band**, at the Winterland Ballroom, San Francisco, on Thanksgiving Day 1976, is released in US cinemas.

1991 'Greetings from **Tim Buckley**', a tribute concert to the late singer-songwriter who died in 1975, takes place at St Ann's Church, New York. Buckley's then-unknown son Jeff performs 'I Never Asked to Be Your Mountain', written by his father for him and his mother Mary.

27 APRIL

1971 **Dave and Ansell Collins** become the second Jamaican act to top the UK singles charts, two years after Desmond Dekker's 'Israelites'. The drummer on the duo's song 'Double Barrel' is 18-year-old **Sly** Dunbar, who will later form a dynamic rhythm section with bassist **Robbie** Shakespeare.

1973 ROTD: **Stealers Wheel**'s Gerry Rafferty deliberately performed 'Stuck in the Middle with You' as a pastiche of Bob Dylan's vocal style. It reaches US #6 and UK #8, and nearly 20 years later soundtracks a shocking scene in the movie *Reservoir Dogs*.

2018 ROTD: Perhaps the best-known track on *Dirty Computer*, the fourth album by **Janelle Monáe**, is 'Make Me Feel', and she reveals that none other than Prince 'helped me come up with sounds . . . before he passed on to another frequency'.

APRIL 28

1963 19-year-old Andrew Loog Oldham and booking agent Eric Easton go to the Crawdaddy Club in Richmond to see **The Rolling Stones** and make a successful offer to manage the band.

1969 ROTD: The eponymous first album by Chicago Transit Authority. Thereafter, the band will simply call themselves **Chicago** with most of their albums assigned only a number; 'If You Leave Me Now' will appear on *Chicago X*, and by 2022, they will reach *Chicago XXXVIII: Born for This Moment*.

1994 ROTD: Underpinned by a nagging four-bar sample from Michael McDonald's 'I Keep Forgettin'', **Warren G and Nate Dogg**'s 'Regulate' single will reach US #2 and UK #5.

29 APRIL

1968 The age of Aquarius dawns: *Hair*, generally regarded as the first rock'n'roll musical, opens on Broadway. Several recording artists appear in the production's original run including Meat Loaf and Vicki Sue Robinson.

1980 'Geno' by **Dexys Midnight Runners** reaches UK #1. The song owes its title to the fact that the band's frontman, Kevin Rowland, was inspired to become a singer at the age of 15 after seeing Geno Washington live at the Railway Hotel, in Harrow, in 1968.

1996 ROTD: *Casanova* by **The Divine Comedy**. It is the band's most ambitious album to date, partly because Setanta Records are able to provide a bigger budget thanks to the international success of Edwyn Collins' 'A Girl Like You'. Its track 'Songs of Love' is made by adding words to the familiar theme tune of cult comedy series *Father Ted*.

30 APRIL

1957 Between 10 a.m. and 1.45 p.m., **Elvis Presley** records 'Jailhouse Rock' in West Hollywood, California.

1978 On the Sunday of Britain's very first May Day Bank Holiday weekend, an estimated 100,000 people march from London's Trafalgar Square to Victoria Park in Hackney – soundtracked by the group Misty in Roots – to watch **Rock Against Racism**'s concert of punk and reggae: Carnival Against the Nazis.

The concert can trace its roots back to 1976 when Rock Against Racism (RAR) was founded. With a low profile to begin with, the movement saw a marked increase in support when several established rock artists expressed some sympathy for the bigoted views of Enoch Powell and the National Front – most notoriously Eric Clapton on stage in Birmingham that summer.

This gave rise to a regular RAR fanzine, the emergence of smaller local campaigning groups around Britain, and the recruitment of more musicians to back the cause, culminating in the concert itself: the headline band is The Clash, with the rest of the bill comprising Patrik Fitzgerald, X-Ray Spex, Sham 69's Jimmy Pursey, the Tom Robinson Band and, from Handsworth in Birmingham, Steel Pulse.

1988 In Dublin, 20-year-old Canadian singer **Celine Dion** wins the Eurovision Song Contest, singing the Swiss entry, 'Ne Partez Pas Sans Moi', which beats the UK's entry 'Go' by Scott Fitzgerald by just one point.

1993 At 12.15 p.m., the UK's first national commercial pop radio station, **Virgin 1215**, goes on the air on medium wave. The first song played is a specially recorded cover of 'Born to Be Wild' by INXS.

MAY

1 MAY

1956 ROTD: 'I Walk the Line'/'Get Rhythm', recorded at Sun Studios a month ago, will become the first single by **Johnny Cash** to cross over from the country-and-western charts to the *Billboard* pop charts, where it peaks at #17.

1991 For the first time, **BBC Radio 1** becomes a round-the-clock station. Whispering Bob Harris's midnight show is extended from two to four hours in length, while early breakfast host Gary King's start time is moved back from 5 to 4 a.m.

1998 The final episode airs of Channel 4's *Father Ted*, featuring a cameo appearance in the opening scene from 'Father **Brian Eno**'.

2 MAY

1979 At the Rainbow Theatre, London, **The Who** play their first live show since the death of drummer Keith Moon the previous September. Replacing Moon is Kenney Jones, formerly of Small Faces and Faces.

1980 Singer and lyricist Ian Curtis plays what will prove to be his final concert with **Joy Division** at Birmingham University. Just over two weeks later, Curtis will die at the age of 23. The set opens with 'Ceremony', which will be recorded by the surviving band members as **New Order**'s first single in 1981.

1989 ROTD: While **The Cure**'s *Disintegration* and **Simple Minds'** *Street Fighting Years* are the day's obviously big album releases, **The**

Stone Roses' influential self-titled debut will make a quieter start (#32), eventually rising to #19 in January 1990, and reaching the top 10 only in 2004.

3 MAY

1967 Gary Leeds, Scott Engel and John Maus, aka **The Walker Brothers**, announce they are splitting, with singer Scott Walker establishing himself as a solo artist within the year. (The trio will reform for two albums between 1976 and 1978, as well as the hit single 'No Regrets'.)

1986 **Dolly Parton** relaunches Silver Dollar City in Pigeon Ridge, Tennessee, as a new theme park called Dollywood.

1993 ROTD: The abrasive, tense *Rid of Me* (UK #3), recorded with Steve Albini in Minnesota, is **PJ Harvey**'s second LP, and her first for Island Records. Aside from the hit single '50 Foot Queenie', there's also a cover of Bob Dylan's 'Highway 61 Revisited'.

4 MAY

1968 The day after her 18th birthday, Welsh singer **Mary Hopkin** wins ITV's *Opportunity Knocks*. Fashion model Twiggy, who's watching the show, contacts Paul McCartney, suggesting Hopkin as a signing for The Beatles' new Apple record label.

1970 During a protest against the Vietnam War at Kent State University, four demonstrators are shot dead by the National Guard of Ohio. Two of them (Jeffrey Miller and Allison Krause) are friends of Jerry Casale, who later says that their deaths 'galvanized my creativity, infusing it with an existential anger and urgency'. Eventually, by 1973, the tragedy leads Casale and fellow student Mark Mothersbaugh to co-found the group **Devo**.

1973 ROTD: 'Can the Can' by Detroit-born singer and bass guitarist **Suzi Quatro** will top the UK charts in June and make her a bigger star across Europe and Australia than in her native America.

1979 It feels fitting that on the day Margaret Thatcher becomes the British Prime Minister, the first single is released by 2-Tone Records – a label that will paint a vivid and often critical reflection of life during the first half of her premiership through its mix of new wave and ska.

'Gangsters' by The Special A.K.A. (soon to be known simply as **The Specials**) is about the 'gangsters' of the music business, and takes specific aim at their former manager, Bernie Rhodes, who stopped the group touring for five months. It introduces itself with a sample of Prince Buster's 'Al Capone' – 'a musical quotation' as founder member Jerry Dammers later phrases it, while lead singer Terry Hall's two vocal takes (one 'bored', the other 'angry') are combined. On the flip side is an instrumental originally entitled 'The Kingston Affair', but later renamed 'The Selecter' after the band who recorded it.

To begin with, 5,000 copies of 'Gangsters'/'The Selecter' are pressed. Just three days later, John Peel plays it on Radio 1, and in August, the record will become a national hit, eventually peaking at UK #6. The Selecter, too, with Pauline Black on vocals, will themselves reach the top 10 in November, with 'On My Radio'.

5 MAY

1967 ROTD: The song began as 'Liverpool Sunset' but Ray Davies of **The Kinks** soon retitles it, not least because of his childhood memories of being taken to the 1951 Festival of Britain on the South Bank of the Thames. 'Waterloo Sunset' will reach UK #2, one of the best-loved songs of the decade.

1977 **The Crucial Three** form in Liverpool. Though they will never record anything together in their short six-week spell as a group, it is a significant moment for post-punk music in Britain. Singer Ian

McCulloch (it's his 18th birthday), guitarist Pete Wylie and bassist Julian Cope will all go on to front successful British post-punk bands, respectively **Echo & the Bunnymen**, **Wah!** and **The Teardrop Explodes**.

1981 'Stand and Deliver' by **Adam and the Ants**, boosted by a lavish promotional video starring Adam Ant in spectacular highwayman's costume, enters the UK charts at #1 and stays there for five weeks.

2019 ROTD: Nobody seems to know for certain the full line-up of producer Dean 'Inflo' Cover's new British funk, soul and R&B collective **Sault**, who debut with 5, but they will certainly be prolific, releasing 11 albums of material by the close of 2022.

6 MAY

1965 After a **Rolling Stones** concert in Clearwater, Florida, is curtailed after only four songs due to an attempted stage invasion by members of the audience, Mick Jagger sits by the pool at the Jack Tar Harrison Hotel and pours his frustration into the lyrics of a new song. They already have a Keith Richards guitar riff, and four days later, in Illinois, the group records '(I Can't Get No) Satisfaction'.

1983 One week before the release of their debut single, 'Hand in Glove', **The Smiths** open for the Sisters of Mercy at the University of London. Rough Trade publicist Scott Piering persuades Radio 1 producer John Walters to accompany him — and it leads to the quartet's first BBC radio session.

2018 ROTD: While Donald Glover guest hosts TV's *Saturday Night Live*, 'This is America', about the epidemic of gun violence in the US, is released under his alter ego of **Childish Gambino**. The song will rocket to US #1.

7 MAY

1956 BOTD: Anne Beckingham in Beckenham. As **Anne Dudley**, she will perform sporadically as the pianist on the BBC's *Play School* between 1978 and 1980 before going on to become an Oscar-winning composer for *The Full Monty*'s original soundtrack. She will also become a string arranger and frequent collaborator with producer Trevor Horn, with whom she will also work on ABC's 'The Look of Love' (ROTD in 1982). Together they will form Art of Noise the following year.

1968 Reginald Dwight, 21-year-old member of the band Bluesology, legally changes his name – taking his new first name from the group's sax player **Elton** Dean, and his new surname from singer Long **John** Baldry.

1985 ROTD: 'Kayleigh', which will become the biggest hit single (UK #2) for British rock group **Marillion**.

8 MAY

1965 In an alley near London's Savoy Hotel, director D. A. Pennebaker shoots the opening of his **Bob Dylan** documentary film, *Dont Look Back*. During the sequence, which is designed to be a film accompaniment to 'Subterranean Homesick Blues', Dylan displays a series of cue cards featuring some of the song's lyrics.

1984 ROTD: **Billy Ocean**'s 'European Queen'. Though it proves to be a flop at this stage, the song will become a much bigger hit later in the year when its US version, 'Caribbean Queen', hits #1 on *Billboard*. Also ROTD: the Hi-NRG pop of 'The Upstroke' by Agents Aren't Aeroplanes is the first production collaboration between Mike **Stock**, Matt **Aitken** and Pete **Waterman**.

1994 In the early hours of Sunday morning (3–5 a.m.), Annie Nightingale hosts Radio 1's first *Chill Out Zone* for coming-down clubbers.

9 MAY

1960 ROTD: After a few minor US hits in the 1950s, 'Only the Lonely' (US #2, UK #1) will establish Tennessee singer-songwriter **Roy Orbison** as an international star, beginning a run of 22 top 40 hits in the US and 26 in the UK during the 1960s alone.

1974 In two shows at the Harvard Square Theatre in Cambridge, Massachusetts, 24-year-old **Bruce Springsteen** and the E Street Band perform as the opening act for Bonnie Raitt. Music critic Jon Landau sees the second show and notes the presence of a new song, 'Born to Run', which he describes as having 'a *Telstar* guitar introduction and an Eddie Cochran rhythm pattern'. Landau's write-up will appear in *The Real Paper* dated 22 May – the day after Springsteen happens to be in the studio recording the 'Born to Run' backing track. The critic's review of the Cambridge show is headlined 'Growing Young with Rock and Roll' and contrasts the detachment and routine of what a rock critic's job often means with the rarer occasions when it's worth it: 'I saw rock and roll future and its name is Bruce Springsteen . . . There is no one I would rather watch on a stage today.'

A year later, Springsteen will say of Landau's review: 'He floored me. He had laid it out for people to see . . . and it gave me a lot of hope.' By then, Jon Landau will have joined his management team, and become the *Born to Run* album's co-producer.

1980 ROTD: Following a trio of disco albums, **Grace Jones** makes her debut for Chris Blackwell's Island label with *Warm Leatherette*, recorded at Compass Point in the Bahamas with the likes of Sly & Robbie and guitarist Barry Reynolds. It reinvents a number of songs: Mute Records boss Daniel Miller's title track; Roxy Music's 'Love is the Drug'; and Chrissie Hynde's 'Private Life'.

1998 In Birmingham, **Dana International** wins the Eurovision Song Contest for Israel with the song 'Diva'. After her victory, she reprises her performance, this time in a costume of bird feathers designed by Jean-Paul Gaultier.

10 MAY

1982 ROTD: Something for everyone, frankly: **The Birthday Party**'s *Junkyard*; **Duran Duran**'s *Rio* album; 'Temptation' by **New Order**; and *Tropical Gangsters* by **Kid Creole**.

1999 ROTD: *Remedy* by **Basement Jaxx**. The first album by duo Felix Buxton and Simon Ratcliffe is one of the liveliest, most colourful dance records of the time. Among its four hit singles is 'Red Alert', which reaches UK #5.

2019 ROTD: Toni Watson, from the Australian state of Victoria, releases her electropop anthem 'Dance Monkey' under the moniker of **Tones and I**. As well as topping the charts in her homeland for an unprecedented 24 weeks, it will become a UK #1 for 11 weeks.

11 MAY

1981 ROTD: **Kraftwerk**'s *Computer World*, their first LP for three years, also heralds their return to live work for the first time since 1976, as they effectively tour a portable version of their Kling Klang Studio. (Reputedly, Kraftwerk did not have a computer during the making of the album.)

1993 ROTD: Formerly a founding member of the 1980s group 'Til Tuesday, Virginia singer and songwriter **Aimee Mann** enrols as a solo artist with the critically acclaimed *Whatever*.

1998 ROTD: 'Overdue', 'Cave', 'Coma' and 'Escape' form the EP *Muse*, from the Devon trio of the same name. It is their first release.

12 MAY

1965 **Wilson Pickett** comes to record at Stax Studios in Memphis. Given advance notice of Pickett's session, guitarist Steve Cropper revisits the 1962 single 'I Found a Love' by The Falcons, which features Pickett on lead vocal. Hearing the phrase 'in the midnight hour' in its lyrics, Cropper then teams up with Pickett to write and record the famous song that bears the same title.

1967 ROTD: *Are You Experienced?* by the **Jimi Hendrix Experience**, and 'A Whiter Shade of Pale' by **Procol Harum**. Meanwhile, at London's Queen Elizabeth Hall, **Pink Floyd** unveil their new quadrophonic speaker system for a full surround-sound experience. The event is called 'Games for May' and Syd Barrett writes a song by that name, soon to be retitled 'See Emily Play' as the next Floyd single.

1992 ROTD: The breakout hit from the movie *Mo' Money* is 'The Best Things in Life Are Free' sung by **Luther Vandross and Janet Jackson** (US #10, UK #2).

13 MAY

1977 ROTD: As its title suggests, **Donna Summer**'s *I Remember Yesterday* LP is a celebration of past musical trends from the 1940s to the 1960s – before inventing the sound of 'the future' on its final track: 'I Feel Love'.

1985 The **Parents Music Resource Center** (PMRC) meets for the first time. Created to address concerns about the content of albums and videos, the organisation came into being after Tipper Gore, wife of Senator Al, bought a copy of Prince's *Purple Rain* for their daughter, and heard the record's most explicit song 'Darling Nikki'. At around the same time, she found their children watching the promo video for Van Halen's 'Hot for Teacher'.

The first act of the PMRC is to produce a list that they brand 'The Filthy Fifteen', containing songs that reference sex and masturbation, violent imagery, drug and alcohol use, and the occult. The artists and tracks on the list tend either towards heavy rock (Judas Priest, Mötley Crüe, Black Sabbath, Twisted Sister) or pop and R&B (Prince, Sheena Easton's 'Sugar Walls', Madonna's 'Dress You Up' and Cyndi Lauper's 'She Bop').

The list comes with a proposal that record companies in the US should introduce a voluntary ratings system for music, in the same vein as cinema ratings: X for profanity or sexually explicit lyrics; V for violent imagery; O for occultism; and D/A for drugs/alcohol. Eventually the Recording Industry Association of America agrees to compromise by putting 'explicit' stickers on contentious albums.

The artists under scrutiny receive support from perhaps unexpected quarters: John Denver comments that when he first released 'Rocky Mountain High', he had to battle with radio programmers who assumed the song was a paean to drug taking; and Dee Snider of Twisted Sister points out that the band's song 'Under the Blade' was less about sadomasochism, and more about undergoing surgery.

1991 ROTD: Having been painstakingly cleared for samples, **De La Soul**'s second LP, *De La Soul is Dead*, forces an end to their Daisy Age image, but is no less ambitious than their previous work.

14 MAY

1972 Ready to throw in the towel after three underperforming albums, **Mott the Hoople** have been persuaded by long-time fan David Bowie to persevere just a little longer. On this day, the band agree to record his song 'All the Young Dudes' and head into the studio. It will become their first hit in August (UK #4). By then Bowie is a star and will later perform it himself on the Ziggy Stardust live tour.

1982 ROTD: **Adam Ant** goes solo with 'Goody Two Shoes', and **Madness** make a veiled homage to the buying of condoms in their 12th single, 'House of Fun'. Both singles will make it to UK #1.

1984 ROTD: Even if *Smash Hits* gives it a drubbing review – 'an absolutely dreadful comeback' – 'Wake Me Up Before You Go-Go' will give **Wham!** their first #1 in the UK and US.

2003 ROTD: What is that horn sample from on **Beyoncé**'s 'Crazy in Love'? Well, I'll tell you. It's from the opening of The Chi-Lites' 1970 hit, 'Are You My Woman (Tell Me So)'.

15 MAY

1969 On tour in Berkeley, **The Four Tops**' Renaldo Benson witnesses police attacking anti-war protestors and wonders, 'What is happening here?' With the help of songwriter Al Cleveland, he begins work on a song that will be reworked by **Marvin Gaye** a year later as the socially aware anthem 'What's Going On' (US #2 in 1971 but, incredibly, never a hit in the UK).

1970 ROTD: **Free**'s 'All Right Now', written backstage after a disastrously apathetic student gig in Durham, will spend five weeks at UK #2. Meanwhile, in Detroit, **Edwin Starr** covers the anti-war Whitfield–Strong song 'War', already released as an album track by The Temptations but reportedly denied single status in case the group's more conservative fanbase was alienated. Starr's version goes to US #1.

1988 Technically it's not just **Wet Wet Wet** who reach UK #1 with 'With a Little Help from My Friends'. It's officially a double A-side, thus meaning chart-topping glory for **Billy Bragg and Cara Tivey**'s 'She's

Leaving Home'. Both tracks come from the multi-artist *NME* LP of Beatles covers, *Sgt Pepper Knew My Father*, with all proceeds going to the charity Childline.

Further down that same chart, at UK #65, is 'Fairplay', the first chart entry from **Soul II Soul**, whose roots on the London music scene date back almost 10 years. At their kernel is Hornsey-born Trevor Beresford Romeo (better known as Jazzie B) whose first paid gig as a soul and reggae DJ was at 14 years of age in the week of the 1977 Silver Jubilee under the name Jah Rico.

By 1982, after a period as a studio tape operator for, among others (and of all people), Tommy Steele, Romeo had co-founded the Soul II Soul umbrella organisation to connect several disparate ideas: a specially created sound system, a clothing brand, a Camden record shop, a label, and the group itself. The name also came from his partnership in all these enterprises with Philip 'Daddae' Harvey – 'not just because of the music we played,' Romeo later recalls, 'it also stood for . . . two souls moving together.'

'Fairplay', which features Rose Windross on lead vocals, was recorded in 1987 at Covent Garden's Africa Centre, where the band hold a regular Sunday-night club night, frequently raided by police, with arrests and confiscation of equipment. These experiences later inspire their first massive hit in 1989: 'In order to stay strong we had to *keep on moving*.'

1990 ROTD: Newcomer **Mariah Carey** showcases most of her many octaves on 'Vision of Love', which by August will become the first of her 15 US #1 hits during the 1990s.

16 MAY

1966 ROTD: If *Pet Sounds* marks a slight downturn in **The Beach Boys'** commercial fortunes Stateside (a modest #10 on *Billboard*), in the UK it will become their most successful LP so far, peaking at #2. Plus **Janet Jackson** is BOTD.

1972 'Metal Guru' provides Marc Bolan and **T. Rex** with their fourth and final UK #1.

1994 ROTD: Senegalese singer **Youssou N'Dour** teams up with **Neneh Cherry** for '7 Seconds', sung in French, English and the West African language Wolof. Though it barely makes the US Hot 100, it reaches UK #3, and from 13 August begins an unprecedented 16-week run at the top of the French singles chart.

17 MAY

1966 After performing a solo acoustic set at Manchester's Free Trade Hall, Bob Dylan returns to the stage with backing group The Hawks for the 'electric' set. Just before their final song, a single audience member — upset at what he perceives to be Dylan's departure from his folk roots — heckles him with the word 'Judas!'. Dylan replies, 'I don't believe you . . . you're a liar!' before introducing 'Like a Rolling Stone' and saying to the band, 'Play it fucking loud!'

1978 The disco comedy *Thank God It's Friday* opens in US cinemas. **Donna Summer** and **The Commodores** both feature on its soundtrack, while there are early acting roles for Jeff Goldblum and Debra Winger.

2019 ROTD: *Divinely Uninspired to a Hellish Extent* by the 22-year-old Glaswegian singer-songwriter **Lewis Capaldi** will become the best-selling British album in 2019 *and* 2020.

18 MAY

1964 **The Animals** record the traditional folk number 'The House of the Rising Sun' with producer Mickie Most. While touring with Chuck Berry, the group had added the song to their live set after frontman Eric Burdon heard it being sung in a Newcastle club by Northumbrian folk artist Johnny Handle. It will become a UK #1 in July – and a US #1 in September (albeit drastically edited there for length).

1975 Chaos breaks out at Mallory Park in Leicestershire where 50,000 fans have gathered to watch Slade, The Rubettes, and headlining act the **Bay City Rollers**.

The Rollers are at the peak of their popularity: 'Bye Bye Baby' has just been UK #1 for six weeks, the biggest-selling single of the year. The band are flown in by helicopter, but such is the intensity of their fanbase that they are forced to land on an island in the middle of a lake. This does not stop their fans, who proceed to try to wade and swim through the lake to reach them. Many of them have to be rescued. Meanwhile Tony Blackburn, covering the event for BBC Radio 1, is circling proceedings in a speedboat being steered by a man in a Womble costume.

1992 ROTD: 'Raving I'm Raving' by **Shut Up and Dance** is available in the shops for only one day after composer Marc Cohn objects to the sampled inclusion of his song 'Walking in Memphis'. It enters the UK charts at #2 but survives only another week in the top 100.

19 MAY

1938 BOTD: Brian Keith Flowers in Isleworth. As **Herbie Flowers** he will go on to have a career unlike any other: bass guitarist on dozens of sessions – that's him on 'Space Oddity', 'Walk on the Wild Side' and 'Rock On'; founder member of the groups Blue Mink and Sky; and composer with Kenny Pickett (from The Creation) of 'Grandad' for Clive Dunn.

1976 John Peel's last record tonight – 'Judy is a Punk' by the **Ramones** – marks the beginning of his late-night Radio 1 programme's affiliation with punk rock.

1996 *The Simpsons* episode 'Homerpalooza' is broadcast on the US's Fox Network, in which Homer Simpson tries to gain some credibility with his kids by attending a music festival. Guest voices come courtesy of Cypress Hill, Peter Frampton and Smashing Pumpkins, plus Sonic Youth, who also perform a new arrangement of Danny Elfman's *Simpsons* theme.

2014 ROTD: Norway's **Röyksopp** and Sweden's **Robyn** join forces for a five-track EP, *Do It Again*, with a video for its title song filmed in Mexico. The more reflective ten-minute 'Monument' has been partly inspired by the Juliana Cerqueira Leite clay sculptures at a London art gallery.

20 MAY

1967 On the BBC Radio Light Programme's *Where It's At*, Kenny Everett interviews **The Beatles** about their upcoming album *Sgt. Pepper's Lonely Hearts Club Band* and plays several extracts from it — although *not* 'A Day in the Life' as the BBC has just banned it from airplay due to the references to drugs in its lyrics.

1996 ROTD: **Manic Street Preachers'** *Everything Must Go* — their first since the mysterious disappearance of Richey Edwards — while the **Super Furry Animals'** *Fuzzy Logic* is their first album for the Creation label.

2016 ROTD: With guest appearances from Nicki Minaj, Macy Gray, Lil Wayne and Future, **Ariana Grande**'s *Dangerous Woman* takes its title from Egyptian novelist Nawal El Saadawi's 1975 work, *Woman at Point Zero*.

21 MAY

1964 R&B vocal group **The Drifters** are forced into a last-minute personnel change following the sudden death overnight, believed to be an overdose, of 27-year-old frontman Rudy Lewis. Scheduled to record a new song 'Under the Boardwalk' at Atlantic Studios, the band find themselves looking for a replacement for Lewis, who was himself a replacement for Ben E. King when he left the line-up in 1960 to begin his solo career.

In the end, the spot goes to band member Johnny Moore, who will continue as permanent lead singer well into the 1970s, when they enjoy a string of British hits. During the 'Under the Boardwalk' session, The Drifters also record a tribute to the departed Lewis: 'I Don't Want to Go on Without You', this time with band member Charlie Thomas singing lead.

1979 ROTD: **Orchestral Manoeuvres in the Dark**'s 'Electricity' is a homage to Kraftwerk's 'Radioactivity', and is released as a one-off single with Manchester label Factory as FAC 6.

1990 ROTD: Exactly 11 years later, 'World in Motion' by **New Order**, but credited to ENGLANDneworder (FAC 293), which will become Factory's first and only UK #1 single. Recorded with several members of the England national football team (notably 'rapper' John Barnes), and released during the 1990 Football World Cup, the song began life in 1988 as the instrumental theme to the BBC2 youth current affairs series *Reportage*.

22 MAY

1970 ROTD: Spending seven weeks at #1, **Mungo Jerry**'s 'In the Summertime' will become the UK's biggest-selling single of the year, and one of the biggest-selling singles worldwide, with sales estimated at over 30 million copies.

1979 'Sunday Girl' by **Blondie**, written by lead singer Debbie Harry and guitarist Chris Stein, reaches UK #1. It is unusual for the time for one album to contain four UK top 20 hits, but the group's *Parallel Lines* has already spawned 'Picture This', 'Hanging on the Telephone' and 'Heart of Glass'.

1980 ROTD: *Diana* by **Diana Ross**. Recorded with Bernard Edwards and Nile Rodgers of Chic, but remixed, edited and with re-recorded vocals, her final record for Motown will become her best-selling solo LP. Featuring three major hits ('Upside Down', 'I'm Coming Out' and 'My Old Piano'), it will be reissued in 2003 with Chic's original mix as a bonus disc.

1995 ROTD: 'Common People' by **Pulp**, which will enter the UK charts at #2 but fail to overtake Robson & Jerome's 'Unchained Melody'. In the US, **TLC**'s 'Waterfalls', with a young CeeLo Green on backing vocals, will go on to top the *Billboard* Hot 100.

23 MAY

1966 Starting tonight, and for the next three months, **The Doors** become the resident house band at the Whisky a Go Go nightclub in Los Angeles, opening for such outfits as Them, Captain Beefheart and His Magic Band, and Love.

1975 ROTD: 'I'm Not in Love' by **10cc**. Six minutes in length and featuring tape-looped multi-tracked vocals, the track's whispered middle section is delivered by Kathy Redfern, the group's secretary, at Strawberry recording studios.

1999 'Sweet Like Chocolate' by **Shanks & Bigfoot**, with vocalist Sharon Woolf, becomes the first UK garage track to reach #1.

2004 Nearly 30 years after his death, **Nick Drake** scores his first top 40 hit single when 'Magic' (intended for inclusion on *Five Leaves Left* in 1969) is remixed with a newly recorded string arrangement by Robert Kirby. Accompanying it is a Drake all-time classic: *Bryter Layter*'s 'Northern Sky'.

2019 At the Ivor Novello Awards, **Richard Ashcroft** accepts a gong for Outstanding Contribution to British Music, and during his speech reveals that the songwriting credits and royalties for perhaps his best-loved song have reverted to him and him alone.

'Bitter Sweet Symphony' was the first major hit for Ashcroft and his former band **The Verve** in the summer of 1997 (UK #2, US #12). But he was soon to relinquish all royalties because of its distinctive use of a string melody from an instrumental cover of The Rolling Stones' 'The Last Time', made by the Andrew Oldham Orchestra in 1965. Although copyright holders Decca Records gave permission, the Stones' then manager, the late Allen Klein, did not. As a result, Mick Jagger and Keith Richards became credited as co-writers, even though they had not actually composed the string melody in question.

Twenty-two years on, Jagger, Richards and Klein's son Jody have ruled in favour of Ashcroft, who is now credited as sole composer once more. According to *Billboard* magazine, the song has generated nearly $5 million in publishing revenue.

24 MAY

1974 ROTD: **Sparks'** *Kimono My House*, which opens with 'This Town Ain't Big Enough for Both of Us', currently at UK #3, and set to rise to #2 a week later.

1991 *Madonna: Truth or Dare* is given a full worldwide release. Outside America, Alek Keshishian's two-hour documentary film about the singer's 1990 'Blond Ambition' tour will be known under the title *In Bed with Madonna*.

1999 ROTD: *The Man Who* by **Travis**. They are one of two Glaswegian bands (the other being Texas) to take their name from Wim Wenders' 1984 film *Paris, Texas* – in their case, after Harry Dean Stanton's character of Travis Henderson.

25 MAY

1961 ROTD: Tamla Records in Detroit releases 'Let Your Conscience Be Your Guide', written and produced by Berry Gordy, and the first solo single by session drummer and singer **Marvin Gaye**. Though it fails to chart nationally, by the end of the decade, Gaye will have scored 28 hits on the US top 40.

1973 ROTD: Richard Branson's company Virgin releases its first two albums: *Flying Teapot* by **Gong** has the catalogue number V2002; V2001 is *Tubular Bells* by **Mike Oldfield**.

1984 ROTD: The melancholy but defiant 'Smalltown Boy' by **Bronski Beat** introduces the general public to Jimmy Somerville's unique falsetto voice. The song quickly rises to UK #3.

1998 ROTD: Irish foursome **B*witched** enjoy immediate commercial success with 'C'est La Vie'. Contrastingly, a three-track EP called *Safety* by a quartet of University of London students attracts limited attention. It is the first record released by **Coldplay**.

26 MAY

1967 ROTD: *Sgt. Pepper's Lonely Hearts Club Band*. The fading final E major chord of 'A Day in the Life' is still not *quite* the end of **The Beatles'** new album; first comes a high-frequency tone designed to annoy dogs (a Lennon wheeze), and then the sound of a locked groove of laughter and backwards nonsense.

1987 ROTD: As you might have guessed, **ABC**'s 'When Smokey Sings' is not a tribute to the band who gave us 'Living Next Door to Alice', but to soul legend Smokey Robinson.

1993 While accepting the Ivor Novello Award for Song of the Year (for 'Stay'), Siobhan Fahey announces that **Shakespears Sister** are splitting up. This comes as news to the other member of the duo, Marcella Detroit, and the two do not speak for another 25 years.

27 MAY

1977 ROTD: 'God Save the Queen' by the **Sex Pistols**. Aside from a couple of preview spins on John Peel's late-night programme and on Charlie Gillett's BBC Radio London show, the song is otherwise excluded by all British broadcasters, radio and television, BBC and commercial. Several high-street chains – Woolworths, WHSmith, John Menzies and Boots – refuse to stock the single. Even the TV advert is banned. Nonetheless, it will enter the singles charts at #11, and in the week of Queen Elizabeth II's Silver Jubilee celebrations, it will reach #2 on the BBC chart and #1 on the *NME* chart.

'The BBC's objections,' says Virgin press officer Al Clark, 'revolve principally around the phrase "fascist regime". If this country isn't one, then one of the first principles of democracy is that the band should be free to sing that line on radio and television.'

Instead, the Pistols' exposure is largely confined to the music press. In *ZigZag* magazine, Rotten reveals one of his current favourite live acts: Shakin' Stevens and the Sunsets.

1986 ROTD: 'Happy Hour', jolly sounding but sharply anti-sexist, is **The Housemartins**' third single, which will hit UK #3 within a month. Paul Heaton (vocals) and Fatboy Slim (bass) in the same group! Imagine that!

2022 On the same day that **ABBA**'s run of *Voyage* shows open in London – with its four members represented in hologrammatic form – **Kate Bush**'s 'Running Up That Hill' begins an unexpected comeback when it is used prominently in the fourth season of the Netflix drama *Stranger Things*. Largely driven by streaming and radio play, the song, which reached UK #3 and US #30 on its original 1985 release, will peak at UK #1 and US #3.

28 MAY

1971 ROTD: **Rod Stewart's** third solo album, *Every Picture Tells a Story*, features covers of Tim Hardin's 'Reason to Believe', Arthur Crudup's 'That's Alright (Mama)', and an original by Stewart and guitarist Martin Quittenton called 'Maggie May'.

1974 The **Portsmouth Sinfonia** play the Royal Albert Hall. Co-founded in 1970 by the composer **Gavin Bryars**, the experimental orchestra is designed to give inexperienced but enthusiastic players the chance to perform classical pieces such as Rossini's *William Tell* Overture or Strauss's 'Blue Danube'. At one point, it features **Brian Eno** on clarinet (he is also the producer on the Sinfonia's first two albums).

1981 The **Clash** begin a run of live shows at Bond's International Casino in New York's Times Square. Each show features a different opening act. Tonight, it's **Grandmaster Flash and the Furious Five**.

29 MAY

1942 In Los Angeles, Irving Berlin's 'White Christmas', a then-unusual example of a secular seasonal song, is recorded by **Bing Crosby** in less than 20 minutes. Merry Christmas.

1997 DOTD: At the age of just 30, **Jeff Buckley** accidentally drowns while swimming in the Wolf River Harbor near Memphis. PJ Harvey, Juliana Hatfield, Rufus Wainwright and Chris Cornell will all write tribute songs to Buckley's memory.

1998 **TLC** and **Backstreet Boys** have both turned down recording it, but **Britney Spears** today records '. . . Baby One More Time'. She has prepared for the session by listening to Soft Cell's version of 'Tainted Love'. 'I wanted my voice to be kind of rusty,' she says.

30 MAY

1966 ROTD: 'One thing is certain,' the *Evening Standard* says of **The Beatles'** 'Paperback Writer': 'Ella Fitzgerald [who has covered 'Can't Buy Me Love'] and all the gang of real singers will not be rushing off to record their cover versions. Real singers sing about love.' The song is in fact a deliberate attempt *not* to write a love song. (The 'noise' at the end of its B-side, 'Rain', is John Lennon's voice played in reverse.)

1989 ROTD: **Cliff Richard's** 100th single, 'The Best of Me' (UK #2), makes the headlines, but 'Back to Life (However Do You Want Me)' by **Soul II Soul featuring Caron Wheeler**, which will soon spend a month at #1, will be better remembered.

2005 ROTD: **James Blunt's** 'You're Beautiful', recorded in Los Angeles while the British singer-songwriter was actor Carrie Fisher's lodger. Fisher is also responsible for the name of Blunt's debut album, *Back to Bedlam*, which will become the biggest-selling album of the noughties in the UK.

31 MAY

1956 In Lubbock, Texas, **Buddy Holly** and his drummer Jerry Allison go to see the new John Ford western, *The Searchers*, in which John Wayne's character has a habit of saying the phrase 'that'll be the day'. The Liverpool band **The Searchers** will also name themselves after the film.

1976 **The Who** become known as 'the loudest band' when their stadium show at The Valley in south-east London is measured at 126 decibels.

1993 Alan McGee approaches **Oasis** to sign them to his Creation label, after they insist on adding themselves to a bill of 18 Wheeler, Boyfriend and Sister Lovers at King Tut's Wah Wah Hut in Glasgow.

(Oasis play four songs: 'Rock 'n' Roll Star', 'Bring It on Down', 'Up in the Sky', and a cover of 'I Am the Walrus'.)

1999 ROTD: 'Bills Bills Bills', about dates who won't pay their own way, will become the first of **Destiny's Child**'s four US #1 singles.

JUNE

1 JUNE

1959 The first episode of *Juke Box Jury* is aired on BBC Television. The show, which has been running in the United States for several years, features a panel of 'judges' who listen to newly released recordings, and pass comment on them, deciding on whether they are 'hits' or 'misses'. Given that promotional videos lie a good way in the future, and what remains is a static half-hour of the judges nodding their heads roughly in time to piped-in music, you might feel the show is more suited to the radio. And that's where it began in the 1940s, hosted by its creator, DJ Peter Potter. Perhaps the most televisual element lies in the show's surprise twist: at least one of the recording artists being assessed is waiting backstage . . .

The BBC version is hosted by former newsreader David Jacobs, and its theme tune ('Hit or Miss' by The John Barry Seven) will itself become a hit. Over the next nine years, a variety of celebrities will appear as judges — recording artists and disc jockeys but also actors, entertainers, and the occasional titled figure (on 24 October 1964, the line-up is Sid James, Stones producer/manager Andrew Loog Oldham and the Marchioness of Tavistock). Three special 'group' editions are also broadcast: The Beatles (7 December 1963), The Stones (4 July 1964) and The Seekers (24 December 1966).

As well as inspiring numerous record review shows, including the video votes on Saturday morning shows *Superstore* and *Going Live!* and BBC Radio's *Roundtable*, *Juke Box Jury* itself will be revived twice. Noel Edmonds hosts the 1979 version, in which a sullen John Lydon will walk off the set before the end, while Jools Holland will preside over two further series in 1989 and 1990.

1972 'People Need Love' is the first single from the Swedish quartet **Björn & Benny, Agnetha & Anni-Frid**, before they decide to rearrange their initials into something more compact.

1997 The *Chicago Tribune* newspaper publishes an essay by Mary Schmich headed 'Advice, like youth, probably just wasted on the young'. Subsequently it forms the heart of 1998's 'Everybody's Free (to Wear Sunscreen)' by **Baz Luhrmann**, a UK #1 in 1999.

2 JUNE

1981 **Prince** performs his first-ever British concert, at the Lyceum in London. Among those watching is comic performer, naturalist and funk enthusiast Bill Oddie.

1987 **Whitney Houston** returns to the UK #1 spot with 'I Wanna Dance with Somebody (Who Loves Me)'. The song's writers, George Merrill and Shannon Rubicam (who also wrote 'How Will I Know') will later record another song Houston's record label turned down: 'Waiting for a Star to Fall' (under the name **Boy Meets Girl**).

2008 ROTD: 'One Day Like This' by **Elbow** is what you might call a 'sleeper' hit. Peaking only at UK #35 on its original outing, it will eventually reach #4 after the group perform it at the London 2012 Olympics.

3 JUNE

1964 With **Ringo Starr** indisposed due to tonsillitis, Shubdubs drummer **Jimmie Nicol** replaces him in The Beatles touring band for the next 13 days, performing with the group in Denmark, the Netherlands, Hong Kong and Australia.

1970 A **Kinks** show in New York is cancelled because Ray Davies must fly to London to re-record one line of new single 'Lola'. The BBC has a no brand-names policy, and so 'Coca-Cola' is replaced with 'cherry-cola'. The single reaches UK #2.

2013 ROTD: 'Royals' by **Lorde**. A critical examination of extravagance, consumerism and celebrity lifestyle, the title of the track came to Auckland teenager Ella O'Connor when she saw an archive photograph of the US baseball player George Brett wearing the shirt of his team, the Kansas City Royals. It will top the New Zealand, US and UK charts and sell 22 million copies.

4 JUNE

1966 **Janis Joplin** travels from Texas to San Francisco to become the new lead singer of psychedelic rockers **Big Brother and the Holding Company**. They play their first concert together six days later.

1976 The **Sex Pistols** play the Free Trade Hall, Manchester. A remarkable proportion of those spectating will go on to form bands: Howard Devoto and Pete Shelley (Buzzcocks), Ian Curtis, Bernard Sumner and Peter Hook (Joy Division), Mark E. Smith (The Fall), Morrissey (The Smiths), and even Mick Hucknall (The Frantic Elevators, and eventually Simply Red).

1979 ROTD: 'Good Times' by **Chic**. Meanwhile the 112 members of the University of Southern California's Trojan Marching Band are recorded at the Los Angeles' Dodger Stadium as part of **Fleetwood Mac**'s track 'Tusk'.

5 JUNE

1974 As her first single, **Patti Smith** radically reworks 'Hey Joe' at Electric Lady Studios, adding a spoken word section about the recent kidnapping of heiress Patty Hearst by the Symbionese Liberation Army.

1975 **Pink Floyd** are busily recording their *Wish You Were Here* album at Abbey Road Studios, when they realise that the shaven-headed stranger who has been watching them is in fact **Syd Barrett** who left the group in 1968. Coincidentally, the centrepiece of the album is a tribute to Barrett: 'Shine On You Crazy Diamond'.

2006 ROTD: **Snow Patrol**'s 'Chasing Cars', which, despite peaking at only UK #6, will be announced in 2019 as the 21st-century's most played record on British radio, ahead of 'I Gotta Feeling' by Black Eyed Peas and 'Happy' by Pharrell Williams.

6 JUNE

1981 The first issue of the heavy rock and metal magazine *Kerrang!* is published. Featuring Angus Young of AC/DC on its cover, it is included free as a 'Heavy Metal Special' with the weekly paper *Sounds*.

1988 ROTD: **Nick Cave and the Bad Seeds**' 'The Mercy Seat', about a man facing execution by electric chair, will become one of Cave's defining songs. Twelve years later it will be re-interpreted by **Johnny Cash**.

1994 ROTD: Although it is far from the first 'jungle' single, it will be the first to cross over into the pop charts: 'Incredible' by **M-Beat** featuring 19-year-old **General Levy** will reach the UK top 10 by autumn.

7 JUNE

1976 *New York Magazine* publishes an article by Irish rock journalist **Nik Cohn** entitled 'Tribal Rites of the New Saturday Night', about the working-class disco scene away from Manhattan's East Side. 'The new generation takes few risks,' Cohn writes. 'It graduates, looks for a job, endures. And, once a week, on Saturday night, it explodes.'

Robert Stigwood, then manager of the Bee Gees, reads the piece and suggests that it would make an interesting film. Cohn duly writes the first draft of what will become *Saturday Night Fever*, but it is considered a little too dark, even considering what will end up in the final X-certificate cut in 1977.

Twenty years after the film's release, Cohn will reveal that his article was not entirely non-fictional. By way of research, he had gone to the 2001 Odyssey discotheque in Bay Ridge, but encountered a fight, was thrown up on, and beat a hasty retreat. Short of material, he decided to base his magazine piece instead on the characters he had known in Derry, and then in West London, drawing on his memories of a mod to create the character of Vincent in his article, who in turn became John Travolta's character Tony Manero in the movie. 'It reads to me as obvious fiction,' Cohn told the *Guardian* in 2016, on the essay's 40th anniversary. 'In the 60s and 70s, the line between fact and fiction was blurry . . .'

The article is not Cohn's first impact on popular culture. His love for pinball games inspired The Who's single 'Pinball Wizard' in *Tommy*, and it has been claimed that David Bowie based his Ziggy Stardust persona on Cohn's 1967 novel *I Am Still the Greatest Says Johnny Angelo.*

1979 Building on an idea conceived by music industry stalwarts Kenny Gamble, Dyana Williams and Ed Wright, President Jimmy Carter designates June as the first Black Music Month and holds the first such event at the White House with invited guests such as Chuck Berry and Billy Eckstine. Still celebrated to this day, it is now called **African American Music Appreciation Month.**

1993 ROTD: 'Human Behaviour' by **Björk**. The song is considered by most fans to be the Icelandic singer's first solo release, after the break-up of The Sugarcubes, but the truth is that she made and released a whole album when she was aged only 11, which has since been given the name *Björk*.

8 JUNE

1969 With his contributions to **The Rolling Stones** albums diminishing and his reliance on narcotics increasing, 27-year-old Brian Jones is dismissed from the group. The following day, Jones announces his intention to embark on solo work, but within one month he will be dead, having drowned in his swimming pool.

1984 The film *Beat Street*, co-produced by Harry Belafonte, opens in US cinemas. Among the artists making cameo appearances are Afrika Bambaataa, Arthur Baker, Kool Moe Dee, Doug E. Fresh and Grandmaster Melle Mel & the Furious Five.

1992 ROTD: **The Orb** issue a single, 'Blue Room', with a version on CD that lasts just a few seconds short of 40 minutes, the maximum running time for chart eligibility. It reaches UK #8, and the band appear on *Top of the Pops* playing chess . . . to a three-minute edited version, obviously.

9 JUNE

1972 ROTD: **Hawkwind**'s 'Silver Machine' was recorded live in February at the Roundhouse, but songwriter Robert Calvert has been too ill to re-record his lead vocal for the single release. Eventually bass guitarist Lemmy Kilmister steps in. The single reaches UK #3.

1977 ROTD: Female vocal trio **The Emotions** have been recording artists since 1964, but 'Best of My Love', written by Earth Wind & Fire's Maurice White and Al McKay, will give them international success (US #1, UK #4).

1987 *The Roxy* launches on ITV. Conceived by the channel as a rival to *Top of the Pops*, featuring studio performances and videos and based around the MRIB's Network Chart, the show's ratings soon dip and the experiment lasts just 10 months.

10 JUNE

1961 BOTD: Twin sisters **Kelley and Kim Deal** in Ohio, eleven minutes apart. Kim will become bass player with Pixies, and then form the Breeders in 1989, where she will be joined three years later by her guitarist sister.

1967 While **The Monkees** begin recording Goffin and King's 'Pleasant Valley Sunday' in Hollywood, the two-day **Magic Mountain Rock Festival** begins in San Francisco. Generally regarded as the first major music event of the 1967 'Summer of Love', the bill on day one includes The Doors, Canned Heat and Dionne Warwick.

1985 ROTD: *Steve McQueen*, **Prefab Sprout**'s second LP, sees them work for the first time with producer Thomas Dolby after he revealed himself to be a fan of one of their singles, 1984's 'Don't Sing', on Radio 1's *Roundtable*.

Most of the songs on *McQueen* date back several years. 'I just remember them as pub songs that we used to play in pubs,' says singer-songwriter Paddy McAloon. 'To Tom they were all fresh.' But there are a few newer McAloon compositions. 'When the Angels' is a tribute to the late Marvin Gaye, while 'When Love Breaks Down' (the album's breakout single, but only on re-release) was composed in June 1984 with the working title 'Old Confetti' just after the group came back from a European tour.

Steve McQueen will reach a comparatively modest UK #21, but is thought by many to be the group's masterpiece. In America, after a complaint from the late actor's estate, it is retitled *Two Wheels Good*.

11 JUNE

1970 ROTD: **The Spinners**' 'It's a Shame'. Co-written by Stevie Wonder, Lee Garrett and Syreeta Wright, and with G. C. Cameron on lead, it will become the vocal group's biggest hit for Motown (US #14,

UK #20). In Britain, to avoid confusion with the Liverpudlian folk group of the same name, they are credited as The Motown Spinners, and later – after they sign to Atlantic in 1972 – as The Detroit Spinners.

1988 To raise awareness for the anti-apartheid cause, the **70th Birthday Tribute Concert for Nelson Mandela** (who is at the time incarcerated in Pollsmoor Prison, Cape Town) is staged at Wembley Stadium. The concert makes a star of Tracy Chapman, who is unexpectedly asked to play her set twice. Also appearing are Whitney Houston, UB40, Salt-N-Pepa, Stevie Wonder, Eurythmics and Sting, plus numerous entertainment figures and speakers.

2002 The first season of *American Idol* begins broadcasting on the Fox network. It will be won by 20-year-old **Kelly Clarkson**.

2013 ROTD: 'No More Dream' by **BTS**. It is believed that Jimin, one-seventh of BTS (an abbreviation of Bangtan Sonyeondan, which translates as Bulletproof Boy Scouts) has the number '13' tattooed on his left wrist as a symbol not only of the day of his birth (13 October 1995) but also the year of the band's public debut.

Together with J-Hope, Jin, Jungkook, RM, Suga and V, Jimin had been selected in 2010 by producer and record executive Bang Si-Hyuk with a bold intention: to overturn the all-powerful studio system and its stifling management and recording contracts. Bang's plan was to give the band more space for self-expression and to create their own music and lyrical content, and the single accompanying their first album, *2 Cool 4 Skool*, exemplifies this intention. At a time when South Korea's education system has been pressuring students to aim for top universities, the song suggests that they should focus instead on doing what they love.

From here on in, BTS – and other K-pop groups – will be encouraged to question their own status as pop stars and celebrities, express their own thoughts and opinions, and above all, present themselves as human beings.

12 JUNE

1952 A fortnight after her eighth birthday, **Gladys Knight** performs the Nat King Cole song 'Too Young' at Madison Square Garden in the national finals of the *Original Amateur Hour* contest. Launched in 1934, the radio show has already unearthed the talent of Frank Sinatra, who sang as part of The Hoboken Four, and it will continue running on radio and then TV until 1970, discovering stars such as Ann-Margret, Irene Cara and José Feliciano.

Because the contest is at that time decided through write-in votes, Knight will discover only in July that she has won $2,000, but there is some sour reaction to her win, as the only African American competitor on the show. 'The trophy was bigger than I was,' she will tell Oprah Winfrey in 2017. 'So they asked some of the other contestants . . . if they would come and stand with me and just help me hold the trophy.' The parents of the other competitors forbade it – but help was at hand. 'Sometimes the lead person in any situation can set the pace.' That person was the host of *Original Amateur Hour* – Ted Mack.

In the September after her victory – while celebrating her older brother Bubba's birthday – Gladys will decide to form a group with him, to be managed by their cousin James 'Pip' Woods. 'He was our manager in the beginning,' Bubba will relate. 'We didn't have any money to pay him, so we decided to "honor" him by naming the group **The Pips**.'

1981 ROTD: Two of the most enduring songs of the early 1980s. **The Specials'** 'Ghost Town', which is as much about tensions within the band as the state of Britain, proves to be the final single (and UK #1) that features their full original line-up. Soon Neville Staple, Lynval Golding and Terry Hall will leave to form Fun Boy Three, who will have seven UK top 20 hits. Also ROTD: 'Our Lips Are Sealed' by **The Go-Go's**, co-written by Hall and the quintet's Jane Wiedlin, will reach US #20.

1989 ROTD: Ian Broudie, up to now, is best known for production work (Echo & the Bunnymen, Icicle Works, The Fall) but **The Lightning Seeds'** 'Pure' will give him his first hit single in his own right (UK #16, US #31).

13 JUNE

1969 **The Rolling Stones** announce **Mick Taylor**, guitarist in John Mayall's Bluesbreakers, as the replacement for Brian Jones. Taylor will stay with the group until the end of 1974.

1978 From the soundtrack of the screen version of the musical *Grease*, 'You're the One That I Want' by **John Travolta and Olivia Newton-John** hits UK #1, remaining there for some nine weeks.

1995 ROTD: *Jagged Little Pill*, **Alanis Morissette**'s third album, marks a radical departure from the 21-year-old's former teen-pop image in her native Canada. Like Debbie Gibson in the US, Morissette had previously been permitted to compose her own songs, but something was missing, and only when she joined forces with LA-based writer-producer Glen Ballard (best known for co-writing 'Man in the Mirror' for Michael Jackson) did she find the ideal collaborator for her ideas.

Morissette was signed to Maverick Records, the company co-founded by Madonna in 1992, on the basis of three songs: 'Perfect', 'You Oughta Know' and 'Hand in My Pocket'. Maverick's A&R man was sold just thirty seconds into 'Perfect'. (Ironically, 'Perfect' wasn't even released as one of *Jagged Little Pill*'s six international hit singles.) The demos were sufficiently impressive that they were said to make up 80 per cent of the released album. 'Musically and cerebrally,' Morissette recalled of the 1994 sessions, 'Glen and I were so on the same wavelength . . . It was all very visceral and fast.'

The album will go on to sell 33 million copies worldwide.

14 JUNE

1967 The Beatles begin recording 'All You Need is Love' in London, after being asked to provide a song with a universal message to the world. Meanwhile **The Monkees** start work in a Hollywood studio on 'Daydream Believer', written by The Kingston Trio's John Stewart.

1968 ROTD: The 17-minute title track of **Iron Butterfly's** debut LP began as 'In the Garden of Eden' a love song from Adam to Eve, but when a decidedly merry-on-wine singer and organist Doug Ingle played his composition to the band, its slurred lyrics gave rise to its new title: 'In-A-Gadda-Da-Vida'.

1999 ROTD: The **Super Furry Animals** describe *Guerrilla* — with three of their best-loved singles, 'Northern Lites', 'Fire in My Heart' and 'Do or Die' — as 'a disposable pop album that's too good to throw away'.

15 JUNE

1965 In New York, **Bob Dylan** begins recording 'Like a Rolling Stone'. It takes him two days to get it right, not least because he has to boil the song down from what he later describes as 'this long piece of vomit, 20 pages long'.

1978 The Undertones record guitarist John O'Neill's 'Teenage Kicks' at Wizard Studios in Belfast. The first half of its title is taken from the MC5's 'Teenage Lust'; the second half from the chorus of The Rolling Stones' cover of 'Route 66'.

1999 ROTD: **Santana's** *Supernatural* is a mix of rock, Latin and African music, which in 2016 will become part of the new AQA GCSE Music curriculum in the UK.

2018 ROTD: *Oil of Every Pearl's Un-Insides*, nominated for a Best Dance/Electronic Album at the Grammys, is what turns out to be the only album from Scottish singer **Sophie** (1986–2021), who discards her anonymity and comes out as transgender on its opening track, 'It's Okay to Cry'.

16 JUNE

1967 The first night of the three-day **Monterey International Pop Festival** begins with LA band The Association, followed by a bill including Lou Rawls, Beverley Martyn, Eric Burdon's New Animals, and headliners Simon and Garfunkel, who perform an acoustic set.

1972 ROTD: Two British albums that will inspire generations of future musicians to form bands: the self-titled debut by **Roxy Music** and **David Bowie**'s *Ziggy Stardust and the Spiders from Mars*.

1979 Madness record their first single – 'The Prince', a tribute to Prince Buster – in Highbury, north London. Backed with their cover of Buster's 'Madness', it will be their sole release on 2-Tone Records, before signing with Stiff.

17 JUNE

1967 The *New Musical Express* publishes an advertisement from Liberty Records looking for songwriting and recording talent. The ad is answered by Reginald Dwight, based in London, and Bernie Taupin, a lyricist from Lincolnshire. Although neither of them passes their audition at Liberty, Dwight is given an envelope of Taupin's lyrics to take away, whereupon a writing partnership begins that will catapult Dwight to stardom as **Elton John**. Incredibly, despite all of their intervening success, it will take exactly 23 years before the pair's 'Sacrifice'/'Healing Hands' gives John his first solo UK #1 in 1990.

1983 ROTD: *Synchronicity*, **The Police**'s fifth and final album, trailed by the 'Every Breath You Take' single, will top the US album charts for

17 weeks. Exactly two years later, in 1985, lead singer **Sting** releases his first solo LP, *The Dream of the Blue Turtles*.

1996 'I felt I had so much more ground to cover,' **Beck** will later say about *Odelay* (US #16, UK #17), his long-awaited major label follow-up to 1994's *Mellow Gold*. Home to three international hits – 'Where It's At', 'Devil's Haircut', 'The New Pollution' – the album is an eclectic blend of hip hop, funk and roots, but the artist denies that it is born out of an impatience akin to channel surfing. 'I'm not bored with anything I'm doing. The public consciousness is moving to a point where we can assimilate two or three things at the same time.' Besides, although he is interested in the roots of music, he wants to keep developing. 'There's a need to not keep yourself in a world populated by antiques.'

With *Odelay* (its title is inspired by a Latin American cry of joy) Beck aims to transplant the spirit of celebration in Mexican music. He also claims that he and co-producers The Dust Brothers were subliminally influenced by the two albums being recorded in the studios on either side of theirs. One was by Black Sabbath. The other was by The Muppets.

18 JUNE

1966 Bass guitarist Paul Samwell-Smith quits **The Yardbirds** during a concert at Queen's College, Oxford. An audience member called Jimmy Page agrees to take over, and continues in the group until its dissolution in 1968. Samwell-Smith goes into record production, notably for Cat Stevens.

1980 ROTD: **Diana Ross's** 'Upside Down', written and produced by Bernard Edwards and Nile Rodgers of Chic, will become her final solo US #1.

1988 Depeche Mode play the 101st and final concert of their 'Music for the Masses' world tour at the Rose Bowl in Pasadena, California.

In 1989, the show will be released as a double live LP, *101*, and as a documentary film directed by D. A. Pennebaker.

19 JUNE

1923 BOTD: Initially an actor, presenter and interviewer for ITV, in 1968 **Muriel Young** will become a producer in young people's music television at Granada in Manchester. Among her credits will be *Lift Off With Ayshea*, *Shang-a-Lang* (starring the Bay City Rollers) and what becomes Marc Bolan's final work, the *Marc* series in 1977.

1981 ROTD: Despite its title, the live LP *No Sleep 'Til Hammersmith* by **Motörhead** was not recorded in London at all, but predominantly at Newcastle's City Hall. The following week, it becomes their only UK #1 album.

2000 ROTD: With an instantly memorable sample, taken from Chic's 1982 single 'Soup for One', 'Lady (Hear Me Tonight)' by French duo **Modjo** will become a worldwide smash, and a UK #1.

20 JUNE

1963 **Martha and the Vandellas**, with Martha Reeves on lead vocals, record 'Heat Wave' at Hitsville Studio A in Detroit. In 1964, it will be nominated for Best Rhythm and Blues Recording at the Grammys – the first time that a Motown group will receive such a nomination.

1975 ROTD: **Neil Young**'s *Tonight's the Night*, recorded in 1973, pays tributes to his guitarist Danny Whitten and roadie Bruce Berry, both of whom had recently died drug-related deaths. Meanwhile, **Talking Heads** begin a weekend of shows opening for the Ramones at CBGBs in New York.

1989 ROTD: 'Love Shack' by **The B-52's**. Produced by Don Was, the single will finally break the band as a top 40 act in the US (#3), four years after the death of their founder member Ricky Wilson. In 1990, it will reach UK #2.

21 JUNE

1974 ROTD: Issued in the UK before the US, 'When Will I See You Again' is arranged as a succession of questions, and will take **The Three Degrees** all the way to UK #1 in August.

1975 In a year when he is said to have sold an estimated 2 per cent of all worldwide music, **Elton John** plays Wembley Stadium and devotes the second half of his set to a track-by-track performance of his newly released LP, *Captain Fantastic and the Brown Dirt Cowboy*.

1997 ROTD: *Happy End of the World* by Tokyo's **Pizzicato 5** will become their biggest international success, and lead them to play live in the USA and Europe for the first time. The duo (vocalist Maki Nomiya and DJ Yasuharu Konishi) had first come to prominence outside Japan when their 'Twiggy Twiggy Twiggy vs James Bond' was included on the soundtrack to Robert Altman's 1994 movie *Prêt-à-Porter*.

22 JUNE

1971 ROTD: *Blue* by **Joni Mitchell**. 'There's hardly a dishonest note in the vocals,' Mitchell later says of the album, which features some of her most powerful and confessional songs: 'Carey', 'River' and 'All I Want'. 'I had no personal defences. But the advantage of it in the music was that there were no defences there either.'

1974 David Bowie performs at the Cobo Hall in Detroit. It is the first gig that one 15-year-old in the audience has ever attended. Her name: **Madonna** Louise Ciccone.

2008 Coldplay's single 'Viva la Vida' becomes #1 in the UK. Its title, which translates as 'Long Live Life', is inspired by an inscription added by artist Frida Kahlo to her final painting, 1954's *Watermelons*.

23 JUNE

1972 On the day that Smokey Robinson plays his final concert as lead singer with the Miracles in Washington DC (his replacement is Billy Griffin), The Osmonds record 'Crazy Horses', their only hit with Jay Osmond on lead vocals. Although it is about ecology and the environment, the song is banned by the South African government who assume it to be about heroin.

1987 16-year-old Tiffany Derwish begins a two-month-long tour of US shopping malls, performing in a presentation called 'The Beautiful You'. It proves to be an extraordinarily effective build-up to the launch of her first single, the chart-topping 'I Think We're Alone Now'.

1997 ROTD: The Mercury Prize-winning *New Forms* (UK #8) by Bristol DJ Roni Size and Reprazent, which combines drum and bass with jazz.

24 JUNE

1966 The Battle of the Bands at the Hollywood Bowl is won by The Richard Carpenter Trio, featuring 16-year-old drummer Karen Carpenter.

1982 In an appearance on *Top of the Pops*, Shalamar's Jeffrey Daniel wows the audience with a demonstration of bodypopping and moonwalking. The band's single 'A Night to Remember' goes on to rise from #25 in the UK charts to #5. On the same day, in the new issue of *Smash Hits*, singles reviewer Neil Tennant (later of Pet Shop Boys fame) awards the 'Single of the Fortnight' accolade to 'Wham! Rap', the first single by Wham!, which – for now – fails to chart.

1995 At the Glastonbury Festival, The Stone Roses (unavailable after guitarist John Squire is injured in a cycling accident) are replaced as Saturday night headliners by **Pulp**, who premiere 'Mis-Shapes', 'Disco 2000' and 'Sorted for Es and Wizz', and finish with what else but their recent UK #2 smash hit 'Common People'. The crowd appear to be word perfect.

25 JUNE

1969 **Sly and the Family Stone** record 'Hot Fun in the Summertime' (US #2), the same day that **The Hollies** record 'He Ain't Heavy, He's My Brother' (UK #2, and UK #1 in 1988) at Abbey Road Studios in London, with session player Elton John on piano.

1982 ROTD: *The Lexicon of Love* by **ABC**. The band's debut album comes after several years performing as post-punk outfit Vice Versa – with singer Martin Fry joining their line-up as a keyboardist after interviewing them for a fanzine he was editing called *Modern Drugs*. After Fry had heard Kevin Rowland of **Dexys Midnight Runners** say, 'Everything I do will be funky from now on', he and his fellow band members decided it was time 'to get our funky outfit together' under the new name of ABC, but feared that 'we'd be beaten to the punch'.

Looking for a new producer to work with on the album, the band brought in Trevor Horn after admiring his work on Dollar's 'Hand Held in Black and White'. Horn in turn was hooked by Martin Fry's lyrics, which reminded him of disco, 'but in a Bob Dylan way', packed with wry wordplay.

Subsequently, when ABC and Horn were in the studio recording one of the album's later hit singles 'The Look of Love', David Bowie happened to drop by and suggested adding in some answering machine messages. 'We went with the bit where I rant a little speech about finding true love,' says Fry, 'which, funnily enough, was heavily influenced by Iggy Pop's monologue in "Turn Blue".' Which was produced by David Bowie . . .

Ironically, for all of ABC's fears about being beaten to the punch, Dexys Midnight Runners have already moved on from the idea of funk to something else entirely: an emotionally powerful blend of soul and Irish-tinged music (thanks in part to the addition of a string section of Helen O'Hara and Steve Brennan, known as the Emerald Express). On the same day that ABC release *The Lexicon of Love*, arguably the defining album of the year, Dexys put out their new single, 'Come On Eileen'. A startling exercise in catharsis, it will become the best-selling UK single of 1982, and establish itself as a standard, played at every wedding you will ever attend.

1982 Also ROTD: With his fifth album, *Night and Day*, British singer, songwriter and musician **Joe Jackson** has relocated to New York. 'Steppin' Out', its breakout song, will become his only top 10 single in both the UK and US.

1990 ROTD: 'New Art Riot', a four-track EP on the Damaged Goods label, is the first release by Blackwood quartet, **Manic Street Preachers**. It is made *Melody Maker*'s single of the week.

2000 For the first time since 'Tears on My Pillow' a decade earlier, **Kylie Minogue** makes it to UK #1 with 'Spinning Around'. It is the start of a remarkable career resurgence, in which her next 13 singles will all reach the top 10.

26 JUNE

1963 In a Newcastle hotel room, John Lennon and Paul McCartney write most of a new song. The following day, back in Liverpool, they will finish it. Within a week, they will record it. And in August, they will release it. 'She Loves You' will become **The Beatles**' biggest-selling single in the UK.

1979 Tubeway Army begin a four-week run at the UK #1 spot with 'Are "Friends" Electric', making a star of lead singer **Gary Numan**.

1995 ROTD: *Exit Planet Dust* by **The Chemical Brothers**. The album's name is a reference to the act's previous name, The Dust Brothers, which they are forced to change when it turns out there is another act of the same name in America. When choosing their new name, they take inspiration from one of the tracks on the album, 'Chemical Beats'.

27 JUNE

1970 Though billed in the local Cornish press under their former name of Smile, **Queen** play their first gig under their new name and with new lead singer Freddie Mercury, at Truro's City Hall.

1983 ROTD: During the first hot British summer since, inevitably, 1976, **Bananarama**'s 'Cruel Summer' will reach UK #8, while **Wham!**'s debut LP *Fantastic* (which contains 'A Ray of Sunshine' and next single 'Club Tropicana') will be a UK #1.

2010 'California Gurls' by **Katy Perry** (featuring rapper Snoop Dogg) becomes UK #1. Inspired by the release of Jay-Z and Alicia Keys' 'Empire State of Mind' the year before, the single's spelling of 'Gurls' is a reference to 'September Gurls' by Big Star, whose lead singer Alex Chilton has died just a couple of months earlier.

28 JUNE

1970 Michael Eavis attends the Bath Festival of Blues and Progressive Music where he sees **Led Zeppelin** and Donovan – who at one point covers 'I Know an Old Lady Who Swallowed a Fly' – and decides to organise his own festival: the Pilton Festival, staged in September, and the birth of what will become known as **Glastonbury**.

1987 A one-off surprise guest at **Peter Gabriel**'s Earl's Court live show: when he performs 'Don't Give Up', **Kate Bush** shows up.

2009 The new UK #1 is 'Bulletproof' by **La Roux**, the support act on Lily Allen's spring tour.

29 JUNE

1973 In Osaka, **Ian Gillan** plays his final show as lead singer of **Deep Purple**, having already given advanced notice by letter to quit months earlier. He will form the Ian Gillan Band in 1975.

1983 After **John Peel** announces on BBC Radio 1 that he is hungry, he receives a mushroom biryani during his programme from **Billy Bragg**, who also sends a copy of his new LP, *Life's a Riot with Spy vs Spy*. A grateful Peel plays a track off it, 'The Milkman of Human Kindness', although initially at the wrong speed.

1989 Chart favourites since 1985, **Pet Shop Boys** only now begin their first-ever live tour, starting out in Hong Kong, and later visiting Japan and the UK, with the saxophonist Courtney Pine and a series of accompanying short films directed by Derek Jarman.

30 JUNE

1972 ROTD: *School's Out*, the fifth album by shock rockers **Alice Cooper**, and their breakthrough release. It is a masterpiece of LP packaging: a mock-up of a school desk covered in graffiti, which flips up. The record inside is wrapped in paper underwear, although this idea is soon dropped when it is deemed to be a fire hazard.

1975 It is announced that **The Jackson 5** will be leaving Motown to sign with the CBS label Epic. Jermaine Jackson will stay at Motown as a solo act, with the younger Randy Jackson replacing him.

1978 Four hours before supporting The Clash at Friars in Aylesbury, Coventry band The Automatics change their name to **The Specials**.

1986 ROTD: *True Blue* by **Madonna**, which is destined to become the year's best-selling LP. One track was offered to Michael Jackson for his *Bad* album ('La Isla Bonita', prior to Madonna's written contribution), but he turned it down.

JULY

1 JULY

1956 **Elvis Presley** appears on Steve Allen's NBC TV variety show, and finds himself singing 'Hound Dog' to an actual basset hound.

1970 **T. Rex** record 'Ride a White Swan' at Trident Studios with producer Tony Visconti, who loops the final ad-libbed vocal section to extend the track past the two-minute mark. It will become their and his breakthrough hit, peaking at UK #2 in January 1971.

1979 The first portable music cassette recorder, the Sony TPS-L2, or the **Walkman**, goes on sale in Japan. Sony has been a pioneer in technology since the late 1940s when the company launched as Tokyo Telecommunications and Engineering Industries. It first specialised in military communications technology before exploring alternative avenues, particularly in entertainment and lifestyle. The portability of the transistor, and in the 1970s, the ghetto blaster for outdoor use, became hugely popular. But the Walkman has specifically come about because Sony's honorary chairman Masaru Ibuka wanted a smaller tape-playing device for his business journeys. Engineer Shizuo Takashino set to work by taking the existing Sony Pressman (a Dictaphone used by news reporters and journalists), replacing the recording machinery and speaker with a stereo amplifier, and adding headphones.

It will be three months before Walkman sales take off, and it begins to be sold abroad. In the US, where it will hit the shops for Christmas 1979, it will be known as the Sound-about. In Australia and Sweden, it will be called the Freestyle. In the UK, from summer 1980, it will be called the Stowaway – leading Heaven 17 to issue a cassette-only release, *Music for Stowaways*.

In its first 10 years on sale, 50 million Walkmans will be sold, and a further 150 million personal stereos developed by other companies. It is believed its success in Japan is a reaction to the pressures of city life, and people's desire to create their own personal space and fill it with sound of their own choice.

1983 ROTD: *Synchro System* by **King Sunny Adé and his African Beats**. Their first LP to be recorded in London, it will not only become one of *NME*'s top 10 albums of the year, it will also secure the first-ever Grammy nomination for a Nigerian act.

1985 ROTD: The opening track of German pop quartet **Propaganda**'s lavish *A Secret Wish* (UK #16) sets music to Edgar Allan Poe's 1849 poem 'A Dream Within a Dream'.

2 JULY

1973 After only two **Roxy Music** albums, **Brian Eno** leaves the group to pursue solo projects, and subsequently proclaims their next Eno-less LP, *Stranded*, to be their best.

1980 Scottish singer **Sheena Easton** is profiled on BBC1's documentary series *The Big Time* alongside footage of her recording her debut single, 'Modern Girl'. Within two months, she will have two tracks – 'Modern Girl' and '9 to 5' – in the UK top 10, and the following year the latter track will reach #1 in the US, where it is retitled 'Morning Train (Nine to Five)' to avoid confusion with the recent Dolly Parton single.

1990 ROTD: 'Wash Your Face in My Sink', based around a sample of 'Hang on Sloopy' by Count Basie, is the first single from King Lou and Capital Q aka Toronto hip hop duo **Dream Warriors**.

2021 ROTD: Birmingham's **Laura Mvula** returns with her third album, *Pink Noise*, her first album in five years. Like its predecessor, *The Dreaming Room*, it will win an Ivor Novello Award for Best Album.

3 JULY

1969 ROTD: *Unhalfbricking* by **Fairport Convention**. Between recording and releasing the album (their second for Island Records) the band's 19-year-old drummer Martin Lamble has died in a road accident. Perhaps its most enduring song remains Sandy Denny's 'Who Knows Where the Time Goes?' Also ROTD (and also on Island): **Nick Drake**'s debut, *Five Leaves Left*.

1973 An announcement comes from '**Ziggy Stardust**' on the stage of the Hammersmith Odeon, London: 'Of all the shows on this tour, this particular show will remain with us the longest, because not only is it the last show of the tour, but it's the last show that we'll ever do. Thank you.'

1985 **Pet Shop Boys** make their first TV appearance, on the ITV children's pop quiz *Poparound*, hosted by Gary Crowley, performing their debut single for Parlophone, 'Opportunities'. Though it will go on to be a hit a year later, it will for only now reach UK #116.

2006 ROTD: After circulating some demos on MySpace, **Lily Allen**'s first single, the pop-reggae-tinged 'Smile', will become a UK #1.

4 JULY

1966 ROTD: Two of the musical inspirations for 'Summer in the City' by **The Lovin' Spoonful**: the sound of George Gershwin; and Mussorgsky's tense *Night on Bald Mountain* (as heard in the 1940 Disney film *Fantasia*).

1969 ROTD: **The Rolling Stones'** 'Honky Tonk Women'. Issued the day after the death of their former guitarist Brian Jones, it will prove to be the last of the band's eight UK #1s. Also out today: 'Give Peace a Chance' by **John Lennon** and **The Plastic Ono Band**, recorded in a Montreal hotel a month earlier.

1994 ROTD: **The Prodigy** return with *Music for the Jilted Generation*, a reaction in part to the popularity and even criminalisation of parts of the rave scene in Britain. It becomes a UK #1 album.

5 JULY

1954 As the UK experiences its first day without food rationing for 14 years (when restrictions on meat are lifted), **Elvis Presley** records his debut single, a cover of Arthur Crudup's 'That's All Right' at Sun Studios in Memphis.

1997 Irked by the music industry's tokenistic presentation of female artists, Sarah McLachlan has organised the first **Lilith Fair** festival, which begins its seven-week tour today in the Washington town of George, with Suzanne Vega, Tracy Chapman, Sheryl Crow, the Indigo Girls, Emmylou Harris and over 50 other artists.

2015 Belgian DJ and producer **Lost Frequencies** hits UK #1 with 'Are You with Me'. Because the unveiling of the following week's chart is brought forward from Sunday to Friday (in order to synchronise release dates across the global music industry), the single is #1 for only five days, earning it the dubious distinction of being the shortest-lived UK chart-topper.

6 JULY

1957 As skiffle sextet **The Quarrymen** prepare to perform at the St Peter's Church garden fete in Woolton, Liverpool, tea chest bass player Ivan Vaughan introduces his student friend **Paul McCartney** to the band's lead singer and guitarist, **John Lennon**.

1964 Exactly seven years later, *A Hard Day's Night*, the first film starring **The Beatles** – the biggest group on the planet – premieres at the London Pavilion.

1979 ROTD: **The B-52's'** self-titled first album. It comes out on the same day as their second single, the 'Peter Gunn'-aping 'Planet Claire'.

1983 ROTD: Asked to create a half-hour soundtrack album for a Paris art exhibition called Orrimbe, **Jean-Michel Jarre** decides to print just one copy of the resulting *Music for Supermarkets*, which is sold at auction for 69,000 francs. (The album is also broadcast in full on Radio Luxembourg and Jarre encourages home tapers everywhere to record it.)

7 JULY

1968 The Yardbirds' farewell gig takes place in Luton's College of Technology in Bedfordshire. Guitarist Jimmy Page is expected to embark on solo work, but instead forms The New Yardbirds with three new members: Robert Plant, John Paul Jones and John Bonham . . .

1980 In Japan, the **Yellow Magic Orchestra**, featuring **Ryuichi Sakamoto**, replace themselves at #1 in the albums chart, when *Multiples* takes over from *Solid State Survivor*.

1991 'Everything I Do (I Do It for You)' by **Bryan Adams** begins a (still unbeaten) 16-week reign at the top of the UK charts, during which time the following six singles reach #2: 'Now That We've Found Love' by Heavy D and the Boyz; 'More Than Words' by Extreme; 'I'm Too Sexy' by Right Said Fred; 'Let's Talk About Sex' by Salt-N-Pepa; 'Wind of Change' by Scorpions; and 2 Unlimited's 'Get Ready for This'.

8 JULY

1967 **The Jimi Hendrix Experience** perform the first of seven shows as the opening act for **The Monkees** in Florida, North Carolina and New York state. The two bands get along well, but audience reaction is less convivial, and the Experience soon bid an amicable farewell.

1996 ROTD: It begins with the sound of Mel B's approaching footsteps and Geri's laughter. 'Wannabe' by the **Spice Girls** is finally available to buy after several weeks of TV and radio promotion (from *The Big Breakfast* to *Surprise Surprise*), and will top the UK charts for seven weeks.

2016 ROTD: *Wildflower* ends a 16-year wait for a second **Avalanches** album, complete with guest appearances from Kevin Parker (Tame Impala), Father John Misty, MF Doom and The Flaming Lips' Jonathan Donahue.

9 JULY

1965 ROTD: **Sonny and Cher's** 'I Got You Babe' is Sonny Bono's answer song to Bob Dylan's 'It Ain't Me Babe'.

1971 Michigan rockers **Grand Funk Railroad** play a sold-out show at Shea Stadium, New York, only the second group to do so (after, inevitably, The Beatles). The 55,000 tickets reputedly sold out in just three days.

1981 Released as a single in March, **Phil Lynott's** 'Yellow Pearl', co-written by Midge Ure, becomes the theme to *Top of the Pops*. The record finally reaches the top 20 in its own right in 1982.

2001 ROTD: **Yeah Yeah Yeahs'** self-titled first EP on the band's own Shifty label. Also making her recording debut today is Moscow-born American singer-songwriter **Regina Spektor** with *11:11*.

10 JULY

1981 ROTD: **Spandau Ballet's** 'Chant No. 1 (I Don't Need This Pressure On)' is a musical tribute to a favoured haunt, the London funk club Le Beat Route. Horn backing comes from Britfunk group Beggar and Co.

2007 ROTD: *Marry Me*, titled after a catchphrase in the TV sitcom *Arrested Development*, becomes the first album release from Annie Clark under the name **St Vincent**. Clark was previously a member of the capacious Dallas-based group The Polyphonic Spree.

11 JULY

1969 ROTD: 'Space Oddity' by **David Bowie**. Five days later, despite its themes of alienation and doom, the song will feature briefly in the BBC's coverage of the Apollo 11 mission to the Moon. In October, it will climb to UK #5; and when reissued in 1975, it will reach UK #1.

1980 ROTD: *Searching for the Young Soul Rebels* by **Dexys Midnight Runners** begins with tiny snatches of 'Smoke on the Water', 'Holidays in the Sun' and 'Rat Race', and ends with Kevin Rowland singing a section from 'Everything I Do Gohn Be Funky' by Lee Dorsey.

1988 ROTD: 'The Only Way is Up' by **Yazz and the Plastic Population**. In 1980 it had been an obscure single by the Mississippi-born soul artist Otis Clay. Thanks to producer Coldcut's remake, it will become the UK's second-best-selling single of the year.

12 JULY

1962 Brian Jones, Mick Jagger, Keith Richards, Ian Stewart and Dick Taylor play the Marquee Club in London. All they need is a name, and

Jones is drawn to the opening song on a Muddy Waters compilation, entitled 'Rollin' Stone'.

1979 The **Disco Demolition Night** takes place at Comiskey Park in Chicago. Organisers have invited people to show up with disco records, which will then be destroyed in an explosion. In a nadir for the 'Disco Sucks' movement, the event descends into a riot, with fires breaking out, six people injured and 39 arrested.

2019 ROTD: **Ed Sheeran's** cast of collaborators for his *No. 6 Collaborations Project* includes Cardi B, Justin Bieber, 50 Cent, Dave, Skrillex, Eminem, Bruno Mars . . . and **Camila Cabello**, whose own new single with **Shawn Mendes**, 'Señorita', hits UK #1 on this day.

13 JULY

1954 British pop music changes forever. No, really. A couple of songs shy of completing the recording of an album for Decca Records called *New Orleans Joys*, the **Chris Barber Jazz Band** visit the nearest pub to discuss how to proceed. Soon enough, they decide to record some live material as a 'breakdown group'. In other words, the brass section will take a break, while trombonist Barber will switch to double bass and take centre stage alongside washboard player Beryl Bryden and the band's Glaswegian guitarist **Lonnie Donegan**.

Donegan doubles up on the session as a singer, performing a song written in 1929 by Clarence Wilson, who had worked for the Rock Island railway company in the US. 'Rock Island Line' had already been embellished and popularised on record by **Lead Belly** in 1937, and in Britain by George Melly in 1951. But Donegan's recording will unexpectedly become a hit single in 1956 when Decca is on the lookout for something homegrown with the same kind of mass appeal as Bill Haley's 'Rock Around the Clock'. Not only does 'Rock Island Line' reach UK #8 and even US #8, it almost single-handedly popularises the skiffle craze in the UK.

1985 'Global jukebox' **Live Aid**, beamed by satellite to 150 countries, attracts 72,000 visitors to Wembley Stadium, London, and nearly 90,000 to Philadelphia's JFK Stadium, with performances from Status Quo, Queen, Sting, Phil Collins, U2, David Bowie, Sade, Dire Straits, Elton John, George Michael, Paul McCartney, Led Zeppelin, Tina Turner, Duran Duran and Bob Dylan. Meanwhile, other countries around the world contribute too. In Sydney, an Oz for Africa bill is topped by INXS. In The Hague, BB King contributes from the North Sea Jazz Festival, while Russian rock band Autograph play two songs in Moscow.

1987 ROTD: 'Roadblock' by **Stock Aitken Waterman**. Reacting to criticism that all of their songs sound the same (a pop-oriented approach that was often deemed by some in club circles to lack credibility), the songwriting and production trio release their new single as a white label with no accompanying information at all. After it provokes feverish excitement among a number of DJs, they then take great delight in revealing the truth.

2020 **Olivia Rodrigo**'s diary entry for today begins: 'I got my drivers license today, a very highly anticipated achievement.' It inspires her debut single 'Drivers License', which will become a worldwide smash in 2021.

14 JULY

1973 **The Everly Brothers** split up during a disastrous concert in Buena Park, California, when an inebriated Don is unable to play or remember the lyrics to their songs. Phil smashes his guitar and storms off. The brothers will reunite 10 years later at London's Royal Albert Hall.

1977 After refusing to give airtime to 'God Save the Queen' earlier in the year, the BBC decide that the **Sex Pistols** can perform 'Pretty

Vacant' (up from UK #45 to #7) on *Top of the Pops*. But Johnny Rotten's delivery is as full of subversion as ever.

1999 ROTD: The first album from Mancunian DJ Andrew Carthy, or **Mr Scruff**: *Keep It Unreal*. A whimsical and highly entertaining mix of breakbeat, trip hop and electronica, its best-known track, 'Get a Move On!' samples Moondog's 1969 tribute to Charlie Parker, 'Bird's Lament'.

15 JULY

1982 **Dexys Midnight Runners** (UK #31 and rising) present 'Come On Eileen' on *Top of the Pops*. Meanwhile, ABC in America televises *Vietnam Requiem*, a documentary about the conflict which, when screened by ITV in the UK in late 1984, has its commentary heavily sampled by producer Paul Hardcastle for his worldwide hit '19'.

2010 Exactly 15 years after **Robbie Williams'** abrupt departure from **Take That**, it is announced that he has rejoined the reformed quartet for one album and one album only, the already recorded *Progress*.

2012 'Doing it not right is right' is the philosophy of Jae-Sang Park, a 34-year-old veteran of the Seoul hip hop scene who records and performs under the name of **Psy** (short for 'Psycho'). On this day, the video for his new single, 'Gangnam Style' – an amusing and affectionate tribute to the upmarket lifestyle of his home city – is uploaded to YouTube, and proves to be an addictive clip. People can't stop watching it. Its accompanying dance, a kind of horse trot, is also part of the appeal.

Within five weeks, nearly 50 million people have viewed it on YouTube and it becomes the number one clip on iTunes, inspiring parodies in South Korea and the USA, and getting an airing at the Stockholm Pride parade. By the end of 2012, over 1 billion people will have seen the video, and Psy will have appeared with Madonna and her dance troupe on stage. It all comes as a surprise to Psy, who tells the press that the video was not targeted at foreign countries: 'It was for local fans. My goal was to look uncool. I achieved it.'

But then Psy has never quite fitted into the South Korean pop scene. On releasing his first album, 2001's *Psy from the Psycho World!*, he was nicknamed 'The Bizarre Singer' due to his unusual appearance and dance moves.

16 JULY

1982 A three-day festival called 'A World of Music, Art and Dance', or **Womad** for short, begins for the first time in Shepton Mallet, Somerset, where a rock bill of Peter Gabriel and Echo & the Bunnymen is augmented by performers from China (singers and dancers Tianjin), Nigeria (highlife exponent Prince Nico Mbarga), Jamaica (trombonist Rico) and India (the Dhrupal Singers).

1984 ROTD: *Diamond Life* by London-based group **Sade**, fronted by singer Sade Adu, will sell 10 million copies worldwide, buoyed by hit singles 'Your Love is King' and 'Smooth Operator'.

1990 BOTD: Ayodeji Ibrahim Balogun in Lagos, Nigeria. As Afrobeat star **Wizkid**, he will become the first Nigerian artist to chart in the US in 2016 when he collaborates with Canadian hip hop's **Drake** on the worldwide #1, 'One Dance'.

2021 ROTD: *All Over the Place* by **KSI**. The London rapper's second album, which features a litany of guest stars including Craig David, Anne-Marie, Yungblud and Digital Farm Animals, will enter the UK album charts at #1.

17 JULY

1974 The **Moody Blues** announce they have converted Decca's Studio One in north London into Threshold Studios (named after their own record label, formed in 1970), which houses the world's first quadrophonic sound studio, Westlake Audio.

1975 Island Records founder Chris Blackwell is present at the London Lyceum gig by **Bob Marley and the Wailers**, which is being recorded for a live album. One of the stand-out songs of the set is the seven-minute 'No Woman No Cry', already familiar to many in its studio recording from 1974's *Natty Dread*.

Edited down to four minutes as a single, 'No Woman No Cry' will be a rare example of a song that becomes far better known in its live version. It soon reaches UK #22, but will reach #8 in 1981 following Marley's death at the age of only 36.

The song's credited writer is one Vincent Ford, who at that time is running a soup kitchen for the malnourished and homeless in the Trenchtown ghetto of Kingston, Jamaica, and has known Marley since their childhoods. Some will later suggest that this is an example of Marley attempting to avoid the restrictions that come with putting his own name to a publishing contract. Others such as journalist Vivien Goldman will wonder if the song emerged from a creative conversation between Marley and Ford – or maybe simply that 'Bob wanted him to have the money'. Whatever the reason, in 1987, a court decision will eventually award full control over the song to the Marley estate.

1981 ROTD: Two very different cover versions, both of which will hit UK #1. **Shakin' Stevens'** rockabilly revival of 'Green Door', first a hit for Jim Lowe in 1956, will have an almost immediate impact. Slower to take off is 'Tainted Love' from Leeds electronic duo **Soft Cell**, first recorded by Gloria Jones in 1964 and a cult Northern soul classic, but it will go on to sell a million in Britain and spend 43 weeks on the *Billboard* Hot 100, peaking at #8.

18 JULY

1978 **Def Leppard** play their first-ever gig, at an end-of-term dance held by Westfield School in Mosborough in their home city of Sheffield. They encore with a cover of Thin Lizzy's 'Jailbreak'.

1980 ROTD: *Closer* by **Joy Division**. The album is issued exactly two months after the death of the band's lead singer and lyricist Ian Curtis. Its funereal sleeve was conceived prior to Curtis's death and its co-designer Peter Saville expressed concern about its suitability: 'We've got a tomb on the cover of the album!' But the band didn't want to change the design that they – including Curtis – had agreed upon together.

1991 The very first **Lollapalooza** festival is held in Tempe, Arizona, before embarking on a tour of the US for the next six weeks. On the bill is headlining act Jane's Addiction, plus Siouxsie and the Banshees, Living Colour, Nine Inch Nails and Ice-T's rock band Body Count.

19 JULY

1966 A 46-piece orchestra is waiting for **Frank Sinatra** to show up for a recording session, but Frank isn't coming. Riding high in the charts with 'Strangers in the Night', and in the middle of filming *The Naked Runner* in London, he has flown to Las Vegas to marry the 21-year-old star of TV's *Peyton Place*, Mia Farrow. Rather than cancel the session, writer-producer Jerry Ragovoy contacts the Philadelphia-born singer **Lorraine Ellison**, and she, with that full orchestra, creates one of the all-time great dramatic soul ballads: 'Stay With Me'.

'When the time came for me to come out to record,' Ellison recalls in 1974, 'the guys [in the orchestra] just fell apart – Frank sure had changed!'

Though 'Stay With Me' will become a classic – covered by The Walker Brothers, Bette Midler, Janis Joplin and Duffy – Ellison's version with its blaze of voice and orchestra will prove hard to top.

Nonetheless, it enjoys only modest success, reaching US #11 on the R&B chart, only #64 on the Hot 100, and failing to chart at all in the UK.

1968 ROTD: **Family**'s *Music in a Doll's House*. The album causes The Beatles to rethink the title for their next album, which they were planning to call 'A Doll's House'. It will eventually be released in a plain white sleeve with no title or cover art, leading to it being unofficially referred to as the 'White Album'.

1983 Paul Young, previously hitless on the UK charts save for the 1978 novelty hit 'Toast' with the group Streetband, reaches #1 with a downtempo cover of 'Wherever I Lay My Hat (That's My Home)', first released by Marvin Gaye in 1962.

20 JULY

1974 A one-day 'Bucolic Frolic' event is held in Knebworth Park, Hertfordshire, marking the start of the **Knebworth rock festivals**. Appearing are The Allman Brothers, The Doobie Brothers, Van Morrison, the Mahavishnu Orchestra, The Sensational Alex Harvey Band and Tim Buckley.

1979 ROTD: 'Reasons to Be Cheerful (Part 3)' by **Ian Dury and the Blockheads**. Dury later explains the thinking behind what is one of the great 'list' songs, saying that it was inspired by the way that The Beatles put 'just a load of nice people' on their *Sgt. Pepper* sleeve. The flip side, 'Common as Muck', offers another list – this time of celebrities with working-class roots.

1998 ROTD: The **Spice Girls**' 'holiday romance' single, 'Viva Forever' – and the last to feature the just-departed Geri Halliwell. Released on the same day, 'Music Sounds Better with You' (UK #2) technically makes **Stardust** one of the great one-hit wonders, although one of the trio, Thomas Bangalter, is of course responsible for many more hits as half of Daft Punk.

21 JULY

1978 ROTD: 'Top of the Pops' by Edinburgh new wavers **Rezillos**. Satirising the music industry in general and the BBC pop show in particular, the single reaches UK #17 and – inevitably – sees the band perform on the show. Songwriter Jo Callis will later join The Human League for their commercial zenith in 1981.

1981 ROTD: **Luther Vandross**, former lead singer with the group Change, goes solo with 'Never Too Much', which tops the US R&B singles chart, but will become a UK top 40 single only when remixed in 1989.

2016 ROTD: 'Human' by Rory Graham, or **Rag'n'Bone Man** (so named because of Graham's love for the sitcom *Steptoe and Son*), will initially become a massive hit in Germany, where it tops the chart for 12 weeks. It will finally break through in Britain (#2 at Christmas 2016) after being covered by UK *X Factor* contestant Emily Middlemas.

22 JULY

1977 ROTD: According to **Elvis Costello**, the songs on his debut LP, *My Aim is True*, are composed entirely from 'revenge and guilt'. He is backed on the album by US country rock band Clover, who for contractual reasons are uncredited – though they do get referred to as The Shamrocks in some publicity. (Clover's keyboard player Sean Hopper will subsequently form The News with singer Huey Lewis.)

1980 US soul trio **Odyssey** reach #1 in the UK with 'Use It Up and Wear It Out', despite missing the charts completely in their homeland. The song's composers are Sandy Linzer (responsible for many

Four Seasons hits) and L. Russell Brown (whose surprising past credits include Dawn's 'Tie A Yellow Ribbon').

1996 ROTD: 'I Am, I Feel', produced by Dave Stewart of Eurythmics, becomes the first of several hits for **Alisha's Attic**: Shelly and Karen Poole, the daughters of 60s pop star Brian Poole.

23 JULY

1973 At 5 p.m., Alan Freeman hosts the first BBC Radio 1 live Roadshow from Newquay in Cornwall. It marks the start of a touring event that will feature many of the station's presenters entertaining live crowds around the country during the months of July and August – an event that will be repeated every year until 1999.

1984 ROTD: In between Wham!'s first two #1 singles comes **George Michael**'s introduction as a soloist, 'Careless Whisper'. Based on his teenage experiences, and written with Andrew Ridgeley, its demo versions in early 1982 predated Wham!'s chart career.

1996 ROTD: *Tidal* by 18-year-old New Yorker **Fiona Apple**, whose breakout single 'Criminal' will win a Grammy for Best Female Rock Vocal Performance.

24 JULY

1964 ROTD: One of the all-time great debut singles, 'She's Not There' by **The Zombies**, partly based by composer and keyboard player Rod Argent on a John Lee Hooker song called 'No One Told Me'. The record's producer, Ken Jones, will later become the composer and bandleader for many TV themes of the 1970s and 80s: *Sykes*, *Only When I Laugh*, *The Paul Daniels Magic Show*, and *Aspel and Company*.

2011 A few weeks before releasing his second mixtape, *Thursday*, the secretive 21-year-old producer, singer and musician Abel Tesfaye – who first released music on YouTube two years before – publicly reveals his identity as **The Weeknd** at a hotly anticipated Toronto gig.

2022 At 78 years of age, **Joni Mitchell** makes a spectacular live comeback at the Newport Folk Festival, her first live set in over 20 years.

25 JULY

1980 ROTD: **Adam Ant** unveils his new incarnation of **the Ants** – guitarist Marco Pirroni, bassist Kevin Mooney and the effective dual drumming of Merrick and Terry Lee Miall – on 'Kings of the Wild Frontier', which first lucks out at UK #48 but will soar to #2 the following spring.

1983 ROTD: **Metallica**'s brand of heavy metal and thrash punk is captured on vinyl for the first time on the LP *Kill 'Em All*. Two weeks later, the frenetic 'Whiplash' is extracted from it as a single.

1989 ROTD: Having turned their back on their 'frat hip hop' period at Def Jam, the **Beastie Boys** return on the Capitol label with producers The Dust Brothers, on the more experimental but staggering *Paul's Boutique*, containing over 100 samples (some of which originate from their own previous output).

26 JULY

1968 On the day that **The Jackson 5** sign to Motown Records, the scheduled release of **The Rolling Stones**' LP *Beggars Banquet* is postponed when their Decca label objects to the sleeve: a toilet wall daubed with graffiti. The LP will finally be released in December in a plain cream cover, but later CD reissues will feature the original – instantly recognisable – artwork.

1974 ROTD: *Rock Bottom* by **Robert Wyatt**. Released the year after his disastrous fall from a window in London, which left him permanently paralysed from the waist down, some people assume that the songs are a direct reaction to the accident itself. Yet Wyatt had already begun working on the record before that, completing it only after a lengthy stay in hospital.

Previously the drummer of jazz-rock fusion group Soft Machine and later Matching Mole, Wyatt was forced to go solo by the practicalities of his life after the accident in June 1973, thereby showcasing his inimitable, vulnerable voice. 'If anything, being a paraplegic helped me with the music,' he later tells Q magazine, 'because being in hospital left me free to dream, and to really think through the music.'

As a whole, the album is less directly about his accident and convalescence, and more about his relationship with his wife, the artist Alfreda Benge, which is celebrated on the record's euphoric opener, 'Sea Song'. Once the LP is released, Virgin Records ask for a single, and Wyatt unexpectedly charts with a cover of The Monkees' 'I'm a Believer' (UK #29).

1982 ROTD: **The League Unlimited Orchestra**'s *Love and Dancing* is producer Martin Rushent's reworked dub/instrumental version of The Human League's *Dare*. In a pre-digital age, Rushent has painstakingly constructed the record by manually editing tape – there are over 2,600 edits. It reaches #3 in the UK LP charts.

27 JULY

1973 ROTD: *New York Dolls'* self-titled first album. The mix of glam and punk in the band's live shows is successfully captured on record by producer Todd Rundgren. Its sales are low on release, but the LP becomes a huge influence on punk rock in both America and the UK.

On the same day comes 'Rock On' by **David Essex**. Although it will be his only hit in the US, it will help shape the style of R.E.M.'s 'Drive' nearly 20 years later.

1983 ROTD: **Madonna**'s debut LP of the same name. Although it will yield three major international hits – 'Holiday', 'Lucky Star' and 'Borderline' – it will take over a year to reach the *Billboard* top 10.

1987 ROTD: 'Never Gonna Give You Up' by **Rick Astley**. Yet another Stock Aitken Waterman composition and production, it will stay at UK #1 for five weeks and become the year's biggest-selling single.

28 JULY

1961 ROTD: 'Johnny Remember Me' by **John Leyton**. Four days earlier, the actor and singer performed the eerie song twice (as fictional rock star Johnny St Cyr) on the ITV department store drama series, *Harpers West One*. The day after its release, it is played to the *Juke Box Jury* panel on BBC TV. Spike Milligan describes it as 'son of "Ghost Riders in the Sky"', and votes it a miss. It will go to UK #1.

1987 ROTD: Instantly memorable for its sampled saxophone screech, taken from the opening of 'The Grunt' by The J.B.'s, **Public Enemy**'s 'Rebel Without a Pause' will give them their first top 40 single in the UK.

2017 ROTD: The 31st and probably final album by **The Fall**, *New Facts Emerge*, which will chart at UK #35.

29 JULY

1959 **The Isley Brothers** record 'Shout (Parts 1 & 2)' in New York. The idea for the opening of the self-penned song comes from two sources: the extended cry of 'We-eee-ll' came from Ray Charles' 'I Got a Woman', while the opening line was ad-libbed by the group during a live performance when their rendition of 'Lonely Teardrops' by Jackie Wilson had brought the audience to their feet in excitement.

1966 Bob Dylan crashes his motorcycle near Woodstock, in New York state, and although he recovers soon after, ceases his touring schedule for nearly eight years.

2016 ROTD: *Viola Beach* by **Viola Beach**. The Warrington rock quartet's only album is posthumously issued, after the deaths in February of the group's four members (Kris Leonard, River Reeves, Tomas Lowe and Jack Dakin) and their manager Craig Tarry when their car fell from a bridge in Sweden. The album enters the UK charts at #1.

30 JULY

1966 Only hours after the England national football team win the FIFA World Cup, Eric Clapton, Jack Bruce and Ginger Baker perform for the first time as **Cream** at Manchester's Twisted Wheel Club.

1990 ROTD: 'Where Are You Baby?', the biggest hit (UK #3) by **Betty Boo** who, as Alison Clarkson, used to be one quarter of the She Rockers, who had supported Public Enemy and De La Soul.

2001 ROTD: *Is This It*, the debut by New York rock band **The Strokes** is first released in Australia, where the group has just toured, and then given a staggered release as they continue their world tour in Japan, the UK and then the US.

31 JULY

1981 ROTD: 'Hand Held in Black and White' is the first of four **Dollar** singles to be produced by Buggles' **Trevor Horn**, and the result leads Horn to be sought out by ABC to produce them.

1989 ROTD: The year's best-selling single in the UK, 'Ride on Time' is **Black Box**'s attempt to make a record 'with the power of Led Zeppelin and Deep Purple, but with a dance beat', according to founder member and rock fan Daniele Davoli. Already a popular record in the clubs of Ibiza, Haçienda DJ Mike Pickering brought it to the attention of his colleagues at the UK record label Deconstruction.

But who is actually singing on this Italo-house anthem? Is it really the model Katrin Quinol, who fronts all their TV appearances? Clearly not. In fact, the voice belongs to US soul singer **Loleatta Holloway**, sampled from her 1980 floor-filler, 'Love Sensation'. To put it mildly, Holloway is not pleased, especially given the work she put into it. 'It was the hardest song I ever sang. I had to do it so many times, I lost my voice.' So begins an extensive legal discussion between Deconstruction, Salsoul (who own the recording of 'Love Sensation') and Holloway.

In mid-September, about halfway through the six-week reign of 'Ride on Time' at UK #1, a remix appears, starring a new voice. Is it Katrin *this* time? Maybe – but while it has never been confirmed, it might also belong to a young British singer called Heather Small, who will go on to front Mike Pickering's 90s hit machine **M People**.

AUGUST

1 AUGUST

1960 At Columbia Records, 18-year-old **Aretha Franklin** starts to leave her gospel roots behind when she records the song 'Today I Sing the Blues' for her first album. But the album, *Aretha*, will not chart when it is released in 1961; indeed the singer will not find crossover success until she signs with Atlantic in 1967.

1971 George Harrison and Ravi Shankar stage two **Concerts for Bangladesh** at Madison Square Garden in New York – one at 2.30 p.m. and the other at 8 p.m. Both Harrison and Shankar perform, as do Bob Dylan, Eric Clapton, Badfinger, Ali Akbar Khan, Billy Preston, Leon Russell and Ringo Starr. Around $250,000 is raised.

1981 Music Television, or **MTV**, launches on cable across the US. The first clip to be aired is 'Video Killed the Radio Star' by Buggles (UK #1, US #40), before the Video Jockeys (VJs) introduce themselves, and we hear the slogan, 'You'll never look at music the same way again.'

The channel has been developed by WNBC radio's Robert Pittman after he noticed *Popclips*, a 1980 series of video clips screened by the Nickelodeon entertainment channel and made by ex-Monkee Mike Nesmith's company Pacific Arts. Pittman in turn created a short-lived format called *Album Tracks*, but audience research confirmed a thirst for a round-the-clock pop music TV service.

At first, the content of MTV is mostly rocky, white and male, per-haps mirroring the output of the genre-specific world of US radio, but by 1983 two major changes of music policy will take place: preference will be given to the imaginative promo videos produced in the UK (leading to the biggest concentration of UK acts on the *Billboard* charts since the mid-60s); and there will be increased coverage of Black acts, most notably Michael Jackson and Prince.

2 AUGUST

1962 As a teenager, he toured with Bobby Vee as 'Elston Gunn'. For a while, he was 'Robert Allen' ('It sounded like the name of a Scottish king'). In the future he'd become screenwriter 'Sergei Petrov' and a couple of (Traveling) Wilburys. But today, Robert Zimmerman officially becomes **Bob Dylan**.

1971 ROTD: 'Uncle Albert/Admiral Halsey' by **Paul and Linda McCartney**. Never released in the UK, the single goes on to top the US Hot 100. The 'Albert' of the title is a fond reference to Paul's own uncle, Albert Kendall, while William 'Halsey' was indeed an admiral in the US Navy during the Second World War.

1988 ROTD: **Salt-N-Pepa**'s *A Salt with a Deadly Pepa*, their second LP, with two reinterpretations of Isley Brothers standards: 'Shake Your Thang' and 'Twist and Shout'.

3 AUGUST

1983 **Prince and the Revolution** perform 'I Would Die 4 U', 'Baby I'm a Star' and the title song of the forthcoming *Purple Rain* movie live, to 1,500 people, at First Avenue in Minneapolis. Recordings of these live renditions will be included as the last three tracks on the 1984 *Purple Rain* album.

1991 Appearing together on BBC1's Saturday morning children's show *The 8.15 from Manchester* (theme music: Inspiral Carpets) are **Take That**, promoting their flop first single 'Do What U Like', and **Blur**, plugging their hardly-flying-out-of-the-shops-either new single 'Bang'. (In October, when the year's *Smash Hits* Readers Poll is published, and pop stars are surveyed in an associated feature, Blur will vote for Take That – still to break through as a hit machine – as the year's 'best dance act'.)

1993 ROTD: *Tuesday Night Music Club* by former Michael Jackson backing singer **Sheryl Crow** has a slow start commercially, but will break through after the 1994 hit single 'All I Wanna Do' (US #2, UK #4).

4 AUGUST

1958 Although *Billboard* has been publishing sales charts since July 1913, and a Top 100 since November 1955, only today does the **Hot 100** (a combination of sales and airplay) premiere. The first Hot 100 #1 is 'Poor Little Fool' by Ricky Nelson.

1964 ROTD: After two misses, **The Kinks** hit third time lucky with 'You Really Got Me', which will become their first UK #1. Ray Davies later says that the song was a tribute to his blues heroes, Lead Belly and Big Bill Broonzy.

1972 ROTD: 'Virginia Plain' by **Roxy Music**. Although it is not unusual for bands of this era to release singles as stand-alone items not replicated on their albums, this exhilarating debut stands out for being recorded *after* the band's first self-titled LP, over three days in July.

The song is born of lead singer Bryan Ferry's long-held obsession with the American Dream and the Pop-Art Movement of artists like Andy Warhol and Roy Lichtenstein. In the 1960s, Ferry had been an art college student in Newcastle, where one of his tutors was Pop-Art pioneer Richard Hamilton. Inspired to create a painting of his own, the young Ferry had chosen to depict Jane Holzer – who acted in several Andy Warhol films – on a pack of cigarettes. And he called the piece 'Virginia Plain'.

When the single 'Virginia Plain' reaches the UK top 10 in September, peaking at #4, Ferry will sum up his feelings of achievement to the *Guardian*: 'Before, everything I did was either body (singing in a student R&B band) or mind (painting and writing). Now they are combined, and I am incredibly happy.'

'Virginia Plain', incidentally, will become one of a select band of hit singles where the title does not appear until the very end of the song. See also: 'Up the Junction' by Squeeze and 'Just Like Heaven' by The Cure.

5 AUGUST

1957 After five years as a local show on WFIL in Philadelphia, and one year after the arrival of presenter and producer Dick Clark, **American Bandstand** is picked up by national broadcaster ABC where it will air weekly for the next 30 years. With a live dancing audience and artists lip-synching to their current hits, it will be a model for *Top of the Pops* in Britain and *Soul Train* in the US.

1993 **Natalie Merchant**, lead singer of **10,000 Maniacs** since their inception in 1981, announces her departure from the group on MTV by saying she 'didn't want art by committee anymore'. Merchant goes solo and the Maniacs continue; their final release together is their *MTV Unplugged* set, recorded in April.

2021 Two days after his 95th birthday, **Tony Bennett** retires from live performance with the recording of the *One Last Time* special with **Lady Gaga**, at Radio City Music Hall.

6 AUGUST

1979 ROTD: Northampton rock band **Bauhaus** as good as invent gothic rock with their nine-minute single 'Bela Lugosi's Dead', issued on the indie label Small Wonder.

1988 A year after its creation for MTV Europe, MTV in America premieres *Yo! MTV Raps*, a weekly hip hop series, with Run-DMC as guest hosts on this first episode.

2001 ROTD: '21 Seconds' by **So Solid Crew**. The single is the result of a challenge that the UK garage act set themselves: to make a single involving 10 different voices, each of which must fill twelve bars of four beats, or 21 seconds.

The idea was partly about great art coming out of restriction, and partly about showing off the diversity of vocalists and rappers in the collective. And it wasn't simply creative democracy but financial democracy too – it meant they all got a composer credit. 'It's not about seeing how many times any one individual can get their face on TV,' the group's MC Harvey says. 'It's about everyone getting their chance.'

The group's expanding and contracting line-up – often up to 30 members – has its roots in a Battersea housing estate in south London. Lisa Maffia, whose three-year-old daughter can be heard on the introduction to '21 Seconds', remembers that she had been in a recording studio only once before: 'The studio was absolutely packed. I was so shy about having to record in front of everyone that I ended up going last.'

7 AUGUST

1989 ROTD: 'Track with No Name' by **Forgemasters**. Coded WAP 1, it is the first release on Sheffield indie label **Warp** Records, future home of Nightmares on Wax, LFO, Aphex Twin, Boards of Canada, Broadcast, and more recently, Bibio and Lonelady.

1995 ROTD: If Happy Mondays ended ignominiously in 1992, Shaun Ryder's next group **Black Grape** begins triumphantly: *It's Great When You're Straight . . . Yeah!* will hit UK #1.

2020 ROTD: 'WAP', **Cardi B** and **Megan Thee Stallion**'s collaboration – probably the most sexually explicit #1 hit to date.

8 AUGUST

1969 ROTD: 'Liquidator' by **Harry J All-Stars**. Recorded in Jamaica by the Harry Johnson-led band and released in the UK on Trojan Records, the instrumental single will climb to #9. In 1972, its introduction will form the basis for the Staple Singers' hit 'I'll Take You There' (US #1). Also on this day, at just after 11.30 a.m., **The Beatles** walk across a St John's Wood zebra crossing, and are photographed for the *Abbey Road* album sleeve.

1974 **Crosby Stills Nash and Young** play the Roosevelt Stadium in Jersey City on the day President Richard Nixon resigns from office in the wake of the Watergate scandal. 'He wanted to widen the war,' David Crosby later tells *Rolling Stone*. 'We wanted to end it. We were elated when he resigned.'

1995 ROTD: Eschewing the lead guitar in favour of the piano, North Carolina trio **Ben Folds Five** debut with their same-titled album. The following year, its extracted single 'Underground' – a witty paean to the underground music scene – will break them overground in the UK (#37) and on Australian radio.

9 AUGUST

1963 'The weekend starts here!' proclaims *Ready Steady Go!*, ITV London's lively new early-evening music show, which launches at 7 p.m.. Among the guests on episode one are Billy Fury and Brian Poole & the Tremeloes.

1983 In the midnight hour, **Holly Johnson**, lead singer of **Frankie Goes to Hollywood**, is ironing and idly watching 1959's *Cover Girl Killer* on ITV, when he is struck by the line 'Surely sex and horror are the new gods in this polluted world of so-called entertainment?' Making a note of it, he will later adapt the words to form part of the lyrics for the band's massive hit 'Two Tribes'.

1986 Queen perform their final concert with Freddie Mercury at Knebworth Park, Stevenage, some of which is captured on the group's live album, *Live Magic*.

10 AUGUST

1979 ROTD: *Off the Wall*, **Michael Jackson**'s first solo album in five years, is unusual for the time in featuring no fewer than four top 10 singles: 'Don't Stop 'Til You Get Enough', the title track, 'Rock with You' and 'She's Outta My Life'. Its producer is Quincy Jones, who met Jackson while working on the movie of *The Wiz*: Jones was arranging the score; Jackson was 'The Scarecrow'.

1987 ROTD: **Midnight Oil**'s 'Beds Are Burning', a song about Aboriginal land rights, will become a worldwide hit, perhaps most tellingly reaching #1 in South Africa. Twenty years later, frontman Peter Garrett, a committed activist on environmental issues, will become a Member of the House of Representatives in Australia for 10 years, then a Minister for Environment, Heritage and the Arts, and then Minister for School Education, Early Childhood and Youth.

1996 Oasis play the first of their two largest gigs (with a combined audience of around 250,000) at Knebworth Park.

11 AUGUST

1962 ROTD: 'Green Onions' by **Booker T. & The M.G.s**. A former B-side, the instrumental will become a soul standard (US #3), but will make it as a UK hit only in 1979 (#7), after it appears on the soundtrack to the *Quadrophenia* film.

1973 At 1520 Sedgwick Avenue, in the Bronx, 18-year-old Clive Campbell, aka **DJ Kool Herc**, provides the musical entertainment at a Saturday night Back to School Jam for his younger sister and the neighbourhood. From his apartment, he uses James Brown LPs to switch from one drum break to another, while adding vocal chants and commentary, essentially a forerunner of rap. The word 'break' is key here: deriving from street slang for 'get excited', it not only describes Campbell's use of music, but also the kind of 'break' dancing it leads to – as performed by 'break-boys and break-girls'.

Campbell was born and raised in the Jamaican capital of Kingston, and by the time his family moved to New York in 1967, he was familiar with the toasting traditions of Jamaican music. As DJ Kool Herc, his brand of DJ'ing and performing skills will influence future hip hop recording pioneers like Grandmaster Flash and Afrika Bambaataa, but unlike them, he will make barely any recordings at all. Apart from a couple of 1990s cameos for Terminator X and The Chemical Brothers, it will be 2019 before he eventually releases an album at the age of 64.

1988 After a live technical gaffe on the part of *Top of the Pops* the previous week, the show welcomes back **All About Eve** for a second chance at performing 'Martha's Harbour'. The single will climb to UK #10.

1997 ROTD: 'Tubthumping', about the 'resilience of ordinary people' in the words of **Chumbawamba**'s Boff Whalley, becomes a surprise worldwide hit (UK #2, US #6) for the Leeds-based politically committed group after a 15-year career.

12 AUGUST

1991 ROTD: **The Prodigy**'s 'Charly' (UK #3) takes its title and some samples from the 1973 series of animated 'Charley Says' public information films. Aimed at youngsters, the Charley in question is a yowling feline character voiced by performer and DJ Kenny Everett.

1992 DOTD: Los Angeles composer **John Cage** at the age of 79. Cage, who believed that music could encompass all kinds of sound and noise, was a major influence on such disparate pop practitioners as Sonic Youth, Frank Zappa, Brian Eno and Radiohead. Three years after his death, Anglo-French band Stereolab will record the song 'John Cage Bubblegum'. And at Christmas 2010, Cage's own work will reach UK #21, thanks to the re-release of his 1952 track '4'33"'. It is his most notorious (and often misunderstood) piece, in which no instruments are played and listeners are encouraged to listen to the sonic environment instead.

1996 Opening for Alanis Morissette in Buffalo, New York, **Radiohead** preview their forthcoming album, *OK Computer*. On the same day, Swedish pop group **The Cardigans** release *First Band on the Moon*, containing their biggest international hit, 'Lovefool' plus their reinterpretation of Black Sabbath's 'Iron Man', a couple of years after covering another of the rock band's tracks 'Sabbath Bloody Sabbath'.

13 AUGUST

1952 'Hound Dog' is recorded for the first time in Los Angeles by Willie Mae **'Big Mama' Thornton**. It comes only a day after 19-year-old writers Jerry Leiber and Mike Stoller have written the song, based on a commission from bandleader and producer Johnny Otis, who is looking for a hit for Thornton.

At first, Thornton sings the song, which is about a woman rejecting a man who wants her to take care of him ('hound dog' is a slang term in use at the time), as a ballad. But Leiber and Stoller persuade her to interpret it differently, in a way that matches her 'brusque and badass personality'. 'We wanted her to growl it,' Stoller will tell *Rolling Stone* in 1990. Warming to the prospect, Thornton decides to 'sing the words and join in some of my own', notably in a call-and-response section over Pete Lewis's guitar solo. She transforms the song, and both Leiber and Stoller will rank it among their favourite recordings of their work.

Released in February 1953, the single will top the US R&B charts for two months, selling over 500,000 copies – although, in common with so many other key rock'n'roll recording sessions, Thornton herself will never get rich from it, earning only $500 from the session. However, one of her own compositions, 'Ball and Chain' will later be covered by Janis Joplin. Meanwhile, in 1956, 'Hound Dog' will become a worldwide smash for Elvis Presley.

1989 **Scorpions** visit Moscow to play the Music Peace Festival – an experience that encourages singer and songwriter Klaus Meine to write the group's international hit of 1991, 'Wind of Change'.

2004 **Björk** performs 'Oceania' as part of the Olympic Games opening ceremony in Athens. She composed the song – part of her vocals-only next album, *Medúlla* – after taking a university course on Greek mythology.

14 AUGUST

1967 At 3 p.m. the Marine Broadcasting Offences Act comes into effect, and 'A Day in the Life' by The Beatles becomes the last record to be broadcast on **Wonderful Radio London**. The station, which operated from a ship anchored off the Essex coast, has been broadcasting since December 1964, reaching an audience of some 12 million listeners in the UK. Many of its DJs will join the BBC's soon-to-be-launched pop station, Radio 1.

1991 **Oasis**, previously known as The Rain, play their first gig at the Boardwalk in Manchester, supporting Catchmen and Sweet Jesus. Liam Gallagher's brother Noel, not yet in the group, has been touring the US as a roadie with Inspiral Carpets, and offers to write the songs for them.

2000 ROTD: **Sophie Ellis-Bextor**, ex-lead singer with guitar band theaudience, turns to the dancefloor with **Spiller's** 'Groovejet'. It beats

Victoria Beckham to a UK #1, and heralds an illustrious solo career for Ellis-Bextor.

15 AUGUST

1965 'At Shea Stadium,' John Lennon later remembers of **The Beatles'** concert at the New York venue, 'I saw the top of the mountain.'

1974 During a promotional trip of the UK, **The Osmonds** co-host *Top of the Pops* with Noel Edmonds. The following day, their #1 single 'Love Me for a Reason' is released.

1988 ROTD: 'I'm Gonna Be (500 Miles)' by **The Proclaimers**. Describing the song as 'a statement of faith', Auchtermuchty's Craig and Charlie Reid wrote it in a spare hour while waiting for a lift to take them to a gig in Aberdeen. The song will peak at UK #11, but will go to #1 in places as far apart as Iceland, Australia and New Zealand.

And then there will be its surprising second act. In the early 1990s, when Mary Stuart Masterson is filming the romcom *Benny & Joon*, director Jeremiah Chechik will ask her to bring in some favourite songs for a painting scene. One of her choices will be '500 Miles' to which Chechik responds: 'Man, this is too perfect. A romantic song about someone who will walk a thousand miles, act crazy, do anything for true love.'

The box-office success of *Benny & Joon* in 1993 will lead to '500 Miles', previously a college radio staple but no bigger, climbing to US #3 exactly five years after its first UK release. In 2007, the Reids will also re-record it for Comic Relief with Peter Kay and Matt Lucas (UK #1). And it is still a crowd anthem at the brothers' beloved Hibernian FC.

16 AUGUST

1962 ROTD: 'I Call It Pretty Music, But the Old People Call It the Blues' is the first-ever single by Motown's latest signing, 12-year-old

Little **Stevie Wonder**. In the UK, meanwhile, Pete Best's two-year stint as drummer with **The Beatles** comes to an end; Ringo Starr is his replacement.

1969 Coinciding with the second day of the Woodstock festival, the **Growth Summer Festival** takes place in Beckenham, Kent, featuring Lionel Bart, Bridget St John and The Strawbs. Compering proceedings, and performing a short set, is David Bowie.

1977 DOTD: The King is Dead. RIP 42-year-old **Elvis Presley**.

1980 **Rainbow** headline at the first Monsters of Rock Festival at Castle Donington. It proves to be drummer Cozy Powell's last gig with the group – in a week that also sees Jah Wobble leave Public Image Ltd, and Jools Holland part ways with Squeeze.

1981 Over a year since the death of Ian Curtis, **Joy Division** unexpectedly score their second #1 single in New Zealand, following up 'Love Will Tear Us Apart' with 'Atmosphere'.

17 AUGUST

1971 Tony Blackburn, BBC Radio 1's breakfast show host, called it. He campaigned to have a **Diana Ross** album track called 'I'm Still Waiting' released as a single by Motown in the UK, and today it begins a four-week spell at #1.

1987 ROTD: **New Order**'s *Substance*, an almost complete collection of the group's 12-inch single releases ending with their current single, 'True Faith'. On the same day, Iceland's **Sugarcubes** release their extraordinary first 45, 'Birthday' in the UK.

1992 ROTD: **Take That**'s *Take That and Party*. Featuring five top 10 singles in its running order, the album will stay in the UK charts for

18 months, peaking at #2. Meanwhile, Walthamstow's **East 17** debut with their 'House of Love' single, their first of 12 top 10 hits.

18 AUGUST

1978 ROTD: 'Hong Kong Garden', a diatribe against the racist skin-heads who used to harass a Chinese restaurant in Chislehurst, is the first **Siouxsie and the Banshees** single (UK #7), and the first of many, many major hits for producer Steve Lillywhite.

1986 ROTD: **Bon Jovi**'s commercial fortunes improve with third album, *Slippery When Wet*, thanks in part to notable collaborations with Kiss, Cher and Bonnie Tyler songwriter **Desmond Child** on two of its tracks: 'You Give Love a Bad Name' and 'Livin' on a Prayer'.

1997 ROTD: 'Brimful of Asha' by **Cornershop**. The duo of Tjinder Singh from the West Midlands and Ben Ayres, who grew up in Newfoundland, Canada, began releasing records in the early 1990s, with a view to overturning Asian stereotypes and tropes (not least in their group's name). This release of 'Brimful of Asha' will peak at only UK #60, but a slightly sped-up remix by Norman 'Fatboy Slim' Cook will propel it all the way to #1 in February 1998.

The song is the pair's tribute to Indian cinema, especially the Hindi film industry in Mumbai, and to Indian recorded music, of which filmi music and playback singing is an integral part. 'Asha' is famed singer Asha Bhosle, who is described in the song as 'sadi rani': 'our queen' in Punjabi. Appearing on literally thousands of recordings, Bhosle's singing career began as a ten-year-old in 1943, when she contributed to the Marathi film, *Majha Bal*, before her first Hindi cinema credit, 'Saawan Aaya' (in the film *Chunariya*) in 1948. Earlier in the 1990s, she even made the UK charts herself, albeit uncredited, on 'Bow Down Mister' by Boy George's band Jesus Loves You.

Despite the popularity of 'Brimful of Asha', a succession of hit singles does not follow for Singh and Ayres. But, over 20 years later, on albums such as 2020's exemplary *England is a Garden*, Cornershop will continue to offer some of the most acerbic, witty and imaginative pop music in Britain.

19 AUGUST

1969 Following the weekend's three-day Woodstock festival, Jimi Hendrix, Jefferson Airplane and **Joni Mitchell** appear on Dick Cavett's ABC-TV talk show, where Mitchell performs a newly written song, simply called 'Woodstock'.

1981 Neil Tennant (then in publishing) and architecture student Chris Lowe meet by chance in a hi-fi shop on London's Kings Road. They soon start writing and recording songs as **Pet Shop Boys**.

1986 Radio 1 unveils its new top 40 and the sound of Chicago house music breaks through in the UK, when 'Love Can't Turn Around' charts at #36, ultimately peaking at #10. Appearing on *Top of the Pops* a few weeks later, its singer, the remarkable Darryl Pandy, will end his performance rolling around on the studio floor. The man behind the hit is **Farley 'Jackmaster' Funk**, otherwise known as 24-year-old Farley Keith Williams. Like other members of the Hot Mix 5 DJs in Chicago, he has built his reputation by enhancing and embellishing records in the clubs with drum machines, keyboards and sequencers. The Roland 808 drum machine is a particular favourite of his, which he miked up to add a bit of punch to some Philly soul records. It has proved to be a big hit with the crowds.

For this, his breakthrough hit, Farley has produced a rewrite of 'I Can't Turn Around', an Isaac Hayes disco record from 1975. It won't be long before the house sound will transcend the clubs and infiltrate chart pop in the form of acts such as Stock Aitken Waterman, Pet Shop Boys and Madonna.

2008 ROTD: *The Fame*, the debut album by New York singer-songwriter Stefani Germanotta, aka **Lady Gaga**, which highlights her love of electropop and dance music — especially on tracks like 'Poker Face' and 'Just Dance'.

20 AUGUST

1982 ABBA gather at Stockholm's Polar Studios to record a song about an ordinary day in the life of an ordinary woman. 'The Day Before You Came' turns out to be the fruit of their final session as a group until the late 2010s. Its reputation will grow, but on its original release the single will struggle to UK #32.

1984 ROTD: The hidden gem of 'William It Was Really Nothing' by **The Smiths** lies on its 12-inch version: a hypnotic seven-minute bonus cut of a track called 'How Soon is Now?' Such is the song's impact that it will become a single A-side, and will chart in its own right five months later.

1995 At just before 7 p.m., BBC Radio 1's chart show reveals that 'Country House' by **Blur** has become their first UK #1, outselling **Oasis**'s 'Roll with It', after both have been on sale for six days.

21 AUGUST

1961 ROTD: 'Please Mr Postman' by **The Marvelettes**. By December the track, which features a young Marvin Gaye on drums, will become the first US #1 for the Motown label. Also on this day, in Nashville, producer Owen Bradley begins recording the Willie Nelson song 'Crazy' with **Patsy Cline**.

1976 **Eddie and the Hot Rods** top the bill at the Mont de Marsan punk festival in south-west France, supported by the Pink Fairies and The Damned. Among those attending is 21-year-old **Ian Curtis** and his wife Deborah.

1981 ROTD: Three top-notch singles: 'Passionate Friend' by **The Teardrop Explodes**; 'Souvenir' by **OMD** (with a total lyric of under 50 words); and **Altered Images'** 'Happy Birthday'.

22 AUGUST

1969 ROTD: **Santana's** organic combination of psychedelia, Latin rock and jazz fusion is released on record for the first time. The LP, also called *Santana*, takes off after the release of two singles, 'Jingo' and the 1970 US top 10 hit 'Evil Ways'.

1993 ROTD: 'Mr Vain' by the German group **Culture Beat** becomes the first UK #1 single since the 1950s not to be available as a 45rpm 7-inch vinyl single; it is issued on three formats, 12-inch vinyl, cassette and CD.

2000 ROTD: Composed by Diane Warren, produced by Trevor Horn and performed by **LeAnn Rimes**: 'Can't Fight the Moonlight', from the film *Coyote Ugly*, underperforms in the US at first, but tops charts in 12 other countries including the UK and Australia.

23 AUGUST

1970 After four albums, **Lou Reed** quits the Velvet Underground for a solo career, departing with a final live appearance at Max's Kansas City club in New York.

1994 ROTD: Manhattan quartet **Luscious Jackson** – their name a pun on the Texan-born basketball player Lucious Jackson – debut on the Beastie Boys' label Grand Royal with their album, *Natural Ingredient*. On the same day, the **K Foundation**, who as the KLF had split up and deleted their back catalogue two years earlier, burn £1 million on Jura in the Inner Hebrides, in what is described as a 'work of performance art'.

2007 Sixty-year-old Queen guitarist **Brian May**, BSc graduate in Maths and Physics from Imperial College London in 1968, is awarded a PhD in astrophysics from the same institution.

24 AUGUST

1964 Cilla Black becomes the first *Desert Island Discs* castaway on BBC Radio 4 to select a track by **The Beatles** (namely 'Love Me Do') as one of her eight records. She also chooses her own recording of 'Anyone Who Had a Heart' as her 'favourite', which may not quite be in the spirit of the programme.

1987 ROTD: Exactly five years after the release of their *Chronic Town* EP, **R.E.M.**'s 'The One I Love' will become the band's first single to reach the US top 10, perhaps because some listeners hear the title line without absorbing the full lyrical content, which is more concerned with manipulation than love-song material.

1995 Microsoft introduces **Windows 95**. Its start-up jingle has been composed by **Brian Eno**, ironically on a Mac.

25 AUGUST

1967 ROTD: Written by Roy Wood, 'Flowers in the Rain', a UK #2 single, will land **The Move** in the High Court when as part of their management's promotion, a postcard is circulated showing a cartoon of a naked Harold Wilson in bed with his secretary. The prime minister sues, and the resulting settlement means that all royalties from the song — to this day — go to charity.

1997 ROTD: **All Saints** — so called because two of the group members, Shaznay Lewis and Melanie Blatt, had begun as backing singers at Sarm West studios by London's All Saints Road — debut as a quartet with 'I Know Where It's At'. The song, sampling Steely Dan's 'The Fez', was previewed two weeks earlier on the BBC's *National Lottery Live* show, and peaks at UK #4.

2003 ROTD: 'Milkshake' by New Yorker **Kelis** Rogers. Boasting an addictive playground chant, and plentiful use of percussion instruments like the darbuka and the manjira, it is another landmark recording from the Neptunes (production duo Pharrell Williams and Chad Hugo). In the same month a survey of British radio airplay reveals that songs worked on by the Neptunes account for an incredible 20 per cent of the output (largely via their work for Britney Spears, Jay-Z, Usher, Justin Timberlake and Beyoncé). Kelis, who defines the song title as 'what gives us our confidence and what makes us exciting', had been working with the Neptunes since her debut album in 1999, but had started collaborating with other producers too because, in her words, 'People had started messing with me ... "Is she REALLY any good without The Neptunes?" And so I was like, "I'll take that challenge."' Her follow-up single to 'Milkshake', for example, is 'Millionaire', which sees her collaborate with André 3000, one half (alongside Big Boi) of Atlanta hip hop act **OutKast**.

Just as the Neptunes' Pharrell Williams was a big fan of white rock bands like Coldplay and Radiohead, so André 3000 was inspired by new wave bands like the Ramones and Buzzcocks, and this influence underpins OutKast's biggest hit, 'Hey Ya', also released today. Although their new double album *Speakerboxxx/The Love Below is* issued under their collective name of OutKast, it is effectively comprised of two solo albums by Big Boi and André respectively. Both expand far beyond hip hop in purely sonic terms and encompass a free-flowing range of musical influences, and both feature a monster smash: 'The Way You Move' and 'Hey Ya'. The latter – Lou Reed's favourite song of the year – manages to be both catchy and idiosyncratic; after all, how many other top-selling hits are based on a 22-beat phrase? Go on, count along.

26 AUGUST

1968 ROTD: The first record released by **The Beatles'** Apple label is the band's own seven-minute-long classic 'Hey Jude'. 'Apple 2' is **Mary Hopkin**'s 'Those Were the Days', produced by Paul McCartney and set to succeed 'Hey Jude' at #1 in the UK. You might think that 'Hey Jude' must therefore be 'Apple 1', but technically that honour belongs to **Frank Sinatra**, who records a sung message in honour of Ringo's wife Maureen under the title 'The Lady is a Champ – But Beautiful'. The one-sided single is never officially released.

1969 ROTD: 'Suspicious Minds', one of the finest **Elvis Presley** singles, which returns him to US #1. But on the same day, his live performance of 'Are You Lonesome Tonight?' at the International Hotel, Las Vegas, all but falls apart when he starts laughing. The soprano backing singer is a pro throughout: it's Cissy Houston, mother of Whitney. (This live recording, subtitled 'the laughing version', is unexpectedly a UK hit in 1982.)

2014 **Kate Bush** performs the first night of *Before the Dawn*, her first full live show since 1979, with a total run of 22 nights at the Hammersmith Apollo in London. Most of the set comes from two albums: 1985's *Hounds of Love* and 2005's *Aerial*.

27 AUGUST

1985 For the second time, 'I Got You Babe' reaches the UK #1 spot, 20 years after Sonny and Cher. If they ever remake the film *Groundhog Day* for the British market, the 6 a.m. alarm call will be **UB40 featuring Chrissie Hynde**.

1991 ROTD: They were first known as Mookie Blaylock, after the NBA player, but when the Seattle-based rockers rename themselves **Pearl Jam**, they still call their first LP *Ten* after the number of Blaylock's shirt. The band's popularity in the US rockets during the autumn when they support Red Hot Chili Peppers on tour.

2000 'Music', one of several collaborations with French composer-producer Mirwais Ahmadzaï, becomes **Madonna**'s tenth UK #1 single, and a fortnight later becomes the last (to date) of her 12 US #1s. In the song's promo video Sacha Baron Cohen, in the guise of his Ali G character, makes a cameo as a limousine driver.

28 AUGUST

1963 'Tell them about the dream, Martin!' calls out gospel singer **Mahalia Jackson** to Dr Martin Luther King Jr at the March on Washington DC for Jobs and Freedom, whereupon King's speech extemporises around the theme of 'I have a dream'. As well as other political speakers, Bob Dylan, Peter, Paul & Mary and Joan Baez perform, with appearances from public figures Harry Belafonte, Sidney Poitier, Josephine Baker and Sammy Davis Jr. The event is a catalyst for the passing of the Civil Rights Act in 1964 and 1965's Voting Rights Act.

1994 London pirate radio station **Don FM**, an important outlet for jungle and drum and bass music since November 1992, begins to broadcast legally for the first time. Unable to raise enough advertising revenue to extend its broadcasting licence, the venture will last only four weeks, but a year later, Don will return to pirate status, continuing to broadcast drum and bass, house and techno.

2009 The day before the fifteenth anniversary of *Definitely Maybe*'s release, **Oasis** split up when Noel Gallagher walks out of the band. He goes on to form High Flying Birds, while younger brother Liam founds the group Beady Eye.

29 AUGUST

1958 ROTD: On the day that Michael Jackson is born in Indiana – and, in fact, the day that Lenny Henry is born in the West Midlands – Harry Webb releases his debut single, 'Schoolboy Crush'. But within a couple of weeks, it is clear that the record's flip side is getting all the attention, and producer Jack Good invites Webb, known as **Cliff Richard**, to perform on his ITV music show, *Oh Boy!*, on condition that he sings that flip side: 'Move It'. He does, and will become a regular attraction on the programme.

While most UK rock'n'roll thus far has merely covered US originals, 'Move It' is different and fresh. Its writer, Ian Samwell, is Cliff's guitarist, the two having been regulars at the 2Is coffee bar in London. When a recording session for 'Schoolboy Crush' track loomed, and they still lacked a B-side, Samwell's mind wandered to a recent critical piece in *Melody Maker* – 'So rock'n'roll is dead, is it? Good riddance' – and wrote a defiant riposte in the mould of Chuck Berry and Eddie Cochran. 'Move It' will peak at UK #2, the first of 69 top 10 singles for Cliff Richard.

Oh, and why 'Cliff Richard'? 'Cliff' was word association ('cliff face' and 'rock'), while 'Richard' was a nod to Little Richard, although it was seeing Bill Haley and His Comets live in north London in March 1957 that left Webb in no doubt as to what he wanted to do with his life.

1966 Exactly eight years after the 15-year-old George Harrison joined Lennon and McCartney in the line-up of The Quarrymen, **The Beatles** call time on their regular live work, at Candlestick Park in San Francisco.

2005 ROTD: 'Suddenly I See' (UK #12) is **KT Tunstall**'s tribute to the empowering and enduring influence of Patti Smith on her work, specifically the sleeve of Smith's *Horses*, photographed by Robert Mapplethorpe.

30 AUGUST

1963 At the Berlin Radio Show in West Germany, Philips unveil their new compact musicassette tape. Portable and easy to use, it will become popular for dictation and especially for playing back music.

1975 Sparks guest on BBC Radio 1's *My Top Twelve*, and select a budget album soundalike version of their own song, 'This Town Ain't Big Enough for Both of Us'.

1992 Nirvana headline the Sunday night of the Reading Festival. Kurt Cobain dedicates a new song, 'All Apologies', to wife Courtney Love and his daughter Frances, born just 12 days earlier.

1993 ROTD: On the same day that Nirvana's 'Heart-Shaped Box' is issued across Europe (it is released only in promo form in the US), Creation releases The Boo Radleys' remarkably eclectic *Giant Steps*, while 4AD issues *Last Splash* by The Breeders.

31 AUGUST

1976 ABBA leap from #16 to #1 on the UK singles chart with 'Dancing Queen', where the song will stay for six weeks.

1987 ROTD: On a day that sees new releases from U2 ('Where the Streets Have No Name'), R.E.M. (*Document*) and Michael Jackson (*Bad*, his first album in nearly five years), there's also 'I Owe You Nothing' which flops this time round for Bros, but 10 months later will race to UK #1.

2009 ROTD: Michael Bublé's 'Just Haven't Met You Yet', which becomes his biggest hit in the UK, peaking at #5. He dedicates the song to his partner and future wife, the Argentine actor Luisana Lopilato, who also appears in the song's video clip.

SEPTEMBER

1 SEPTEMBER

1981 ROTD: **Daryl Hall and John Oates'** *Private Eyes* contains two future US #1 singles. The title track is one; the other is 'I Can't Go for That (No Can Do)' – about the power of creative control – which will cross over to urban radio and top the R&B and dance charts.

1990 Nearly five years after its launch as a pirate radio station, **Kiss 100**'s mix of dance and club music begins legal broadcasting in London with host Norman Jay. Its other presenters at this stage include Trevor Nelson and Lisa I'Anson.

1997 Similarly, **XFM** began as a pirate radio station (as Q102 in 1989), but after several years of legal short-term broadcasts, it becomes a permanent fixture in London as of today. On its roster of present-ers: Gary Crowley, Claire Sturgess, and future creators of *The Office*, Stephen Merchant and Ricky Gervais.

2 SEPTEMBER

1985 ROTD: 'Who Needs Love Like That?' – modestly charting at UK #55 – kicks off the most long-lasting and hit-studded project of Vince Clarke (ex-Depeche Mode, Yazoo and Assembly). **Erasure**'s lead singer and Clarke's co-writer is Andy Bell, who answered an ad placed by Clarke in *Melody Maker*.

2013 ROTD: *The 1975* is the Cheshire foursome's chart-topping debut album, which rides the momentum generated by their live performances in London that summer, supporting Bastille, Muse and even The Rolling Stones.

2021 ROTD: **ABBA** return with 'I Still Have Faith in You' and 'Don't Shut Me Down', a preview single for their first album in 40 years: *Voyage*. The latter song will reach UK #9, their first top 10 hit since 1981's 'One of Us'.

3 SEPTEMBER

1968 **Sly and the Family Stone**, already established in the pop charts with 'Dance to the Music' (UK #7, US #8), win NBC's *Showcase '68*, a talent show series for professional acts.

1982 ROTD: Previous singles 'White Boy' and 'I'm Afraid of Me' have floundered, but it will be third time lucky for **Culture Club**, with 'Do You Really Want to Hurt Me?' (UK #1, US #2).

2021 ROTD: The backronym of *Sometimes I Might Be Introvert* (UK #4) is SIMBI, and this album is how Simbi Ajikawo follows up the grime, funk and lavish arrangements of *Grey Area* with an even more ambitious, introspective journey through self-doubt and low-key vindication. As **Little Simz**, she describes herself as 'being this introverted person that has all these crazy thoughts and ideas and theories in my head and not always feeling like I'm able to express it if it's not through my art'. The album will win the Mercury Prize in 2022.

Unlike many rappers, Little Simz prefers to shift between first and third person, and writes for other voices too, notably that of Emma Corrin – whom Ajikawo had spotted during the 2020 lockdown, playing the young Princess Diana in *The Crown* – whose speeches pepper the album.

Ajikawo has also acted on TV (*Spirit Warriors, Youngers, Top Boy*) and there is a dramatic, cinematic feel to her records. She and her producer Inflo do not lean hard on samples, preferring to devise backings and arrangements that artfully and convincingly sound like existing music. The apparent single exception is a Smokey Robinson sample on 'Two Worlds Apart'.

4 SEPTEMBER

1958 Chicago-based soul vocal group **The Impressions**, perhaps best known for the socially conscious 'People Get Ready' (written by singer Curtis Mayfield in 1964), make their national TV debut on ABC's *American Bandstand*, performing 'For Your Precious Love'.

1981 ROTD: **Adam and the Ants'** lavish 'Prince Charming' video co-stars Diana Dors as the Fairy Godmother, and helps propel the single to UK #1 for four weeks.

2004 *The X Factor* premieres on ITV, with a judging panel comprising series creator Simon Cowell, Sharon Osbourne and Louis Walsh.

5 SEPTEMBER

1980 ROTD: An Ian Dury-influenced stream of consciousness about schooldays written by lead singer Suggs, 'Baggy Trousers' will return **Madness** to the UK top three. A memorable moment in the video finds sax player Lee Thompson apparently airborne.

1988 ROTD: **Metallica's** first album for major label Polygram is ... *And Justice for All*, with songs about corruption, the environment, prejudice and, in the case of 'One', the effects of war. It enters the UK charts at #4.

2005 ROTD: Lyrically, 'Fix You' by **Coldplay** (UK #4) was a reaction to Gwyneth Paltrow's grief over the death of her director father Bruce; musically it was partly inspired by Elbow's 'Grace Under Pressure' and 'Many Rivers to Cross' by Jimmy Cliff.

6 SEPTEMBER

1967 In Los Angeles, **Canned Heat** record 'On the Road Again', as a homage to the Floyd Jones blues song of the same name, and with an instantly memorable falsetto vocal from Alan Wilson. On release the following spring, it will climb to US #16 and UK #8.

1983 ROTD: Formerly singer with New York power pop band Blue Angel, **Cyndi Lauper** goes solo with 'Girls Just Wanna Have Fun', a redrafted feminist version of a male perspective song by songwriter Robert Hazard. It takes three months to enter the US charts, but will finally peak at #2, and at UK #2.

1993 ROTD: For **Meat Loaf**'s first album in seven years, he reunites with writer-producer Jim Steinman. *Bat Out of Hell II: Back into Hell* opens with the 12-minute 'I'd Do Anything for Love (But I Won't Do That)', a worldwide #1 single, and the year's bestseller in the UK.

7 SEPTEMBER

1979 ROTD: The J. G. Ballard short story, 'The Sound-Sweep', about the rise of new technology leading to the erasure of past music, is cited as an influence on 'Video Killed the Radio Star' by Trevor Horn and Geoff Downes' **Buggles**. In October it becomes the first UK #1 single for Chris Blackwell's Island label.

1987 ROTD: **Pet Shop Boys** demonstrate that 'West End Girls' and *Please* were no fluke. Indeed, a few songs on their second LP — notably 'It's a Sin' and 'Rent' — were held back from that first album, despite existing in Neil Tennant and Chris Lowe's private repertoire from their early demo tapes. *Actually* (UK #2, US #25) has four major hit singles, but also several songs critiquing and examining government privatisation ('Shopping'), Catholic guilt ('It's a Sin'), urban poverty ('King's Cross') and the coverage and perception of AIDS ('It Couldn't Happen Here'). It can be seen as a series of snapshots about Britain during the time of Prime Minister Margaret Thatcher. It also has some stomping dance tracks on it; the opener, 'One More Chance', is literally the 12-inch mix for an unreleased single, while 'Heart' (UK #1) features a combined vocal sample of Prefab Sprout's Wendy Smith and of Luciano Pavarotti. Yes, in a sense Pavarotti had a bigger chart hit than 'Nessun Dorma' (UK #2, 1990).

The sleeve of *Actually*, which shows Lowe and Tennant (the latter yawning), came from a photograph taken on the video shoot for 'What Have I Done to Deserve This?', which has given their duettist Dusty Springfield her biggest hit single since 1969. The image was intended for the front cover of *Smash Hits*, the pop magazine where Tennant had been assistant editor in 1984–85.

1987 Meanwhile, in one of the more unlikely double bills in music history, the stage is set at the National in Kilburn, London, for an evening with rock'n'roll revivalists **Showaddywaddy** and German industrial noise band **Einstürzende Neubauten**.

8 SEPTEMBER

1957 ROTD: Having departed from R&B group The Dominoes, **Jackie Wilson**'s first single as a solo artist is 'Reet Petite' (UK #8), which helps co-writer Berry Gordy to start his own label, Motown. The song has a surprising resurgence in 1986 (two years after Wilson's death) when it becomes the UK's Christmas #1.

1970 A three-year-old LP track by **Smokey Robinson & the Miracles** called 'Tears of a Clown' climbs to UK #1. Co-written by Stevie Wonder, it's one of the few major pop hits to feature a bassoon, played by the Detroit Symphony Orchestra's Charles R. Sirard.

1980 ROTD: **Kate Bush**'s *Never for Ever* which, the following week, becomes the first album ever by a British female solo artist to reach #1 in the UK. (Note: the UK album charts were first published in 1956.)

9 SEPTEMBER

1977 ROTD: **Iggy Pop**'s *Lust for Life*, his second collaboration with David Bowie, recorded in Berlin, and featuring the title track and 'The Passenger', is released by RCA.

1980 'Feels Like I'm in Love', a disco hit all over Europe for Scottish singer **Kelly Marie** in 1979, reaches UK #1. It was first recorded by songwriter Ray Dorset's group Mungo Jerry as a B-side in 1977 when their original choice of artist, Elvis Presley, died.

2014 ROTD: **U2**'s 13th album *Songs of Innocence* is made available, free, to everyone with an iTunes account – whether they want it or not.

10 SEPTEMBER

1984 ROTD: Two new singles from films, both of which involve **Giorgio Moroder** as co-writer and producer. One is Freddie Mercury's 'Love Kills' (recorded for the new soundtrack of Fritz Lang's *Metropolis*). The other is 'Together in Electric Dreams', for the film *Electric Dreams*, on which Philip Oakey from the Human League provides vocals.

1990 NBC premieres its sitcom *The Fresh Prince of Bel-Air*, establishing rap artist and actor **Will Smith** as a major star.

2005 The final **Destiny's Child** tour, 'Destiny Fulfilled . . . and Lovin' It', reaches its swansong performance in Vancouver, Canada, after which the group breaks up.

11 SEPTEMBER

1977 As a favour to his mother, **David Bowie** participates in the taping of **Bing Crosby**'s TV special, *Merry Ole Christmas*, at Elstree Studios near London. Asked to duet with Crosby on 'Little Drummer Boy', he instead contributes his own countermelody, called 'Peace on Earth'.

1994 After 15 weeks at UK #1, Wet Wet Wet's 'Love is All Around' is replaced by **Whigfield**'s pan-European summer hit, 'Saturday Night'. She is the first artist ever to debut on the UK charts at #1.

2001 Among the albums released in the US this Tuesday morning: Mariah Carey's *Glitter* soundtrack, Ben Folds' *Rockin' the Suburbs*, Jay-Z's *The Blueprint*, and *Love and Theft* by Bob Dylan. But, of course, this is no ordinary Tuesday morning.

12 SEPTEMBER

1966 At 7.30 p.m. (ET), the NBC network airs 'Royal Flush' as part of its Monday schedule, the first of 58 episodes of a new TV comedy series called ***The Monkees***.

1968 At 9 p.m., Patti LaBelle and The Bluebells are among the guests on *Soul!*, the first 'Black Tonight Show', a new variety series aimed directly at African Americans, and which lasts until 1973.

1988 ROTD: 'You should never listen to music as background music. Ever,' says Mark Hollis of **Talk Talk**. In any case, it's hard to imagine *Spirit of Eden* (UK #19), the group's fourth album, being played in that way. Certainly, their record company, Parlophone, isn't entirely sure what to do with its six long tracks.

Two years earlier, Talk Talk had been internationally successful with *The Colour of Spring* album, and the single 'Life's What You Make It', but *Spirit of Eden* – calm but with flashes of intensity – contains no obvious hits. Its influences lie in jazz and classical music: Miles Davis, Claude Debussy, Erik Satie. Talk Talk and producer Tim Friese-Greene were given an open budget and creative control. Guest musicians, such as bassist Danny Thompson and violinist Nigel Kennedy, were encouraged to be spontaneous, although barely 10 per cent of the sessions have made the LP's final cut. Ironically, given that the recording processes were so organic, the music was rearranged afterwards, using digital technology.

Over time, *Spirit of Eden* will sell more than 500,000 copies world-wide, and is a favourite of many artists such as Elbow, Kate Bush, Peter Gabriel, Robert Plant and Charlotte Church.

1989 ROTD: The making of *Floating into the Night*, a collection of col-laborations between singer **Julee Cruise**, composer Angelo Badalamenti and filmmaker David Lynch, began three years earlier with 'Mysteries of Love' on the *Blue Velvet* soundtrack. The album also features 'Falling', soon to be forever associated with TV's *Twin Peaks*.

13 SEPTEMBER

1985 ROTD: **Dexys Midnight Runners'** third LP, *Don't Stand Me Down*, which receives mixed reviews and poor sales, but will later become regarded as a classic. The band premieres 'Listen to This' on this evening's edition of BBC1's *Wogan*.

2001 *Melody AM* by electronic music duo **Röyksopp** enters the LP chart in their Norwegian homeland at #2. It will soon reach #1 there, and become a top 10 album in the UK.

2013 ROTD: **Hozier's** 'Take Me to Church', an exasperated critique of the institution in which it reclaims religious language as the language of love, is the Irish singer-songwriter's debut EP.

14 SEPTEMBER

1979 ROTD: First copies of 'Making Plans for Nigel' by **XTC** (UK #17) offer a bonus foldout board game, called Chutes and Ladders built around the protagonist's mundane and mapped-out life. 'I've had countless Nigels come up to me over the years and say: "That song is my life,"' songwriter Colin Moulding tells the *Guardian* in 2020.

1984 The talking point of MTV's first Video Music Awards is **Madonna**, who unveils her forthcoming single, 'Like a Virgin', and accidentally exposes her underwear while rolling around on live TV. It is her earliest brush with perceived controversy.

1992 ROTD: 'Connected' by **Stereo MCs** becomes a pop-dance crossover, peaking at UK #18 and US #20. It opens with a vocal lift from 'Now That We've Found Love' by Third World, and persists with a bassline from Bo Horne's 'Let Me (Let Me Be Your Lover)'.

15 SEPTEMBER

1970 Last week, it was 'Tears of a Clown'. This week it's 'Band of Gold' by **Freda Payne**, the second UK #1 hit in succession to mention the phrase 'lonely room' in its lyrics.

1986 ROTD: *Blood and Chocolate* finds **Elvis Costello and the Attractions** in their most intimate, raw, stripped-down, ill-tempered and yet most brilliant form. The group will not work together again for eight years.

2003 ROTD: 'Sweet Dreams My L.A. Ex' was recorded by **Rachel Stevens** in the wake of the S Club 7 break-up. An earlier version of the song, about airing details of a former relationship for publicity purposes and said to have been inspired by Justin Timberlake's 'Cry Me a River', had been turned down by Timberlake's own ex, Britney Spears.

16 SEPTEMBER

1977 DOTD: On the same day that La Divina, Maria Callas, dies in Paris, 29-year-old **Marc Bolan** is killed in a car crash in Barnes in south-west London. Bolan had recently finished recording a comeback series for ITV, *Marc*.

1996 ROTD: Notable for being almost entirely built from fragmentary vinyl samples, **DJ Shadow**'s plunderphonic hour-long LP, *Endtroducing . . .*, finds its raw material from all kinds of origins: *Twin Peaks*, *Prince of Darkness*, Tangerine Dream, the 60s band Nirvana, and even Björk and Metallica.

2022 ROTD: *Born Pink* is the second album by Jisoo, Jennie, Rosé and Lisa, aka **BLACKPINK**, and over just eight tracks blends K-pop, hip hop, rock, trap and EDM, while quoting from such disparate sources as Rihanna, the Notorious BIG and Niccolò Paganini. It will become the first album by a female K-pop group to top the US and UK album charts, and by the end of the year, their 2018 song 'DDU-DU DDU-DU' will approach 2 billion hits on YouTube, a record for a K-pop group.

The quartet came together very gradually in South Korea, via a slow-burning auditioning process in the early 2010s. The resulting line-up was revealed at weekly intervals in June 2016, with a debut release 'Whistle' following close behind. The carefully chosen name BLACKPINK was intended to redefine the associations of the colour pink. 'Pink is commonly used to portray prettiness,' said their management, YG Entertainment, 'but BLACKPINK actually means to say that "Pretty isn't everything". It also symbolises . . . great talent.' 'We felt like there's two colours that represented us the most,' Rosé once told US talk show host Jimmy Kimmel. 'We're very girly but at the same time we're very savage too.'

17 SEPTEMBER

1974 In New York, **Janis Ian** records 'At Seventeen', a song about adolescent loneliness that she has created after reading a *New York Times* article which begins with the words 'I learned the truth at eighteen'. Ian knew that 'seventeen' scanned more effectively.

Ian had experienced chart success in America several years earlier; her self-penned 'Society's Child' about an interracial romance, had reached the top 20 in 1967 when she was just 16. But 'At Seventeen' feels so confessional, she wonders if it will cross over. She had been listening to the sorts of artists like Nina Simone and Billie Holiday who 'did write those kind of songs. But pop music and folk music really didn't.' She also found it hard to finish the song, until she brought her own story into it, in the final verse, and to confirm that her own lonely experience was now in the past.

Radio, very male-dominated at the time, could have been a stumbling block – 'Alison Steele was the only female disc jockey I was aware of in New York. So they sent copies of it to all the program directors' wives.'

There was a reference in 'At Seventeen' to a lack of Valentine's cards; in February 1977, the year after the song won a Grammy Award, Janis Ian received 461 of them.

1974 On the same day, **Carl Douglas**'s 'Kung Fu Fighting' – intended as a throwaway B-side recorded against the clock – tops the UK chart. It was produced by Biddu Appaiah, who was a pioneer in the UK disco scene of the 1970s.

1990 ROTD: *Heaven or Las Vegas* by the **Cocteau Twins** (UK #7), from which the single 'Iceblink Luck' has just been Radio 1's breakfast show record of the week.

18 SEPTEMBER

1968 During the 'White Album' sessions, **The Beatles** take a break from recording 'Birthday' to go to Paul's house to watch BBC2's TV premiere (at 9.05 p.m.) of the 1956 movie *The Girl Can't Help It*, starring Jayne Mansfield, Little Richard and Fats Domino.

1978 ROTD: All four members of **Kiss** unload solo LPs: *Peter Criss, Ace Frehley, Gene Simmons, Paul Stanley* (if you played all four albums simultaneously, would it sound like Kiss?). Exactly five years later, in 1983 the group – with a slightly revised line-up – break more new ground by showing up at a photo session without their trademark make up.

1989 ROTD: Who's that shouting 'Guilty!' in the background of 'Drama!' by **Erasure**? Why, it's Jim and William, the Reid brothers from The Jesus and Mary Chain, who happened to be in the neighbouring recording studio at the time.

19 SEPTEMBER

1981 **Simon and Garfunkel** perform together, after often fractious rehearsals between the reunited duo, at a free concert in New York's Central Park. It is recorded for a live album and film, both of which will premiere in February 1982.

1984 While campaigning in New Jersey for his re-election as President, Ronald Reagan namechecks **Bruce Springsteen**'s music (presumably the much misunderstood 'Born in the USA') as offering 'a message of hope . . . so many young Americans admire'. Two days later, on stage in Pittsburgh, a sceptical Springsteen introduces the tale of despair 'Johnny 99' from *Nebraska* with the words: 'I don't think he's been listening to this one.'

1997 **Auto-Tune** software, developed by Antares Audio Technologies, goes on sale as a way for producers to secretly enhance and correct vocal pitch.

20 SEPTEMBER

1964 ROTD: Perhaps the ultimate in 'death discs', 'Leader of the Pack' by **The Shangri-Las** – complete with revving motorbikes and glass-smashing sound effects – will go to #1 in the US and #11 in the UK, where it will be excluded from airplay on the BBC.

1979 When **The Clash's** Paul Simonon smashes his bass guitar onstage at New York's Palladium, photographer Pennie Smith is present. The image will adorn the sleeve for the band's next album, *London Calling*.

1999 ROTD: At long last, there will be a UK top 40 single with Thursday in its title: 'Thursday's Child' by **David Bowie**. The other days of the week have all featured previously, for example: 'Friday on My Mind' (The Easybeats); 'Saturday Night at the Movies' (The Drifters); 'Sunday Girl' (Blondie); 'I Don't Like Mondays' (The Boomtown Rats); 'Ruby Tuesday' (The Rolling Stones); 'Wednesday Week' (Undertones).

21 SEPTEMBER

1971 At 10.55 p.m., BBC2 broadcasts the first episode of *The Old Grey Whistle Test*, a weekly series prioritising album artists, and featuring live performances from a tiny studio. The first episode includes America, Lesley Duncan and an interview with the folk singer Tom Paxton. The series was co-created by Rowan Ayers, the father of Soft Machine singer Kevin.

1978 ROTD: **Chic's** 'Le Freak', the biggest-selling single in the history of Atlantic Records, was written after Nile Rodgers and Bernard Edwards were turned away from Studio 54 on New Year's Eve. According to Rodgers, the refrain 'freak out' began life as 'fuck off'.

2011 **R.E.M.** announce their amicable break-up on their website: 'To anyone who ever felt touched by our music, our deepest thanks for listening.'

2018 Nantes singer-songwriter **Christine and the Queens** continues to defy categorisation on his second album release, *Chris*. First single 'Girlfriend' — a collaboration with Californian funk exponent Dâm-Funk — is an exploration of a woman having 'the right to be too much, and as complex and intricate as a dude could be in a novel'.

Released under the title of 'Damn, dis-moi' in France, it will be judged the song of the year by *Time* magazine.

22 SEPTEMBER

1958 The detective drama series *Peter Gunn* premieres on NBC. Its instrumental signature tune, composed by Henry Mancini, is an early example of a TV theme having rock'n'roll influences rather than jazz. The following year, guitarist **Duane Eddy** takes it into the charts (UK #6, US #27).

1978 ROTD: The genesis of **Funkadelic**'s best-selling single came from the title, and the title came from a gig in Washington DC, which two audience members had described afterwards as 'like one nation under a groove', George Clinton remembered in 2018.

1997 ROTD: **Björk**'s *Homogenic*, her third album, and her first collaboration with Mark Bell from Warp Records' LFO. Although a tribute to Iceland's combination of nature and technology, the album was mostly recorded in Malaga, Spain.

2008 ROTD: 'Human' by **The Killers**, described by Brandon Flowers as 'Johnny Cash meets the Pet Shop Boys'.

23 SEPTEMBER

1966 **The Rolling Stones**' bill-topping set at the Royal Albert Hall is thrown off course in its early stages owing to a mini-riot as fans clamber onto the stage and knock Keith Richards to the floor. One of the band's support acts is the soul revue of **Ike & Tina Turner**, recently in the UK charts with 'River Deep Mountain High'.

1977 ROTD: Having abandoned live performance, **Steely Dan** arguably perfect their studio-based jazz and rock hybrid on *Aja*, which will win them a Grammy Award, inspire a De La Soul sample ('Peg' will become part of 'Eye Know') and give rise to the name of the band Deacon Blue.

1991 ROTD: All out today in UK record shops: *Screamadelica* by **Primal Scream**, *Trompe le Monde* by **Pixies** and **Nirvana**'s *Nevermind*. None of them will be #1 the following week, though: that'll be *Waking Up the Neighbours* from **Bryan Adams**.

24 SEPTEMBER

1969 **Deep Purple** present their 50-minute *Concerto for Group and Orchestra* at the Royal Albert Hall, with the help of the Royal Philharmonic Orchestra under the baton of conductor Malcolm Arnold.

1972 Alan Freeman hosts his final Sunday afternoon edition of the original *Pick of the Pops* series for BBC Radio 1, although he will later host revivals of the show – usually of archive charts – for Capital Radio, and later Radios 1 and 2. One week after Freeman steps down, Tom Browne hosts a new chart show for Radio 1 called the *Solid Gold Sixty* (with the theme tune 'Brother' by CCS).

1982 ROTD: The backbone of *Love Over Gold*, **Dire Straits**' fourth LP, is named after the 80-mile US Highway 24 in Michigan known as 'Telegraph Road'. 'It's the same road,' says Mark Knopfler, who had experienced it from the tour bus, 'and it just went on and on and on forever.' The song fittingly lasts 14 minutes.

25 SEPTEMBER

1970 ABC premieres the musical sitcom *The Partridge Family*, which will run for four seasons and make a star of 20-year-old cast member **David Cassidy**. The inspiration for the series came from the real-life Rhode Island family band The Cowsills.

1975 Kraftwerk appear in a film report on BBC1's science and technology magazine programme *Tomorrow's World*, where they demonstrate the 'machinemusik' and traffic emulation of their recent hit, 'Autobahn'. 'Next year,' says the film's narrator, 'they hope to eliminate the keyboards altogether, and build jackets with electronic lapels, which can be played by touch.'

1981 ROTD: 'Labelled with Love' by **Squeeze**, about a relationship that ended just after the Second World War, has massive cross-generational appeal, and will peak at UK #4. Producer **Elvis Costello** makes the sound of the record even more countrified.

2015 ROTD: 'Writing's on the Wall' by **Sam Smith**, the title song from *Spectre*, will become the first-ever theme from a James Bond film to reach UK #1. (Duran Duran's 'A View to a Kill' (1985) and Adele's 'Skyfall' (2012) had come closest, both #2.)

26 SEPTEMBER

1969 ROTD: The two-part 'Oh Well' by **Fleetwood Mac** is one of the key links between blues rock and heavy metal. 'Part 1' will peak at UK #2. In 1980, a loop of it will form the theme to the award-winning Radio 1 documentary series *25 Years of Rock*, a highly distinctive blend of news footage and music from a given year.

1983 ROTD: Playful, harsh and hypnotic by turns, the EP *Into Battle with the Art of Noise* by **Art of Noise** is the first release from Trevor Horn's new record label, Zang Tumb Tuum (ZTT).

2000 ROTD: **Nelly Furtado**, 21 years old and from British Columbia in Canada, debuts with 'I'm Like a Bird' (US #9, UK #5) – the first of what will be many worldwide hits.

2022 Melissa Viviane Jefferson, better known as **Lizzo**, attends the Library of Congress, Washington DC, to peruse its 1,700-strong collection of flutes. What appeals to her in particular is a crystal flute, patented by Frenchman Claude Laurent in 1806, and made for the fourth US President James Madison in 1813. A clip of the singer goes viral when she plays sections from the 'Carnaval of Venice' and Poulenc's Flute Sonata on the rare crystal instrument. The following night, she is briefly loaned the flute ('it's like playing out of a wine glass') for her concert at Washington's Capital One Arena: 'Nobody has ever heard this famous crystal flute before. Now you have.'

Lizzo, whose own flute 'Sasha Flute' has a dedicated Instagram account, began playing the instrument as a child when her family relocated from Detroit to Houston, and she joined a local marching band, before studying classical flute at the city's university.

27 SEPTEMBER

1968 ROTD: With his love for Ray Charles and Aretha Franklin, Sheffield's **Joe Cocker** slows Lennon and McCartney's 'With a Little Help from My Friends' right down. A UK #1, it only reaches #68 in the US but 20 years later becomes the theme to TV's *The Wonder Years*. It hasn't been used in a John Lewis Christmas advert, though. Yet.

1980 **Kurtis Blow** becomes the first rapper to appear on national TV in the US, performing 'The Breaks' on *Soul Train*.

1999 ROTD: After two minor hits in the UK, Natalie McIntyre will hit big as **Macy Gray** with 'I Try', which in a here-this-week, gone-next-week sales chart, shows unusual tenacity, spending two months in the top 10, despite never rising above #6.

28 SEPTEMBER

1967 ROTD: Though it will become less familiar than Marvin Gaye's version of 'I Heard It Through the Grapevine', **Gladys Knight and the Pips'** take on the song is no slouch. Recorded with The Muscle

Shoals Rhythm Section in June 1967, producer and co-writer Norman Whitfield hoped it would 'out-funk' Aretha Franklin's 'Respect'. It will peak at US #2, topping the R&B chart.

1976 ROTD: Two of the most famous songs on **Stevie Wonder**'s long-awaited double album *Songs in the Key of Life* will not even be released as singles: 'Isn't She Lovely' (dedicated to his daughter) and 'Pastime Paradise' (later adapted by Coolio as 'Gangsta's Paradise'). 'Sir Duke', meanwhile, is of course a tribute to the late Duke Ellington (1899–1974).

1982 Juvenile Birmingham reggae band **Musical Youth** leapfrog from UK #26 to #1 with 'Pass the Dutchie', a more family-friendly take on The Mighty Diamonds' 'Pass the Koutchie'.

1998 ROTD: A band in disarray in the mid-90s, **Mercury Rev** make a dramatic resurgence with *Deserter's Songs*, presumed to be their final album, but which gives them an unexpected second wind. It is the *NME* staff's Best Album of 1998.

29 SEPTEMBER

1987 'Pump Up the Volume' by **M/A/R/R/S** reaches #1 in Britain – a notable achievement not only for an independently made record, but also for one with such an unusual structure. Like 'Jack Your Body' by Steve 'Silk' Hurley earlier in the year, it defies the orthodox architecture of a pop song. While Hurley's record was an insistent near-instrumental punctuated by its title, the M/A/R/R/S track is the result of an experiment to combine the talents of two very different bands who then discover they cannot work together . . .

The story goes that guitar band and dub fans AR Kane wanted to make a dance record, and their label 4AD suggested electronic dance act Colourbox as possible collaborators. Colourbox had brightened up the indie charts in 1986 with their 'Official World Cup Theme' and a cover of Augustus Pablo's 'Baby I Love You So'.

But the two groups were oil and water to each other. In the end, they make only minimal contributions to each other's original song. 'Pump Up the Volume' – crammed with samples over a nagging, repetitive beat, and which gets nearly all the press coverage and radio play – is mostly the work of Colourbox: Martyn and Steve Young (the M and S bit of M/A/R/R/S). 'Anitina (The First Time I See She Dance)' is the AR Kane track by Alex, Rudi and Russell (the A/R/R bit). The two bands fall out. There is no follow-up.

1997 ROTD: Alongside albums from veterans **The Rolling Stones** (*Bridges to Babylon*) and **Bob Dylan** (*Time Out of Mind*, widely regarded as his best in years) today sees **The Verve**'s *Urban Hymns*, **Robbie Williams**' *Life Thru a Lens* (his solo debut), and the second self-titled **Portishead** LP.

2003 ROTD: 'Mr. Brightside', the debut single by **The Killers**. It fails to chart, and on re-release the following spring spends only a month in the UK charts, entering at its peak of #10 (the same peak position as in their US homeland). Yet its persistent popularity in the download and streaming era is unmatched by any other single. In February 2022, it will become the first-ever track to spend 300 weeks on the UK Top 100.

30 SEPTEMBER

1967 At 7 a.m., DJ Tony Blackburn launches **BBC Radio 1** for the second time; he had already launched it for news reporters the day before, the version you always see on documentaries. Blackburn, and his canine sidekick Arnold (spoiler: not in fact a real dog, just a barking sound effect, sorry about that) plays the jazz instrumental 'Beefeaters' by Johnny Dankworth as his theme tune, before playing his first record proper: 'Flowers in the Rain' by The Move.

The introduction of Radio 1 as the BBC's first service of continuous pop had been promised by a Government White Paper in

December 1966, just as they announced plans to outlaw pirate radio (which was where you mostly heard the Swinging Sixties on the radio dial). 'It won't just be a teenagers' programme,' reassured the Postmaster General, Edward Short. 'Many housewives like to listen to "We'll Gather Lilacs". We will try to serve them both.'

Robin Scott, the station's first controller, had written the lyrics to a #1 hit in the 1950s ('Softly Softly' by Ruby Murray), and promised that 'Radio 1 will be like a commercial station without the commercials'. One of the staff producers is John Walters, the trumpeter with the Alan Price Set, and who will from 1969 produce John Peel for 20 years.

Meanwhile, the Light Programme, which features light music and light entertainment, where the BBC's slivers of pop coverage have hitherto lived – *Pick of the Pops, Brian Matthew's Saturday Club, Where It's At* – is now rebranded as Radio 2.

1971 ROTD: Edited down to a three-minute single, it's still nearly two minutes before **Isaac Hayes'** voice enters proceedings on his 'Theme from *Shaft'*. It will go to US #1 and UK #4, and will win Hayes an Academy Award for Best Original Song, the first African American recipient in the category.

1977 ROTD: As ripostes to the 'seen and not heard' order go, few are as confrontational and exhilarating as 'Oh Bondage! Up Yours!' by **X-Ray Spex**, fronted by one of punk's most defining figures, 18-year-old Poly Styrene.

1985 ROTD: While the voice of TV's *Lovejoy* himself, Ian McShane, introduces **Grace Jones** on 'Slave to the Rhythm', Bronski Beat's ex-lead singer Jimmy Somerville unveils **Communards**, with Richard Coles on keyboards, and 'You Are My World'.

OCTOBER

1 OCTOBER

1967 Originally a BBC Light Programme popular music series in 1964–65, *Top Gear* is revived for Sunday afternoon Radio 1, leaning further towards rock. The hosts for the first programme are John Peel and Pete Drummond, and psychedelic band **Tomorrow** – whose frontman Keith West is separately in the top 10 with 'Excerpt from a Teenage Opera' – become the first act to have a specially recorded Radio 1 session broadcast, effectively the first **Peel Session**.

1976 ROTD: Singer-songwriter **Joan Armatrading** will say of 'Love and Affection' (UK #10): 'It was somebody trying to persuade me to be with them, and that's as much as I'm saying about that song.'

1982 ROTD: Ten years after the emergence of Steely Dan, **Donald Fagen** goes solo with *The Nightfly*, digitally recorded but based on Fagen's own formative years in the analogue world of the 1950s and early 1960s. Opening track 'I.G.Y.', for example, remembers the optimism for the tomorrow's world of science and technology imagined in the International Geophysical Year of 1957–58, a scientific project involving 67 countries that examined a total of eleven Earth sciences. The Soviet Union's launch of Sputnik 2 in October 1957 was part of this study.

2 OCTOBER

1959 ROTD: 'Travellin' Light' is Cliff Richard's seventh single, and the first where his backing group The Drifters (by now consisting of Hank Marvin, Bruce Welch, Jet Harris and Tony Meehan) appear under a new name, to avoid confusion with the identically named American vocal group. As **The Shadows**, nine months later they will launch a parallel career as a pioneering instrumental group, beginning with the UK #1 'Apache'.

1971 Previously a regional daily show in Chicago, the musical variety show *Soul Train* begins a 35-year run on selected TV stations in the US, under creator and host Don Cornelius. In 1985 Channel 4 screens a short-lived British version, with Shalamar's Jeffrey Daniel hosting. On the production team is a young researcher named Jonathan Ross.

1974 ROTD: Track two of *Al Green Explores Your Mind*, 'Take Me to the River' is not issued as a single, but becomes one of Green's stand-out songs, and is covered by both Syl Johnson (US #48) and Talking Heads (US #26).

2000 ROTD: For their latest album, **Radiohead** could quite easily have made *OK Computer* again (after all, it had been voted by Q magazine's readers to be The Best Album of All-Time in 1999) but they didn't want to. Tired of the clichés and expectations associated with rock music, they have gone in a completely different creative direction with *Kid A*.

Thom Yorke was smitten with electronic music, and wanted his voice to be one component of the album's musical texture, rather than leading it. Guitarist Jonny Greenwood experimented with string arrangements, and also the ondes martenot, the electronic instrument from the *Star Trek* theme music, which he described as 'a very accurate theremin that you have far more control of'. The mixing desk became an instrument in its own right.

Their producer Nigel Godrich understood the exciting possibilities that can come when a band explores something new that's outside their own background: 'In the same way the Beatles and the Stones wanted to sound like Black American R&B, but couldn't, and produced something special anyway,' he tells *Spin* magazine, 'Radiohead now want to sound like Kraftwerk, but can't, and that's good in the same way.'

The material is not entirely new. 'The National Anthem', in which horns sound like a traffic jam, is something Yorke wrote in his schooldays, while 'Motion Picture Soundtrack' was written prior to 'Creep'. Some pundits are critical of its innovations, but *The Wire* magazine describes it as 'an extraordinary leap into the unknown', and there's enough material left over for a second full album: 2001's *Amnesiac.*

3 OCTOBER

1988 ROTD: The very lyric of 'We Call It Acieed' (UK #3) explicitly stresses the power of acid house music over drug use, but there's a moral panic regardless in tabloid newspapers. After some exposure on *Top of the Pops*, airplay for **D-Mob**'s single will be restricted by the BBC.

1992 On *Saturday Night Live*, **Sinéad O'Connor**, while performing an acapella version of 'War' by Bob Marley, tears up a picture of Pope John Paul II, and says, 'Fight the real enemy!' as a protest about apathy and cover-ups towards abuse in the Church.

2003 The comedy *School of Rock*, in which Dewey Finn, a rock guitarist-turned-supply teacher encourages his pupils to compete in a Battle of the Bands contest, premieres in US cinemas. It stars Jack Black as Finn, with a soundtrack of AC/DC, Led Zeppelin and the Ramones. Finn's flatmate, and the film's co-writer Mike White, will later create and showrun TV's *The White Lotus*.

4 OCTOBER

1968 ROTD: Paul Ryan wrote 'Eloise' – epic in length, approach and scope – to be performed by his brother **Barry Ryan** after hearing Richard Harris's 'MacArthur Park'. In turn, 'Eloise' (UK #2) will be acknowledged by Freddie Mercury as a major influence on 'Bohemian Rhapsody'.

1982 Brit funk band Blue Rondo à la Turk play the Ritz in Manchester. The support band perform four songs: 'The Hand That Rocks the Cradle', 'Suffer Little Children', 'Handsome Devil' and a cover of The Cookies' 1963 song, 'I Want a Boy for My Birthday'. It is the first live showing by **The Smiths**.

1987 The end of crowding round a radio on Tuesday lunchtimes to find out what's #1 this week. The new BBC chart, compiled by Gallup to be 'even more up to date', is moved to Sundays, where 'Pump Up the Volume' is #1 for a further week.

5 OCTOBER

1962 ROTD: On the same day as the premiere of the first James Bond film, *Dr No*, 'Love Me Do'/'P.S. I Love You' is the first **Beatles** single on Parlophone Records. It will reach UK #17, but spend four months in the charts. Twenty years later, it will be reissued, and peak at #4.

1973 ROTD: 'My Coo-Ca-Choo' (UK #2) marks a return to the charts for the singer Bernard Jewry. A decade after his few hits under the name Shane Fenton, and now working in management, he is asked to lip-synch to a song written and sung by Peter Shelley (not Buzzcocks' Pete Shelley). Shelley gives him his new name: **Alvin Stardust**. Stardust will sing all of his subsequent hits (six of them top 10) himself. He is even an early cast member of *Hollyoaks*, in 1995.

1981 ROTD: *Speak and Spell*, named after the educational computer gadget, is **Depeche Mode**'s debut album, and the only one with founder member and songwriter Vince Clarke in the band's line-up.

6 OCTOBER

1969 ROTD: 'I Want You Back' marks the debut on Motown Records of **The Jackson 5**. In January, it will reach #1 on the *Billboard* Hot 100;

as will the one after that ('ABC'); and the one after that ('The Love You Save'); and the one after that ('I'll Be There').

1978 ROTD: 'Rat Trap' by Dublin's **The Boomtown Rats** perhaps has more in common with Bruce Springsteen than punk rock, but nevertheless it will become the first 'new wave' #1 in the UK. Singer Bob Geldof had written the song five years earlier, while working in an abattoir.

1997 ROTD: **Janet Jackson**'s *The Velvet Rope*, in which she confronts the subjects of sexuality, domestic violence and self-esteem. Guest artists on the album include Joni Mitchell and Q-Tip (both on the preview single, 'Got 'Til It's Gone'), and the British violinist Vanessa-Mae.

7 OCTOBER

1977 ROTD: **XTC** from Swindon begin 15 years on Virgin Records with the *3D* EP, and its lead track 'Science Friction'. It was recorded with producer John Leckie at Abbey Road in London.

1986 ROTD: Def Jam, more associated with hip hop up till now, moves into thrash metal circles when its co-founder Rick Rubin produces **Slayer**'s *Reign in Blood*. Its final track, 'Raining Blood' is given a radical makeover 15 years later by Tori Amos.

1996 ROTD: **Toni Braxton** celebrates her 29th birthday with the Diane Warren song, 'Un-Break My Heart'. It will top the US singles chart for 11 weeks.

2008 The Swedish music streaming site **Spotify**, created in 2006, launches in the UK and across several countries in Europe in both free and subscription versions, while securing licensing deals with major companies Universal, Sony BMG, EMI and Warners.

8 OCTOBER

1967 **The Moody Blues**, with Justin Hayward having replaced departed frontman Denny Laine, record Hayward's 'Nights in White Satin' with the London Festival Orchestra and conductor Peter Knight. It forms part of the *Days of Future Passed* LP – regarded as an early foray into progressive rock – and becomes a top 20 single in Britain three times: 1967, 1972 and 1979.

1980 ROTD: **Prince** embraces new wave and punk-funk on his third album, *Dirty Mind*. **Talking Heads**, meanwhile, absorb African music and electronics into their funk-rock sound on their fourth album, *Remain in Light*.

2019 ROTD: From Tokyo, **Babymetal's** collision of metal and J-pop – kawali metal – brings them their widest audience yet on their third album, *Metal Galaxy*. Its #13 peak in the US is the highest ever position for an album in Japanese.

9 OCTOBER

1973 DOTD: The gospel and R&B singer-guitarist **Sister Rosetta Tharpe** dies in Philadelphia from a second stroke at the age of 58. Her 1944 recording, 'Strange Things Happening Every Day' has frequently been regarded as a precursor to rock'n'roll, and she was a huge influence on Little Richard, Johnny Cash, Aretha Franklin and countless others.

1975 Twelve years after the birth of Julian, **John Lennon** becomes a father for the second time on his 35th birthday. Following the arrival of **Sean Ono**, Lennon effectively disappears from the music scene in favour of home life for the next five years.

1981 About to release *Controversy*, his fourth LP, **Prince** and his band are the opening act at The Rolling Stones' first Los Angeles live date for three years, on the recommendation of fan Mick Jagger. But a section of the 94,000 concertgoers at the LA Coliseum do not appreciate this brand of Minneapolis funk-rock, slinging racist and homophobic slurs, and then bottles, cans and food at the stage. 'I got hit in the shoulder with a bag of fried chicken,' Prince bassist Brown Mark remembers, 'then my guitar got knocked out of tune by a large grapefruit that hit the tuning keys.'

Midway through 'Uptown', the fourth number of an agreed five-song set, Prince curtails the performance, but he and the group do reappear at a second Coliseum date two days later. Meanwhile, the real beneficiaries of a support slot at the gigs are The J Geils Band, whose 14-year career is about to yield by far their biggest hit: 'Centerfold'.

1989 ROTD: Glasgow trio **The Blue Nile** break a five-year public silence with an astonishing second album, *Hats*. It yields no hit singles, but is critically acclaimed, reaches UK #12, and one of its songs, 'Let's Go Out Tonight', will be covered by Isaac Hayes.

10 OCTOBER

1966 ROTD: Out today is 'Good Vibrations', the most ambitious single attempted yet by **The Beach Boys** or, well, anyone else. While numerous hit songs are often recorded in one day, this one has taken seven months to make, on and off, between 17 February and 21 September. The group's publicist, Derek Taylor, describes it as a 'pocket symphony', and likens the process of its making to a painter blending oils.

'Good Vibrations' is a song about extrasensory perception, about the cosmic. Brian Wilson, the mastermind behind the record, had in his memory an incident from a childhood outing with his mother when a dog started barking. 'Don't act scared,' his mother warned. 'They pick up the vibes.'

The song – and the record – was constructed like an aural patch-work quilt. 'I had a lot of unfinished ideas, fragments of music I called "feels",' Wilson will later say. 'Each feel represented a mood or an emotion I'd felt, and I planned to fit them together like a mosaic.'

On the last day of recording, Wilson felt vindicated. 'It was a rush. It was everything. I remember saying, "Oh my God. Sit back and listen to this!"'

'Good Vibrations' will become the band's only single to reach #1 in both the UK and US. It was supposed to herald a new equally ambitious full album for 1967. But *Smile* would be abandoned for many decades, and officially completed by Wilson only in the 2000s.

1969 ROTD: A big hit when they supported The Rolling Stones in Hyde Park in July, **King Crimson**'s *In the Court of the Crimson King* – a prog-rock classic – is issued by Island Records (UK #5 and US #28). The sleeve is a self-portrait (in a mirror) of Chelsea Art School graduate (and friend of the band) Barry Godber, who will die at just 23, shortly after the LP's release.

1988 ROTD: The title of a Maya Angelou memoir, 1986's *All God's Children Need Traveling Shoes*, forms the opening line to **Tanita Tikaram**'s second single, 'Twist in My Sobriety', with oboe contributions from Malcolm Messiter (the son of Ian, who created Radio 4's *Just a Minute*). The song is a bigger hit in Europe than the UK (#2 in West Germany, for instance), and the following year is covered by Liza Minnelli.

1994 ROTD: As well as new singles from **Oasis** ('Cigarettes and Alcohol') and **Elastica** ('Connection'), **Suede** return with their second LP, *Dog Man Star* (UK #3), the last to feature original guitarist Bernard Butler.

11 OCTOBER

1946 BOTD: **Daryl Hall**, from Pottstown, Pennsylvania. He will meet **John Oates** in 1967 in a service elevator at the Adelphi Ballroom in

Philadelphia, while a gang riot is breaking out at the venue. The pair are both students at Temple University, where they are respectively members of The Temptones and The Masters. They form a duo in 1970, which will lead to six US #1 hits, among them 'Rich Girl', 'Maneater' and 'Out of Touch'.

1968 ROTD: Best known at this stage for their musical interludes on the proto-Python ITV children's show *Do Not Adjust Your Set*, the **Bonzo Dog Doo-Dah Band**'s 'I'm the Urban Spaceman' is written by the group's Neil Innes, and produced by someone called 'Apollo C. Vermouth'. You'd know him better, though, as Paul McCartney.

1975 *Saturday Night Live* premieres as *NBC's Saturday Night* with its first guest host, George Carlin, and music from Janis Ian and Billy Preston. The programme will spawn The Blues Brothers and Wayne's World, nearly 'reunite' Lennon and McCartney (in 1976), and present over 600 different music acts.

12 OCTOBER

1984 ROTD: Literate pop from **Lloyd Cole and the Commotions** on *Rattlesnakes*, their first of three LPs as a group. Reference points include several novelists: Mailer, de Beauvoir and Adler. Even the album's title has literary origins as a key motif in Joan Didion's *Play It as It Lays*.

1987 ROTD: Already established in the US, Australian rock band **INXS** will finally gain overdue recognition in the UK with *Kick*. All twelve tracks were designed to be singles, and four of them will be: 'New Sensation', 'Devil Inside', 'Never Tear Us Apart' and above all, 'Need You Tonight' (US #1, and UK #2 – but on re-release).

2018 South London rapper **Dave** scores the first rap UK #1 by a homegrown artist in three years with 'Funky Friday', a duet with North

London's Fredo. Released on Dave's own label, its word-of-mouth success is closely linked to social media.

13 OCTOBER

1978 ROTD: A pair of key post-punk 45s: **Public Image Ltd**'s 'Public Image' – John Lydon's first recording since quitting the Sex Pistols; and **The Jam**'s 'Down in the Tube Station at Midnight' – the sleeve displays Bond Street tube, while the track itself refers to a train going through St John's Wood tube.

1979 A month after release, **The Sugarhill Gang**'s 'Rapper's Delight' enters the US R&B charts at #61 (eventually peaking at #4), but the record's mentor has already been in music for 30 years.

Sylvia Robinson, who founded Sugarhill Records, made her first recording in 1950 when she was 14 years old. She took guitar lessons and, with Mickey Baker, released 'Love is Strange' as Mickey and Sylvia in 1956. Later she opened a studio in New Jersey, and in the 70s recorded the seductive 'Pillow Talk' herself after Al Green turned it down, and created 'Shame Shame Shame' for Shirley and Company.

With her son, Robinson attended a New York block party, and loved how the MCs related to the audiences. Then in summer 1979, in a pizza restaurant in New Jersey, she overheard the manager Henry Jackson casually rapping over a disco tune that was playing on the radio. She recruited him, and two of his friends, Guy O'Brien and Michael Wright, and they became Big Bank Hank, Master Gee and Wonder Mike. Then she booked Pennsylvania funk band Positive Force to play 'Good Times' by Chic, that summer's biggest dancefloor hit, and invited the trio to rap over it. At one point, Wonder Mike uses the term 'hip hop' . . .

'Rapper's Delight' – which crosses over to the pop chart (US #36, UK #3 and #1 in Canada, Spain and the Netherlands) – leads to several more hits for the Sugarhill label: 'The Message' and 'White Lines' among them. Robinson, often known as 'Miss Rob' by her signings, also discovers the first female rap group in The Sequence, who release 'Funk You Up' (1979), and whose Angie B will have a second career from the late 90s as neo-soul's Angie Stone.

1981 Ending Adam and the Ants' reign at UK #1 is a highly unusual cover of Lesley Gore's 'It's My Party' by **Dave Stewart and Barbara Gaskin**. Stewart, not to be confused with the Stewart in Eurythmics, had been the keyboard player of **Hatfield and the North** in the mid-1970s, while Gaskin had been the group's backing singer.

14 OCTOBER

1966 After their previous singer, Signe Toly Anderson, quits the group to raise her child, **Grace Slick** performs with **Jefferson Airplane** for the first time, at San Francisco's Filmore West.

1985 ROTD: There can't be many top 20 singles based on the Peter Reich memoir, *A Book of Dreams*, in which Reich recalls helping his father Wilhelm to create a 'Cloudbusting' machine. Fortunately, **Kate Bush** has read and absorbed it.

1991 ROTD: **Saint Etienne's** debut album, *Foxbase Alpha*, is in equal thrall to the nostalgia of 60s pop and the contemporary thrills of 90s club culture. Danceable, eerie and moving – it is all of these things, sometimes simultaneously. It is made by people who have huge record collections. It is also a love letter to London.

Some of its drum samples are common and often used: 'Funky Drummer' and 'When the Levee Breaks'. Other source material is quirky but familiar: a lo-fi excerpt from the TV game show *Countdown*. But the origins of some of its samples will remain mysterious for many years: French radio sports reports; an instructional single about decimalisation in 1971 Britain; Wilson Pickett's version of 'Hey Jude'; a 1969 film called *The Reckoning* ('what you've been waiting for'); a percussion loop from 'Being Boring'. The album's title plays on Moonbase Alpha, the name of the research centre in the 70s TV series *Space 1999*.

Bob Stanley, a music journalist for *Melody Maker*, and keyboard player Pete Wiggs had intended to have different guest singers on each single – that's Moira Lambert from Faith Over Reason on their debut 45, 'Only Love Can Break Your Heart' (which tops the US dance charts) – but they click with Sarah Cracknell, who becomes a full-time collaborator. Thirty years on, they will still be making records together.

15 OCTOBER

1966 The launch of the underground newspaper *International Times* takes place on the opening night of the **Roundhouse** in Camden. Music is provided by 'the Soft Machine', 'the Pink Floyd' and some steel bands.

1990 ROTD: 'She's So High' (UK #48) written in March 1988 by Damon Albarn, Graham Coxon, Alex James and Dave Rowntree, was their first song under the name of Seymour, and is their first single as **Blur**.

2001 ROTD: 'Get the Party Started' by Pink, which establishes **Linda Perry** as a songwriter for other artists; 'Beautiful' by Christina Aguilera will be another Perry creation. Prior to this, she has been best known as the singer with 4 Non-Blondes and their 1993 international hit 'What's Up?'.

16 OCTOBER

1964 **Petula Clark** records 'Downtown' (UK #2, US #1) with producer Tony Hatch, who is still perfecting the lyrics minutes before the session begins. The tune first entered Hatch's mind when he was in New York, gazing towards Times Square. To appeal to both Clark's existing audience and younger consumers, he aimed to 'make a giant orchestra sound like a rock band'.

1973 Nine days after LBC goes on air, **Capital Radio** becomes London's second official independent local radio station, broadcasting music, entertainment and speech 24 hours a day. It launches at 5 a.m. with the national anthem, followed by its first record: Simon and Garfunkel's 'Bridge Over Troubled Water'.

1989 ROTD: A homage to Barry White – not least in its spoken intro – 'All Around the World' has a vocal hook that, as so often with studio activity, came about by accident. **Lisa Stansfield** ad libbed 'I, I, I . . .' in the studio. Within three weeks of release, it's the UK #1.

17 OCTOBER

1978 ROTD: **The Village People**, the village in question being Greenwich in New York, will sell at least 12 million copies worldwide of 'Y.M.C.A.' 'I knew we had something special,' David Hodo, the group's 'construction worker' will say. 'Because it sounded like a commercial. And everyone likes commercials.'

1988 ROTD: Three years after 'The Whole of the Moon' and *This is the Sea*, **The Waterboys** return with a mostly changed line-up under founder Mike Scott, and the strong Celtic music influence of *Fisherman's Blues*. So much material was recorded during the sessions that it will fill a 7-CD box set in 2013.

1994 Six months after the death of Kurt Cobain, Nirvana drummer **Dave Grohl** begins a week of solo recordings at Seattle's Robert Lang Studios, which will be released as the first **Foo Fighters** album, with a full line-up, the following summer. The opening track 'This is a Call' (UK #5) will be described by Grohl as 'a hello and, in a way, a thank you'.

2005 ROTD: The 'next big thing' of indie-rock is a future UK #1: 'I Bet You Look Good on the Dancefloor' from Sheffield's **Arctic Monkeys**. In the US, **Madonna** releases 'Hung Up' (again a future UK #1), only the second single with a legally approved ABBA sample (the first was 'Rumble in the Jungle' by Fugees).

18 OCTOBER

1940 BOTD: Songwriter **Cynthia Weil** is born in New York. Weil and husband Barry Mann will be one of the most prolific writing teams of the 1960s, penning such standards as 'On Broadway' and 'Saturday Night at the Movies' for The Drifters, 'We Gotta Get Out of This Place' for The Animals, and 'You've Lost That Lovin' Feelin'' for The Righteous Brothers. Later, she also writes with the likes of Carole King and Lionel Richie.

1985 ROTD: Organised by Little Steven van Zandt, 'Sun City' by **Artists United Against Apartheid** assembles a vast array of musical figures – from Bruce Springsteen to George Clinton, from Hall and Oates to Run-DMC, from Darlene Love to Miles Davis – all of whom refuse to play South African venues due to apartheid laws.

1993 ROTD: Youth is the producer for what turns out to be the final **Crowded House** album of their original incarnation, *Together Alone*. Meanwhile, *Morning Dove White* is an ethereal, languid masterpiece from Scottish dance act **One Dove**, and brings singer Dot Allison to prominence.

19 OCTOBER

1964 ROTD: *Wednesday Morning, 3 A.M.* (subtitled 'exciting new sounds in the folk tradition') is met with indifference at first, and leads Paul **Simon** to spend a year in England, while Art **Garfunkel** continues studying in New York. But the duo's debut album will fare better after the belated 'electric' revamp of side one's closer, 'The Sound of Silence'.

1987 ROTD: 'Hit the North', which will become one of The Fall's signature sounds, will surprisingly peak at only UK #57. According to Mark E. Smith's co-writer Simon Rogers, the sequencer-sampler features 'a sax note and a bass note from a Gentle Giant record'. Smith: '"Hit the North" has a dual meaning; punish it or go there.'

1998 ROTD: 'Believe' by **Cher**, which introduces the general public to the wonder of Auto-Tune software and boosts the career of co-writer **Brian Higgins**. In the light of its success, he will establish the writer-producer team Xenomania.

20 OCTOBER

1981 The New York musician and performance artist **Laurie Anderson**'s eerie but moving eight-minute single 'O Superman' races to UK #2, assisted by Radio 1 airplay from John Peel by night and Peter Powell by day. The idea for the title came from an 1885 Massenet aria called 'O souverain'.

2003 ROTD: *Frank* by the remarkable 20-year-old singer-songwriter **Amy Winehouse** is partly named in honour of Sinatra, but also to reflect the record's blunt lyrical content. Although it reaches only UK #13 during Winehouse's lifetime, the single 'Stronger Than Me' anticipates the gongs for *Back to Black* by winning an Ivor Novello Award in 2004.

2009 ROTD: **Alicia Keys'** 'Empire State of Mind' was created out of mild homesickness. Songwriters Angela Hunte and Janet Sewell-Ulepic were visiting London in February 2009, but yearned to be in New York. They submitted the song with Jay-Z in mind to his Roc Nation company, where it was turned down, but got a second chance when

Jay-Z's then publisher, EMI's Jon Platt, happened to hear it at a bar-becue. Once Jay-Z was on board, though, they still needed a singer for the chorus.

'There was a first phone call,' Keys will remember, 'and Jay [said], "I feel like I have this record that's going to be the anthem of New York... and it couldn't be the anthem of New York without you."'

In fact, Keys would feel the need to re-record her vocal contribution – in New York. She first recorded it in Los Angeles. 'I think that was the problem. You're not supposed to cut a song about New York in LA. It's just wrong.'

21 OCTOBER

1958 The final studio sessions for **Buddy Holly**, only 22 years old, at Pythian Temple Studios, New York, where he records four songs: 'True Love Ways', 'Moondreams', 'Raining in My Heart' and his posthumous #1 hit, 'It Doesn't Matter Anymore'.

1978 The day after watching *Barbarella*, the late-night film shown on BBC1, John Taylor and Nick Rhodes decide to name their new band as a slight revision of one of its characters: the scientist Dr **Durand Durand**, played by Milo O'Shea.

1983 ROTD: 'The Love Cats' will make **The Cure** top 10 pop stars for the first time, while **The The**'s *Soul Mining* is an album written by Matt Johnson almost entirely from scratch after abandoning a project called 'The Pornography of Despair'. 'Uncertain Smile', a 1982 single, has been re-recorded for the LP with an improvised piano solo from Jools Holland.

22 OCTOBER

1976 ROTD: British punk rock probably starts here, with **The Damned**'s 'New Rose', which borrows its opening spoken line from

'Leader of the Pack'. On its B-side is a riotous remake of Lennon and McCartney's 'Help!'

1991 ROTD: 'I Love Your Smile' from 18-year-old **Shanice** Wilson, which includes not only the saxophone of Branford Marsalis but the background laughter of Janet Jackson.

2021 ROTD: Witty and experimental, unapologetic and accessible, **Self Esteem**'s second album, *Prioritise Pleasure*, completes her move away from her indie roots of Slow Club to pop-dance acclaim.

23 OCTOBER

2000 ROTD: Electronic duo **Lemon Jelly** repackage their three EPs into one album: *Lemonjelly.ky*, sampling easy listening favourites – Nana Mouskouri, Bert Kaempfert, Henry Mancini – and even the voice of John Pearse, the folk guitar instructor on the BBC's *Hold Down a Chord*.

2001 Apple reveals the first version of the **iPod**, with 5GB of storage – a then-unprecedented capacity, in terms of MP3 players, of 1,000 songs.

2007 ROTD: *Raising Sand* unites the voices of **Robert Plant** and bluegrass fiddler **Alison Krauss**, and wins six of Krauss's 27 Grammy Awards.

24 OCTOBER

1980 ROTD: A catalogue of gambling metaphors, which will form the soundtrack to the Young Ones catching a train, and will be the last record Simon Mayo plays on Radio 1 in 2001 – it can only be 'Ace of Spades' by **Motörhead**.

1994 ROTD: One of the year's darker records, 4AD Records' *Geek the Girl*, by singer-songwriter **Lisa Germano**. Germano was previously violinist in John Cougar Mellencamp's band, and played on Simple Minds' #1 hit, 'Belfast Child', in 1989.

1997 At the Rap Olympics in Los Angeles, **Eminem**'s second place is enough to interest an intern from Interscope Records, and his 'Slim Shady' EP eventually finds its way to mentor and producer Dr Dre.

2006 ROTD: While 16-year-old **Taylor Swift**'s first album avoids the rural imagery of some country-and-western music, it does assimilate the influence of confessional lyrics. In November, *Taylor Swift* enters the US album chart at #19.

25 OCTOBER

1968 They are still billed as 'The New Yardbirds' on the poster for tonight's gig at the University of Surrey's Great Hall, then located in Battersea, south London. But they take the stage under the new name of **Led Zeppelin**.

1977 Following eight weeks at #1 in West Germany, Spanish duo **Baccara** sneak a single week at the UK #1 spot, in between David Soul and ABBA, with 'Yes Sir, I Can Boogie'.

1985 Guesting on Channel 4's *The Tube* tonight: R.E.M., The Smiths and – with several songs from *Swordfishtrombones* and new offering *Rain Dogs* – **Tom Waits** live.

26 OCTOBER

1979 ROTD: **The Jam**'s 'Eton Rifles', which sends up the cadet force of Eton College, and which will reach UK #3. Nearly 30 years later, Conservative Party leader David Cameron, an Eton pupil in the corps at the time of its release, will cite it as one of his favourite songs. To which Paul Weller will ask: 'Which part of it didn't he get?'

1998 ROTD: **Robbie Williams'** second album confirms his status as the top male solo artist in the UK. Having sampled the 'You Only Live Twice' melody to underpin 'Millennium', the album is suitably titled *I've Been Expecting You*. It sells 2.5 million copies in the UK alone.

2008 **Girls Aloud** hit UK #1 with 'The Promise', although BBC Radio 2's breakfast host, Terry Wogan, wonders aloud whether it sounds a bit like the *Blankety Blank* theme.

27 OCTOBER

1972 ROTD: Within the packaging of **Stevie Wonder's** new album *Talking Book* is the following message, embossed in braille: 'Here is my music. It is all I have to tell you how I feel. Know that your love keeps my love strong.'

Talking Book is not the first of Wonder's records to demonstrate the depth and breadth of the creative control that he had assumed after his 21st birthday in May 1971; *Music of My Mind* had already established that. But *Talking Book*, crucially, has two hit aces during 1973. Opening track 'You Are the Sunshine of My Life' begins with two couplets from his backing singers: the first from Jim Gilstrap, and the other from Lani Groves. 'Superstition' emerged out of a jam session with guitarist Jeff Beck and will become Wonder's first US #1 hit since 'Fingertips' when he was 13.

Elsewhere, 'Big Brother' is about oppression, and its title does indeed come from George Orwell; Wonder has recently read *Nineteen Eighty-Four*. 'Blame It on the Sun' and 'Looking for Another Pure Love' are co-writes with Syreeta Wright. The two have just divorced as a couple but will continue to work on Syreeta's own LP. 'We lost a little piece of paper,' Wright will say, 'but we gained much more.'

1991 The *Smash Hits* Poll Winners' Party at London Docklands Arena is broadcast live on BBC1 afternoon TV, and Fruitbat from **Carter**

USM rugby tackles host Phillip Schofield following a sarcastic quip. Carter have just had their performance of their new hit single, 'After the Watershed', shortened after apparently kicking a microphone stand off the stage.

2006 ROTD: **Amy Winehouse**'s turbulent relationship and temporary separation from her fiancé provides the troubled foundation for the second and final LP of her lifetime, *Back to Black*. Extracted from the Grammy-winning album will be five major hit singles, and as of 2022, it will have sold nearly 4 million copies in the UK, outstripping everything else in the 21st century save for Adele's *21*.

28 OCTOBER

1962 French television broadcasts coverage of a referendum on how to elect the president. During an interval, it televises a clip of this week's new #1 hit, 'Tous les garçons et les filles' by the 18-year-old singer **Françoise Hardy**. The single, Hardy's first, will keep returning to #1 throughout the winter and even into spring 1963 – 15 weeks on top in all.

1983 ROTD: 'This Charming Man' will rush Mancunian quartet **The Smiths** into the mainstream. Up until now, they have been well-known to followers of the indie charts, where 'Hand in Glove' shone out, and to night-time radio listeners, where they have made one session for David Jensen and two for John Peel.

Their second session for Peel, taped on 14 September 1983 and broadcast a week later, included a preview of 'This Charming Man', which is immortalised on their *Hatful of Hollow* compilation. Johnny Marr wrote the music as an attempt to write something more upbeat and sunnier than what he called his 'Manchester in the rain' disposition. He also wanted the same level of daytime radio airplay being awarded to their Rough Trade label mate, Roddy Frame of Aztec Camera. Singer Steven Morrissey contributed a lyric partly out of a desire to explore unfashionable language, although one line is lifted from the film *Sleuth*.

It had to be a single – Geoff Travis at Rough Trade insisted. On 1 November, it charts at UK #110, a week later it's #55, and when it reaches the top 30, they make their *Top of the Pops* debut. To Morrissey's chagrin, it also leads to a 12-inch dance mix, which showcases Andy Rourke's agile bassline even more prominently.

1997 ROTD: *Zaireeka* by **The Flaming Lips** is a four-disc set with a difference. It is designed so that each disc of contrasting musical components can be played simultaneously or separately on different CD players. Failing to make the cut from the albums' sessions is a Lips classic of the future, 'Race for the Prize'.

29 OCTOBER

1971 DOTD: **Duane Allman** of The Allman Brothers Band, just 24, and widely regarded as one of rock's finest guitarists, dies from his injuries in a motorcycle crash in Macon, Georgia. His final recordings with the group will be collected for their 1972 double album, *Eat a Peach*.

1982 ROTD: SCIENCE! Although 'She Blinded Me with Science' will reach only UK #49, **Thomas Dolby**'s single will unexpectedly hit US #5. This is partly due to heavy rotation on MTV of its video, in which his co-star is the highly British scientist and TV personality Magnus Pyke. SCIENCE!

1990 ROTD: Already popular on import, 'Cübik' by Manchester's **808 State** will return them to the UK top 10. Accompanying track 'Olympic' had been submitted as part of their city's application for the 1996 Summer Games. When the application was unsuccessful (Atlanta won the bid), the group offered it instead as a theme tune to Channel 4's youth show *The Word*.

30 OCTOBER

1961 ROTD: The first single by New York vocal quintet, **The Crystals**. 'There's No Other (Like My Baby)', with Barbara Alston on lead vocals, was recorded in the summer, immediately after their school prom. It is their first top 20 single in America.

1993 As part of BBC Radio 1's radical schedule changes and prioritisation of new music under new station controller Matthew Bannister, Saturday night means *Essential Mix*, a dance music session format that continues to this day. The first essential mixer is Pete Tong.

1995 ROTD: Almost any of the tracks on *Different Class* by **Pulp** could be a single. On the back cover is the message: 'We don't want no trouble, we just want the right to be different. That's all.'

31 OCTOBER

1960 On *Desert Island Discs* on the BBC Radio Home Service, castaway **Cliff Richard** is the first ever to choose an **Elvis Presley** record. He selects 'Heartbreak Hotel' – as will Paul McCartney when he guests on the programme in 1982.

1975 ROTD: Championed by Kenny Everett on London's Capital Radio, the six-minute 'Bohemian Rhapsody' – the first record ever to be UK #1 on two separate occasions – is extracted, unexpurgated, from **Queen**'s *A Night at the Opera* as a single. **Hot Chocolate**'s 'You Sexy Thing', the only record to be a top 10 single in the 1970s, 1980s and 1990s, also comes out today.

2011 ROTD: **Lou Reed**'s final album, the double *Lulu*, based on the work of German dramatist Frank Wedekind, finds him delivering spoken word contributions over instrumental tracks by **Metallica**.

NOVEMBER

1 NOVEMBER

1968 ROTD: *Wonderwall Music*, a mostly instrumental soundtrack album by **George Harrison** that combines Western rock with Indian classical music and instrumentation. It is the first solo LP by a Beatle, just days before the appearance of John Lennon and Yoko Ono's *Unfinished Music No. 1 Two Virgins*, and exactly three weeks before the 'White Album'.

1970 In Gothenburg, the four members of what will become **ABBA** appear on stage together for the first time, as part of a cabaret event called Festfolk, and to icy audience indifference.

1993 ROTD: One track from **Kate Bush**'s *The Red Shoes*, 'Why Should I Love You?' assembles guest vocal contributions from Prince, Lenny Henry and the Trio Bulgarka.

2 NOVEMBER

1965 ITV in London broadcasts *Rod the Mod*, a half-hour documentary about a weekend in the life of the promising 20-year-old R&B singer **Rod Stewart**, currently part of Long John Baldry's band. According to an *Observer* preview of the programme, Stewart claims to enjoy singing but accepts he'll be lucky to last more than a couple of years.

1971 ROTD: With 'Family Affair' fast heading to US #1, **Sly and the Family Stone**'s *There's a Riot Goin' On* takes their sound in a murkier, darker direction, with much use of drum machines and overdubs.

The title track is listed on the record but with a running time of '0:00'; it does not exist as, according to Sly Stone himself, 'I felt there should be no riots.'

1973 ROTD: 'Piano Man' (US #25, and his first hit) is inspired by **Billy Joel**'s time as a pianist and singer under the pseudonym of 'Bill Martin' in an LA bar called the Executive Room, and describes some of the real-life characters who frequented it.

1979 ROTD: The 1970s have been largely wretched for **Marianne Faithfull** – addiction, poverty and homelessness – but she ends the decade with a startling comeback in *Broken English*, a new wave rock record that is not just frank but at times explicit.

1987 ROTD: *Faith*, **George Michael**'s debut LP as a solo artist, fades in with an organ rendition of Wham!'s 'Freedom' before dabbling in rockabilly, R&B, soul and funk. Four of its nine tracks (the title track, 'Father Figure', 'One More Try' and 'Monkey') top the US singles charts.

3 NOVEMBER

1957 ROTD: Dick Clark, the host of TV's *American Bandstand*, suggested to **Danny and the Juniors** and their writers that 'Do the Bop' – a nod to the fast-fading dance fad – could be retitled to reflect the continuing popularity of 'record hops'. 'At the Hop' will hit US #1 in early 1958.

1972 Just a few days before the release of 'You're So Vain', a much-discussed song about three men (only Warren Beatty will be definitively namechecked), its writer and performer **Carly Simon** marries James Taylor. In the late evening, she joins Taylor on stage at his Radio City Music Hall concert. 'I've got a lot to be happy for, tonight,' says Taylor. The marriage will last 11 years.

1977 The night before playing a gig in Edinburgh, **Buzzcocks** are in the lounge and TV room of the city's Blenheim Guest House. *Guys and Dolls* happens to be on BBC2, and Adelaide (Vivian Blaine) utters the line, 'Have you ever fallen in love with someone you shouldn't have? Wait until it happens to you.' The following day, Pete Shelley writes the lyrics to 'Ever Fallen in Love . . . (With Someone You Shouldn't've?)', a year later a UK #12 hit.

1991 The Wonder Stuff, from Stourbridge in the West Midlands, reach UK #1 with a cover of Tommy Roe's 1969 chart-topper 'Dizzy'. The biggest of their nine top 20 singles, the song also appears on the album *I Will Cure You*, released by its guest vocalist Vic Reeves.

4 NOVEMBER

1964 Melbourne folk-pop quartet **The Seekers**, with Judith Durham on lead vocals, record 'I'll Never Find Another You' in London with its writer and producer Tom Springfield, brother of Dusty. In 1965, the single will reach #1 in the UK and Australia, and #4 in the US.

1985 ROTD: 'Holding Back the Years', a 1982 single by Mick Hucknall's band The Frantic Elevators, is reinvented as the third **Simply Red** release. For now, it lucks out at UK #51, but the next year will reach UK #2, US #1, and will eventually be immortalised in a classic *Only Fools and Horses* scene. No, not the one with the chandelier.

1997 ROTD: Canadian country-and-western artist Shania Twain reaches out to the pop market with *Come On Over*. A string of singles – 'Don't Be Stupid', 'You're Still the One', 'That Don't Impress Me Much', 'Man! I Feel Like a Woman!' – help the album ultimately sell over 40 million copies worldwide.

5 NOVEMBER

1971 ROTD: The sparse and plaintive 'It Must Be Love' by the British poet, singer and songwriter **Labi Siffre** (UK #14). Ten years later, he will appear in the video for the **Madness** cover version of the song, which will be a top 10 hit twice (1981, 1992).

1974 ROTD: 'Lady Marmalade' by **LaBelle**, which will go on to top the US charts, although the group will have to change the word 'coucher' to 'danser' when they perform it on TV. As Patti LaBelle will often cheerfully attest, 'I didn't know what it was about.'

1982 Part of the new Channel 4's remit is to provide an alternative to existing programming, and one demographic that has rarely been addressed in any depth is youth. *The Tube*, from 5.15 to 7 p.m. every Friday, is a rock magazine show, with reports, studio performances, interviews and – given that it is aired live – some inevitable surprises and gaffes. Broadcast from Newcastle upon Tyne, it's also an attempt to reinvent the excitement of *Ready Steady Go!* on ITV 20 years earlier. It will run for five series, ending in April 1987.

Although one of its presenters is the journalist Paula Yates, and her co-host Jools Holland is keyboard player with Squeeze, both are relatively new to television. Of their several rotating onscreen colleagues, Edinburgh art graduate Muriel Gray becomes the most regular.

The line-up of guests on episode 1 is varied: local band Toy Dolls perform in the foyer; Pete Townshend and Sting are cross-examined; Mark Miwurdz provides some topical poetry; Heaven 17 play live on TV for the first time. And The Jam, about to go their separate ways, play live on TV for the last time with an eight-song set, including their final single, 'Beat Surrender'.

6 NOVEMBER

1975 The **Sex Pistols** play their first live gig, supporting Bazooka Joe at the St Martin's College of Art. They last only 12 minutes before they are removed. Bazooka Joe's bass player, incidentally, is one Stuart Goddard, a star five years later as Adam Ant.

1984 Chaka Khan's cover of Prince's 'I Feel for You' reaches #1 in the UK, the first to feature a conspicuous sample, namely of Stevie Wonder's 'Fingertips'. Listen out for it at just before the three-minute mark.

Producer Arif Mardin, presently also working with Scritti Politti on *Cupid and Psyche 85*, has been in record production for 20 years. Born in Istanbul, his credits are varied: Hall & Oates' 'She's Gone', 'Pick Up the Pieces' by The Average White Band, and the Bee Gees' 'Jive Talkin''. In fact, it was Mardin who suggested to Barry Gibb that maybe he could sing up an octave, thus essentially helping to create Gibb's distinctive falsetto.

Chaka Khan's time as lead singer with the group Rufus during the 70s had yielded many US hits; solo record 'I'm Every Woman' and her swansong with Rufus 'Ain't Nobody' both chart high in the UK, but 'I Feel for You' is her first chart-topper. Yet she had to be persuaded by Mardin to approve the rap, which she disliked. 'He played me this guy repeating my name over and over again. I was so embarrassed. I thought it was horrible.'

The rapper was Melle Mel, who recorded a section in praise of Khan, initially intended for the middle of the song, but transplanted to the beginning. 'We had an AMS sampler,' Mardin will say in 2004. 'We put Chaka's name in and my hand slipped on the key. So that's how that Chaka-Chaka-Chaka thing happened. Believe me, it was an accident!'

2006 ROTD: **Joanna Newsom**'s *Ys*, named after the mythical Breton city in Brittany, and an exploration of a personal loss and a difficult relationship. A fan of Van Dyke Parks' *Song Cycle* album (1968), Newsom asks him to provide orchestral arrangements. Another influence on the record is Roy Harper's *Stormcock*, so she invites him to perform the whole 1971 album when he supports her at the Royal Albert Hall.

7 NOVEMBER

1969 ROTD: **Led Zeppelin** are an *albums* band. They don't 'do' singles, certainly not in Britain. But internationally, it's a different story. 'Whole Lotta Love' is edited down to three minutes for US radio, and reaches #4. A year later, ironically for a song that isn't a UK single, it is covered by CCS and becomes the *Top of the Pops* theme for over a decade.

1994 ROTD: Sometimes, the attraction of a hits compilation lies in some of it commercially underperforming. *Carry On Up the Charts* by **The Beautiful South** is a case in point. Despite only three of its tracks reaching the top 10, it takes only eight weeks to become the UK's second-best-selling album of 1994, outsold only by **Bon Jovi**'s *Cross Road*.

2005 ROTD: Twelve years after *The Red Shoes*, **Kate Bush** is back with the formidable double album *Aerial*, with tracks about the decimal placings of pi, doing the laundry, and a suite of songs about a single day, *A Sky of Honey*. (It will reach UK #3, outsold by Il Divo and Westlife.)

8 NOVEMBER

1963 ROTD: Just two weeks after it was recorded, 'I Only Want to Be with You' is issued as the first solo single by **Dusty Springfield** (UK #4), after she was excited by the sound of the soul and R&B of American records like 'Tell Him' and 'Don't Make Me Over'.

1968 ROTD: Exactly five years and many top 10 hits later, 'Son of a Preacher Man' (originally composed with Aretha Franklin in mind) will become Dusty's last top 10 hit in the UK for nearly 20 years.

1972 ROTD: *Transformer*, **Lou Reed**'s second LP, and produced by long-time Velvet Underground fans David Bowie and Mick Ronson. The first line of opening track 'Vicious' comes directly from Andy Warhol.

1980 After creative tensions, **The Human League** split into two factions: Martyn Ware and Ian Craig Marsh leave to form Heaven 17 and continue to pursue electronic music; Phil Oakey and Adrian Wright keep the name and push towards poppier climes.

9 NOVEMBER

1966 ROTD: A full decade before forming The Neville Brothers with his siblings, New Orleans R&B singer **Aaron Neville** releases 'Tell It Like It Is', a #1 on *Billboard*'s soul chart and #2 on its pop chart. It will become a civil rights anthem. It will also become a US hit again in 1980, for the Canadian rock band Heart.

1971 The first of **Slade**'s six #1 singles in the UK is 'Coz I Luv You', born out of Noddy Holder and Jimmy Lea's affection for the Hot Club combination of guitarist Django Reinhardt and violinist Stéphane Grappelli.

1992 ROTD: According to one critic, **Aphex Twin**'s entire output is a collision of 'beauty and disturbance', and of calm and disruption. The electronic musician's debut album, the double-set *Selected Ambient Works 85–92*, is less harsh than some of his subsequent releases, but it's haunting all the same. The titles of its tracks are highly unusual (single words with scientific and historical roots) and its samples come from similarly unexpected contexts: Gene Wilder's Willy Wonka, *Robocop*, Public Image Ltd and John Carpenter's *The Thing*. Although it is available only on import at first from Belgium, it develops a cult following, and a sequel, *Selected Ambient Works Volume II* (1994), reaches UK #11.

Richard David James, the man behind Aphex Twin, grew up in Cornwall, and was only in his early teens when he recorded the earliest song on *Selected Ambient Works*, 'i'. He became a DJ and engineering student, releasing his first EP, *Analogue Bubblebath*, in 1991. He records under several other aliases, including AFX, Polygon Window and Caustic Window, and even grazes the top 40 singles chart occasionally during the 1990s.

10 NOVEMBER

1972 ROTD: Over the five years since 'Pictures of Matchstick Men', **Status Quo** have inched away from psychedelia towards a meld of boogie, hard rock and radio-friendly tunes. Beginning with 'Paper Plane' (UK #8), it is a formula that will endure for decades.

1975 ROTD: On the day that **Queen** record the video to 'Bohemian Rhapsody' with director Bruce Gowers, **Patti Smith** releases her debut LP, *Horses*. Smith later acknowledges that its studio sessions with producer John Cale were tense and even confrontational but stressed that the tension had brought the best out of the band's 'adolescent and honest flaws'.

1985 Birkenhead band **Half Man Half Biscuit**, who specialise in amusing diatribes about television, football and provincial British life in general, record the first of many sessions for the BBC, including the first national airings of 'Trumpton Riots' and 'All I Want for Christmas is a Dukla Prague Away Kit'. Their debut LP, *Back in the DHSS*, which tops the UK indie charts, is John Peel's favourite record of the year. As of 2022, they will have issued 15 albums.

2014 ROTD: 'Uptown Funk' sung by **Bruno Mars** and produced by Mark Ronson. Perhaps in a streaming era, it might be more appropriate to talk about clicks rather than sales: by late 2022, its video will have been viewed nearly 5 billion times. A flurry of lawsuits on the subject of musical similarity will ensue: the composers of The Gap Band's 'Oops Upside Your Head', for one, are now officially recognised.

11 NOVEMBER

1964 'It's Not Unusual' is recorded by the as-yet-unknown **Tom Jones** as a demo for the songwriters to offer to Sandie Shaw. But Shaw's response is that Jones should release it instead. In January 1965, he will.

1983 ROTD: **Tina Turner's** interpretation of Al Green's 'Let's Stay Together', recorded with Heaven 17's British Electric Foundation, begins an incredible comeback for the singer (UK #6, US #26), after splitting both personally and professionally from her violent ex Ike in 1976. She had already worked with BEF in 1982 on their LP of covers, *Music of Quality and Distinction, Volume 1*, singing 'Ball of Confusion'.

1991 ROTD: **My Bloody Valentine's** *Loveless* appears in the UK's record shops nearly three years and several recording studio sessions after work had begun on it. (It is their last LP release for over 21 years.) A day later, the band begin a tour of Australia, Japan and the UK, performing shows with the kind of overpowering volume that will never be forgotten by anyone who attends.

12 NOVEMBER

1964 The BBC1 magazine show *Tonight* (just think of it as *The One Show* with your great-uncles) welcomes to the studio a group of youths representing the Society for the Prevention of Cruelty to Long-Haired Men. The most talkative of them is 17-year-old Davie Jones. This is **David Bowie's** first appearance on national television.

1971 ROTD: 'A Horse with No Name' by **America** (UK #3, US #1), of which so many observational stand-up comedians over the years have asked the same question: 'Why didn't they just give it a name?'

1990 ROTD: **The Orb's** 'Little Fluffy Clouds' combines two samples to great effect: composer Steve Reich's *Electric Counterpoint* (performed by guitarist Pat Metheny) and sections from a 1989 promotional interview with the singer Rickie Lee Jones. Meanwhile, **Pet Shop Boys** issue the elegiac 'Being Boring', which despite scraping only a top 20 placing, becomes widely regarded, and not just by Axl Rose – Axl Rose! – as one of their greatest songs.

2021 In Los Angeles, a judge terminates the conservatorship of **Britney Spears** and her estate after nearly 14 years (during which her career has remained as busy as ever). Many of her fans celebrate in public with the words 'Britney is free' and singing her song 'Stronger'. It overturns a decision made in 2008 to deprive the 39-year-old singer of control over her life, finances and career. In the summer of 2021, Spears had described the conservatorship as 'abusive', telling a court that she had had to take medication against her will, as well as perform when she did not want to. Her father, who was one of those running the conservatorship, had been suspended by a judge two months before today's hearing.

Spears herself tweets, 'Good God I love my fans so much . . . Best day ever.' Over the next year, she will announce an upcoming memoir, marry Sam Asghari and return to music, via a duet of 'Tiny Dancer' with Elton John.

13 NOVEMBER

1952 The UK charts' birthday tends to be regarded as 'Saturday 14 November 1952', but the *New Musical Express* is published on a Friday, so technically 13 November 1952 is the date of the first UK chart. How annoying. With 'Here in My Heart', **Al Martino**, perhaps better remembered in the 21st century as Johnny Fontane in *The Godfather*, outsells the likes of Vera Lynn, Frankie Laine, Nat King Cole and Max Bygraves to be the first UK #1.

1989 ROTD: The pairing of **Happy Mondays**' 'Hallelujah' (UK #19, part of the *Madchester Rave On* EP) and **The Stone Roses**' 'Fools' Gold' (UK #8, a double A-side single with 'What the World is Waiting For') brings together the dancefloor and indie rock. Ten days later, both acts are on *Top of the Pops*.

2006 ROTD: After a sold-out comeback tour, Gary, Howard, Jason and Mark release **Take That**'s first new material in over a decade. 'Patience' will hit UK #1 and win the Best British Single award at the Brits.

14 NOVEMBER

1939 BOTD: Composer and electronic musician **Wendy Carlos** will help develop Robert Moog's synthesiser, and popularise it on the Grammy Award-winning *Switched On Bach* collection of 1968 (US #10). She will also compose and rearrange﹐material (Purcell, Beethoven, Rossini) for the electronic score of Stanley Kubrick's 1971 movie of *A Clockwork Orange*, which not only inspired countless musicians and performers, but also the names Heaven 17, Moloko, Campag Velocet and the Korova record label.

1975 ROTD: The most widely heard track on **Brian Eno**'s *Another Green World* will be its reflective, brief title instrumental. It will become the theme music for BBC2's arts strand, *Arena*.

1980 ROTD: 'Fade to Grey' by **Visage** (UK #8), partly thanks to its striking video directed by Godley and Creme, will become a defining single when the New Romantic wave goes from clubland to the charts. Sung by Steve Strange, the lyrics (by Midge Ure) are recited in translated French by Brigitte Arens, whose boyfriend is Visage drummer (and Blitz club DJ) Rusty Egan.

1983 Director John Landis's 14-minute short film for **Michael Jackson**'s 'Thriller' is premiered at a special screening in Los Angeles at the Metro Crest Theater. It will first be televised in the US on MTV on 2 December, and on the same night in Britain at 1.05 a.m. as a late-night exclusive via Channel 4's *The Tube*.

15 NOVEMBER

1969 On waking up in a Waikiki hotel during her first-ever visit to Hawaii, **Joni Mitchell** draws back the curtains, initially admiring with wonder the distant green mountains and a flock of mynah birds . . . only to look down to see a huge car park. 'It broke my heart . . . this blight on paradise,' she later remembers. Her reaction is to write a new song lamenting environmental decline – 'ecology meets rock'n'roll' – and referencing the museum of trees at Foster Gardens, and the all-too-common usage of DDT insecticide (which would be banned in 1972).

Mitchell's first performance of 'Big Yellow Taxi' will take place at Worcester Polytechnic Institute, Massachusetts, on 29 November, and it will appear on her next album, 1970's *Ladies of the Canyon*. Incredibly, it remains her only solo hit single in the UK (#11).

1978 Echo and the Bunnymen debut as a live act at Eric's club in Liverpool. Echo is the name of their temperamental drum machine, and it stars in a 15-minute song called 'I Bagsey Yours' (later to become 'Monkeys' on their first LP, 1980's *Crocodiles*).

1993 ROTD: 'Lipgloss' by **Pulp** is 'about social skills going rusty', says Jarvis Cocker. The first single released by the band on major label Island, it will reach UK #50, which is enough of an incentive for the exhausted Sheffield band (who have endured 10 years of limited success) to keep going.

16 NOVEMBER

1978 On *Top of the Pops*, as **The Boomtown Rats'** 'Rat Trap' replaces 'Summer Nights' by John Travolta and Olivia Newton-John at UK #1 after seven weeks, frontman Bob Geldof commemorates the occasion by tearing up *Grease* posters, before playing a candelabra like a saxophone.

In fact, it's quite a day for historic televised pop. Take your pick, also, from: Sister Rosetta Tharpe on BBC-TV's *Six-Five Special* (1957); a debate on Anglia Television's *Motion* about who's better: Bach or The Beatles (1964); Prog pioneers The Nice on BBC2's *Colour Me Pop* (1968); *James Taylor in Concert* (BBC2, 1970); and Frank Zappa and the Mothers of Invention on BBC2's *The Old Grey Whistle Test* (1971).

1987 ROTD: Written by their manager Tom Watkins and their producer Nicky Graham (who played keyboards on the Ziggy Stardust tour), **Bros**'s 'When Will I Be Famous?' takes two months to reach the top 20, eventually hitting UK #2.

17 NOVEMBER

1973 Leicester octet **Showaddywaddy** appear on ITV's *New Faces*, perform a medley of rock'n'roll classics and win their heat. Also appearing in this series of the talent show are impressionist Les Dennis and the comedian Pete Conway – about to become the father of a certain Robbie Williams.

1978 Following the departure from BBC Radio 1 of Alan Freeman, who will shortly re-emerge on Capital Radio, the *Rock Show* moves from Saturday afternoon to late night on *Friday* with **Tommy Vance**. Under Vance, who will present it for 15 years, the show will be particularly associated with the rise of the New Wave of British Heavy Metal.

1997 ROTD: Heavily promoted as a short film on BBC Television for the past two months (as a celebration of the corporation's diversity), 'Perfect Day' is released as a multi-artist charity single, with proceeds going to Children in Need. Among those who will therefore enjoy their first UK #1 are Shane McGowan, Dr John, Emmylou Harris, Heather Small, Brett Anderson, Laurie Anderson and the song's composer **Lou Reed**.

18 NOVEMBER

1974 ROTD: A concept album about a Puerto Rican man in New York called Rael, *The Lamb Lies Down on Broadway* is packed with American imagery and reference points (from *West Side Story* to Evel Knievel), and marks the final work of **Peter Gabriel** with **Genesis**.

1983 ROTD: '2000 Miles' (UK #15) is forever associated with Christmas, but the inspiration for Chrissie Hynde to write it was the death of **Pretenders** guitarist James Honeyman-Scott at just 25.

1985 ROTD: Quite unlike anything else in 1985, **The Jesus and Mary Chain**'s *Psychocandy* throws together 60s-influenced pop with squealing feedback. It will chart at UK #31 and is highly influential on the indie-rock scene for the rest of the 80s.

19 NOVEMBER

1965 'These Boots Are Made for Walkin'', recorded today by **Nancy Sinatra** in Hollywood, took root in songwriter Lee Hazlewood's mind after seeing her father Frank in the 1963 movie *4 for Texas*, and specifically one line of dialogue: 'They tell me them boots ain't built for walkin'.'

1982 ROTD: The missing link between square dancing and hip-hop culture. 'Buffalo Gals' (UK #9) by **Malcolm McLaren** forms part of his and Trevor Horn's adventures in global music and features the World's Famous Supreme Team. It results in a full album, *Duck Rock*.

1990 ROTD: There were not one but two collaborations between **The Pogues and Kirsty MacColl**. We all know about 1987's 'Fairytale of New York', but there's also their marvellous take on Cole Porter's 'Miss Otis Regrets', part of the *Red Hot & Blue* album made for the Red Hot charity for support and awareness of HIV and AIDS.

20 NOVEMBER

1968 ROTD: One of the curios of Motown's back catalogue: an instrumental LP by **Eivets Rednow**, featuring his takes on such standards as 'Alfie', but also his first-ever entirely solo compositions. He didn't record the whole album backwards, though – that would have been ridiculous.

1969 At King Studios in Cincinnati, Clyde Stubblefield records an eight-bar solo drum part for **James Brown**, who, once it's done, seems to immediately have the title of the record. 'Funky Drummer' will reach only #51 on the US pop chart in 1970, but Stubblefield's eight bars will be sampled by, well, almost everyone.

2000 ROTD: The lyrics to **Eminem's** 'Stan' are made up of: two letters and an angry voice recording to the artist from an obsessive fan; a repeated section from Dido's 'Thank You'; and a final response to the fan's messages from the artist 'in his own voice'. It reaches only US #51, but makes it to UK #1 and is only narrowly pipped for the Christmas #1 by the efforts of Bob the Builder.

21 NOVEMBER

1980 ROTD: The anti-war 'Stop the Cavalry' will return **Jona Lewie** to the UK top three, eight years after he was Terry Dactyl (of The Dinosaurs) on 'Seaside Shuffle'. Though a Christmas-associated hit in Britain due to one line, its anti-war sentiment (both towards the First World War and nuclear apocalypse) will find support across Europe. In France, for instance, it will reach #1 in March 1981.

1994 ROTD: Another one that isn't specifically about Christmas, despite the overdubbing of bells. Tony Mortimer wrote **East 17's** 'Stay Another Day' (UK #1) about the death of his brother, and would in 2019 play piano on a version to raise money for the suicide prevention charity Calm.

2013 ROTD: **Pharrell Williams** wrote 'Happy' with CeeLo Green in mind, but Green's recording would have clashed with his Christmas album – so Williams recorded his own version. It tops the charts everywhere you can think of, although a special mention for France, which will keep it there for 22 weeks.

22 NOVEMBER

1963 As **The Beatles'** 'Twist and Shout' returns to #1 in the UK's EP charts and 'She Loves You' is at #2 (its 12th week in the top three), Parlophone releases *With The Beatles*, their second album of the year. It includes: 'All My Loving'; 'It Won't Be Long'; 'I Wanna Be Your Man' (covered by The Rolling Stones as their latest 45); the first original recorded song by George Harrison, 'Don't Bother Me'; and covers of Chuck Berry's 'Roll Over Beethoven', 'Money' and 'Please Mr Postman'.

In the US, where few people yet know of The Beatles, Philles Records issues *A Christmas Gift for You* — albeit a gift you still have to fork out for. Produced by Phil Spector, of whom Ronnie Spector of The Ronettes would say 'a brilliant producer, but a lousy husband' — which is quite the understatement — the record features covers of favourite Christmas songs by The Ronettes, The Crystals, Bob B. Soxx and the Blue Jeans, and Darlene Love, who premieres 'Christmas (Baby Please Come Home)'. The LP's Wall of Sound arrangements will filter into numerous future Christmas pop records, although few people will know of its existence in the UK until its reissue by Apple Records in 1972.

As usual, *Ready Steady Go!* begins on ITV at 6.15 p.m., with guests The Stones, Gerry and the Pacemakers, Freddie and the Dreamers, and Kenny Lynch. At around 7.15 p.m. (during the ad break of the next programme — the quiz, *Take Your Pick*), viewers in Britain first discover that US President **John F. Kennedy** has been assassinated in Dallas, Texas (he dies just before 1 p.m., Central Standard Time). On 1 February 1964, as The Beatles reach #1 in the US singles chart with 'I Want to Hold Your Hand', a compilation of Kennedy speeches called *The Presidential Years* will peak at #8 on the US album chart.

1974 ROTD: 'Roxette' by pub rock supremos **Dr Feelgood** will fail to reach the British charts, but such is their reputation and following as a live act that their third album, 1976's *Stupidity* (containing a live take), will top the UK album charts. Believe it or not, the Swedish duo **Roxette** did indeed name themselves directly after this song; Per Gessle was a long-time fan.

2010 ROTD: **Nicki Minaj** and **Kanye West** make guest appearances on each other's new albums. Minaj's *Pink Friday* is her debut album; *My Beautiful Dark Twisted Fantasy* is West's fifth.

23 NOVEMBER

1979 ROTD: **Public Image Ltd**'s *Metal Box* is packaged in fiendish fashion: presented as three 12-inch singles, they are packed snugly into a circular metal canister, hard to remove and play, and even harder to preserve. The album itself is well worth the effort, and is swiftly reissued as a standard double LP, a lot more convenient for consumers. On the same day, **Pink Floyd**'s first British single for 11 years, 'Another Brick in the Wall (Part II)', is released, and will hit #1 in time for Christmas.

1992 It is announced that the Manchester independent record label **Factory**, founded in 1978 by Tony Wilson, has gone into administration with debts of £2 million – thanks to a combination of overspending, a recession and lack of sales, most notably for the final Happy Mondays album, *Yes Please!* A completed New Order album, *Republic*, is instead released through the major label Polygram in May 1993.

1992 BOTD: In the same year that her father Billy Ray has scored a worldwide hit with 'Achy Breaky Heart' (US #4, UK #2), which becomes a line-dancing signature song, his daughter Destiny is born in Franklin, Tennessee. As **Miley Cyrus**, she becomes a teenage star actor on Disney's *Hannah Montana* in 2006, while in 2023 her worldwide #1 single 'Flowers' breaks Spotify streaming records with 115 million streams in a single week.

24 NOVEMBER

1969 Breaking away from Chicago psychedelic soul group Rotary Connection, where the upper reaches of her stratospheric voice could be occasionally mistaken for a theremin, **Minnie Riperton** begins recording her debut solo LP, *Come to My Garden*, with a band including Ramsey Lewis and, on drums, Earth Wind & Fire's Maurice White. The album is barely noticed on release in 1970, but becomes an underground classic, especially the much-covered 'Les Fleur'.

1970 Two years after his former group Love Sculpture charted high with their thunderous reworking of Khachaturian's 'Sabre Dance', **Dave Edmunds** reaches UK #1 with a remake of Smiley Lewis's 1955 smash 'I Hear You Knocking'. During the instrumental break, Edmunds namechecks several music legends, and Lewis himself is one of them.

1978 ROTD: **Ian Dury**'s 'Hit Me with Your Rhythm Stick', technically credited to Ian and the Blockheads, and complete with Davey Payne's twin saxophone solo (a homage to the recently deceased Rahsaan Roland Kirk). It's nice to think some of the record's buyers (nearly a million of them) played the single's B-side: 'There Ain't Half Been Some Clever Bastards', a song from Dury's earlier days in Kilburn and the High Roads.

25 NOVEMBER

1984 A charity single to raise money for the malnourished in Ethiopia is recorded with a popstar-studded cast at Sarm West studios, Notting Hill. **Band Aid**'s 'Do They Know It's Christmas?' began as an unrecorded Bob Geldof song called 'It's My World' and was completed with Ultravox's Midge Ure, who also produces the single. The drum sample, by the way, is from the Tears for Fears song, 'The Hurting'.

1991 ROTD: 'Justified and Ancient' (UK #2, US #11), re-recorded by **The KLF with Tammy Wynette**, is subtitled 'Stand By the JAMs' in semi-reference to 1968's 'Stand By Your Man' by the First Lady of Country. 'I know about ice cream vans,' Wynette tells the *NME*, 'but I'd never heard of a 99 before.'

2021 The Disney+ streaming service premieres the first instalment of **Peter Jackson**'s three-part *Get Back*. The series, nearly eight hours long, re-edits unseen footage from **The Beatles**' making of the *Let It Be* album and film in January 1969.

26 NOVEMBER

1976 ROTD: 'Anarchy in the UK', the first **Sex Pistols** single, and their only one to be released by EMI. It will peak at UK #38 in Christmas week.

1993 Shortly after they have passed auditions to be in an 'Irish Take That', and before releasing any records, a seemingly underprepared incarnation of **Boyzone** display their dancing skills live on Gay Byrne's *Late Late Show* in Dublin. Due to the advent of clip shows, it will feel like the most screened thing on television ever.

2007 ROTD: The genesis of 'Call the Shots' by **Girls Aloud** (UK #3) lay in an article Xenomania's Miranda Cooper happened to read about 'the Miranda Complex', a term based on the ambitious lawyer character played by Cynthia Nixon on *Sex and the City*.

27 NOVEMBER

1981 ROTD: On the same day that **The Human League** release their biggest hit and Britain's Christmas #1, 'Don't You Want Me', **Soft Cell** present their debut LP, the offbeat and provocative *Non-Stop Erotic Cabaret*. Recorded in New York, it will reach UK #5 and US #22.

1995 ROTD: **Pulp**'s 'Disco 2000' was written by Jarvis Cocker about his real-life childhood friend Deborah, who as the late Deborah Bone became a major player in the treatment of mental health for young people. Cocker would perform the song at her 50th birthday party in 2013.

2000 ROTD: The fantastically inventive *Since I Left You* by Melbourne group **The Avalanches** is drenched in samples — hundreds, perhaps even thousands of them — and offers something different to the late 90s big-beat fad, opting instead for a lighter echo of 60s pop. It originally peaks at #21 in Australia, but reaches #8 in the UK.

28 NOVEMBER

1969 ROTD: For the new **Rolling Stones** LP *Let It Bleed* a photoshoot was staged involving a cake, which was required to be 'really gaudy', in the words of the woman who made it — the home economist and premier TV cook of the future Delia Smith.

1977 The musical *Elvis*, directed by rock'n'roll TV producer Jack Good, opens in London's West End, with three performers portraying Presley over his lifetime: Tim Whitnall (Young Elvis), PJ Proby (Mature Elvis) and, as Middle Elvis (in other words, the Army and Movie years), 26-year-old Sunsets singer **Shakin' Stevens**. One of the dancers in this original production is future comedy actor and hitmaker Tracey Ullman.

1983 ROTD: Unlike most TV-advertised multi-artist compilations of the time, EMI/Virgin's *Now That's What I Call Music!* aims for minimal filler. Volume 1 in its apparently never-ending catalogue arranges 30 hits from 1983, including 11 of the year's 17 UK #1 singles.

1988 ROTD: **Neneh Cherry**, born in Stockholm and later the stepdaughter of the jazz trumpeter Don, will describe a 'buffalo stance' as 'an attitude you have to have in order to get by. It's not about fashion, but about survival in inner cities and elsewhere'.

'Buffalo Stance' (UK #3, US #3) is her first solo single, but close observers of British pop's fringes have heard and seen her around for several years: touring with The Slits; singing with the post-punk-funk group Rip, Rig and Panic; DJing on the pirate radio station Dread

Broadcasting Corporation; and providing guest vocals for The The (on 1986's 'Slow Train to Dawn').

The history of the strident 'Buffalo Stance' is convoluted. In 1986, duo Morgan McVey released a single called 'Looking Good Diving', one of the very few Stock Aitken Waterman productions of the time to flop. On the B-side was 'Looking Good Diving with the Wild Bunch', which featured Cherry performing a rap interlude. (The Wild Bunch was the group of DJs and musicians in Bristol who would later generate, among others, Massive Attack and Tricky.) Cherry's mix of sung and rapped vocals on her solo remake – co-produced by Tim Simenon of Bomb the Bass – was unusual for the time but soon became common in the work of other artists. Many more hits would follow for Neneh Cherry.

29 NOVEMBER

1962 'Stranger on the Shore' by the Somerset clarinettist **Acker Bilk**, and the instrumental theme to the BBC TV children's serial, spends its 53rd continuous week in the UK top 50, the first single ever to do so. It never betters its UK #2 peak, but in May, it became the first British record to top the US singles charts.

1968 ROTD: Routinely placed high in critics' all-time greatest LPs, **Van Morrison**'s blend of folk, jazz, blues and classical – *Astral Weeks* – sells poorly at first and receives mixed reviews, but is the definition of a steady seller. Incredibly, it has charted in the UK only for one week . . . in November 2015, at #55.

2010 ROTD: 'Rolling in the Deep' is the result of an afternoon writing session between Paul Epworth and **Adele**. The two met the day after she walked away from a relationship, and the song came out of the producer's suggestion that they should write 'a fierce tune' born out of her anger. 'The beat of the song was my heartbeat,' she later says. 'It just built and built.'

30 NOVEMBER

1973 ROTD: **Wizzard's** 'I Wish It Could Be Christmas Every Day' (UK #4), recorded in August, is Roy Wood's attempt to recreate the spirit of Disney music.

1987 ROTD: **Pet Shop Boys** had premiered their reinterpretation of 'Always on My Mind' (UK #1, US #4) in August on an ITV special called *Love Me Tender* to mark the 10th anniversary of Elvis Presley's death – although the song's first-ever appearance on record was by soul singer Gwen McCrae in early 1972. Today, it becomes a stand-alone single for Tennant and Lowe.

2002 ITV broadcasts the 'girls' live final' of *Popstars: The Rivals*. After several weeks of public phone-in votes every Saturday night, Nadine Coyle, Sarah Harding, Nicola Roberts, Cheryl Tweedy and Kimberley Walsh are confirmed as the five members of **Girls Aloud**. They are now pitted against 'rival' group, the all-male One True Voice, for the prize of the year's Christmas #1 single.

DECEMBER

1 DECEMBER

1971 ROTD: Due to copyright complications, **John Lennon and Yoko Ono**'s 'Happy Xmas (War is Over)' is issued in the US a whole year before the UK (#2, 1972, 1980). In *Billboard*'s seasonal singles chart, published separately from its pop Hot 100, it will reach #3, behind Carpenters' 'Merry Christmas Darling' and 'Jingle Bells' by (double-checks), um, 'The Singing Dogs'. Eight years after *A Christmas Gift for You*, it practically single-handedly kick-starts the idea of the modern holiday single.

1976 During November, the **Sex Pistols** have guested on Janet Street-Porter's Sunday morning *The London Weekend Show* and on BBC1's early evening *Nationwide*. But tonight at around 6.30, on Thames's live regional *Today* magazine show in London, and just before *Crossroads*, they are asked by tipsy interviewer Bill Grundy to 'say something out-rageous'. They duly comply.

1980 **Talking Heads**, promoting their *Remain in Light* album, play the first of two nights at London's Hammersmith Odeon. Their support act is promising Irish quartet **U2**.

2 DECEMBER

1986 'The Final Countdown' wasn't designed to be a hit at all, but a way of introducing **Europe**'s live stage shows. Today it reaches UK #1, six months after reigning at #1 for six weeks in the band's native Sweden. The rock band had first come to prominence in 1982 by win-ning the 'battle of the bands' talent contest *Rock SM*.

1993 ROTD: **Salt-N-Pepa** join forces with **En Vogue** for 'Whatta Man' (UK #6, US #3), a revamp and adaptation of 'What a Man' – white Florida singer **Linda Lyndell's** 1968 R&B hit for Stax Records. Its success encourages Lyndell to resume her own singing career, originally halted because of harassment from white supremacist groups.

1997 ROTD: 'Time of Your Life' (Good Riddance)' (UK #11) is, according to **Green Day** bass player Mike Dirnt, the 'most punk' thing they could have recorded. It's their biggest international hit, and ends up soundtracking a *Seinfeld* clips show the following spring.

3 DECEMBER

1965 ROTD: **The Beatles** will monopolise the UK #1 spot over Christmas: *Rubber Soul* is their new album; 'Day Tripper'/'We Can Work It Out' their new single.

1974 **Barry White's** 'The First, the Last, My Everything', which today becomes his sole UK #1, is an embellishment of an unrecorded 1953 song by country-and-western singer Peter Radcliffe: 'You're My First, You're My Last, My In-Between'.

1976 Ahead of a photo shoot for **Pink Floyd's** forthcoming album, *Animals*, a 40-foot-long inflatable pig, which has been moored to the chimneys of Battersea Power Station, breaks away and becomes a hazard for nearby aircraft. (The 'pig' lands in Kent, alarming some real-life cattle, and the image for the final *Animals* sleeve has to be faked.)

2001 ROTD: 'Murder on the Dancefloor', written by **Sophie Ellis-Bextor** with Gregg Alexander (ex-New Radicals), will reach UK #2, blocked from #1 only by Daniel Bedingfield's 'Gotta Get Thru This'.

2018 ROTD: The 'country trap' track 'Old Town Road' is self-released by **Lil Nas X,** who recorded it in Atlanta at the $20-an-hour CinCoYo studio. A few months later, **Billy Ray Cyrus** appears on its remixed version, which will become a global #1.

4 DECEMBER

1956 Johnny Cash, Jerry Lee Lewis, Carl Perkins and Elvis Presley participate in a spontaneous recording session at Sun Studios, Memphis, which has grown out of a Perkins recording. The engineer Jack Clement realises 'I'd be remiss not to record this', but the session will not be released in Europe until 1981 under the title *The Million Dollar Quartet.*

1971 Deep Purple prepare to record their next album, *Machine Head,* in Montreux, while a Frank Zappa concert takes place at the town's casino complex beside Lake Geneva. A flare gun is fired, and the venue burns to the ground, miraculously with no reported casualties. The blaze inspires Deep Purple to write and record 'Smoke on the Water' later that month.

1989 ROTD: If three of the 80s' most significant British pop groups were The Smiths, New Order and Pet Shop Boys, 'Getting Away with It' (UK #12, US #38) is an appropriate way to end the decade, as Johnny Marr, Bernard Sumner, Neil Tennant and Chris Lowe have got together to form the 'supergroup' **Electronic**. Marr and Sumner will make three albums together under the moniker.

5 DECEMBER

1969 ROTD: Having just changed their name from The Iveys, Swansea band and Apple signing **Badfinger's** 'Come and Get It' (UK #4, US #7), sung by Pete Ham, is written by Paul McCartney and featured in the new Peter Sellers film *The Magic Christian.*

1971 Kilburn and the High Roads, fronted by **Ian Dury**, play their first proper gig at the Croydon School of Art, where they share a bill with Thunderclap Newman.

1982 'You write, I'll play.' Immediately following BBC Radio 1's Top 40 countdown, **Annie Nightingale**'s eclectic and lively request show lightens up every Sunday night for the next 11 years. Nightingale previously presented a Sunday afternoon request show for the station between 1975 and 1978.

6 DECEMBER

1977 Recently in the top 10, with '2-4-6-8 Motorway', **The Tom Robinson Band** perform live at the Lyceum in London, their set including a song that, though rarely played on the radio, becomes an anthem for the gay community.

'(Sing if You're) Glad to Be Gay' was originally written by Robinson for him to perform at a Gay Pride rally in Hyde Park in August 1976. Each verse of the song scrutinises a different way in which homophobic attitudes have an everyday impact on the gay community: verse one examines the police; next it's the press; thirdly it's the general public. The fourth and final verse is a call to arms, asking for support for the cause of gay rights.

The live rendition of 'Glad to Be Gay' at the Lyceum becomes part of the next TRB single, the *Rising Free . . .* EP (UK #18) in January 1978, where superficial priority is given to its accompanying song, 'Don't Take No for An Answer'.

1993 ROTD: The seasonal stomp 'I Was Born on Christmas Day' by **Saint Etienne** (UK #37), whose Bob Stanley really *was* born on Christmas Day, features The Charlatans' Tim Burgess on guest vocals. The video, a mock-up of a wedding filmed at a London registry office, co-stars – as bride Sarah Cracknell's father – Richard O'Sullivan from *Man About the House*.

2003 **Elvis Costello** and the Canadian jazz singer **Diana Krall** marry near London. Their first meeting was 'in front of a billion people', in Costello's words, when randomly paired to present the Song of the Year gong at the 2002 Grammy Awards. 'Luckily, we saw our future the same way,' recalls Costello.

7 DECEMBER

1973 ROTD: 'Merry Xmas Everybody' came about thanks to a chance remark from the aunt of **Slade** bass player Jim Lea, who suggested writing the sort of thing 'that'll get played for ever, like "Happy Birthday to You"'.

While Lea and singer Noddy Holder knew that Christmas was the most universal occasion to celebrate in a song, they didn't want gimmicks or clichés. Instead, they dusted off their 1967 song 'Buy Me a Rocking Chair' and reworked it. Lea came up with the first line during a US tour as the opening act for The J Geils Band and Blue Oyster Cult. The rest of the new lyric was then drafted by Holder in a single feverish two-hour writing session at his parents' house back in England.

But the recording of the song was delayed when a tragic car accident in July 1973 killed Angela Morris, the girlfriend of drummer Don Powell and caused him serious memory loss. Powell had to re-learn his drumming skills almost from scratch, and so the band's Christmas song was pieced together layer-by-layer in the Record Plant studio, New York. In the next suite was John Lennon, preparing his next LP, and it was from there that Slade borrowed the harmonium for their new, appropriately Beatlesy, effort. Requiring a particular sort of echo for the singalong chorus, they decided to record the vocals in the Plant's cavernous corridor.

On Tuesday 11 December, 'Merry Xmas Everybody' will become Slade's third UK #1 of 1973 to go straight in at the top spot. In its first four days on sale, it will sell 250,000 copies. Jim Lea's aunt was on to something.

1979 ROTD: **Kurtis Blow**'s ingeniously titled 'Christmas Rappin'' (UK #30) makes him the first rapper to be signed to a major record label (Mercury). Blow's interjection, by the way, in the recitation of 'The Night Before Christmas' – 'Hold it now!' – is lifted by the Beastie Boys for their 1986 single 'Hold It Now, Hit It'.

1987 ROTD: **The Smiths'** final single is the none-less-Christmassy desolate epic 'Last Night I Dreamt That Somebody Loved Me' (UK #30 – everyone's already got the album). **New Order**'s 'Touched by the Hand of God' (UK #20 – not on an album at all) is accompanied by a priceless video in which the group essentially pretend to be Mötley Crüe for four minutes.

8 DECEMBER

1962 **Dionne Warwick**'s 'Don't Make Me Over' enters the US Hot 100 where it will peak at #21, beginning a lengthy association between Warwick, composer **Burt Bacharach** and lyricist **Hal David**: 'Anyone Who Had a Heart', 'Walk on By', 'I Just Don't Know What to Do with Myself' to name just a few.

1965 ROTD: 'California Dreamin'', written by John and Michelle Phillips, has already been recorded by Barry McGuire as an album track, but its backing vocal group (including Mr and Mrs Phillips) impress the record company sufficiently to have their own version made, using the same backing track. It will become the first hit for **The Mamas and the Papas** (US #4, UK #23).

1976 ROTD: Its claustrophobic title song began as something called 'Mexican Reggae' because that's what Don Henley thought the demo sounded like. Apart from compilations, *Hotel California* will become the **Eagles'** biggest-selling album, with sales of over 30 million copies.

1980 When 40-year-old John Lennon is shot dead outside the Dakota Building in New York, a cassette falls out of his pocket that contains the last song he ever worked on.

'Walking on Thin Ice' is in fact a **Yoko Ono** single for which he had played guitar. In the week leading up to his death, they have been working hard on it at the Hit Factory studio. When they completed it, he said to her, 'I think we've just got your first number one, Yoko.'

Yoko Ono thought of a frozen Lake Michigan when writing the song: 'I was just thinking of this woman that is walking Lake Michigan when it is totally frozen, and is walking and walking . . . "Oh, it's ice but I can walk on it." I walk like that in life.'

Lennon told Ono she had to put it out as a single 'right away'. In March 1981, while the charts are packed with posthumous Lennon reissues and new material from the couple's *Double Fantasy* LP, 'Walking on Thin Ice' will manage to creep into the top 40, peaking at #35. Over 20 years on, its alternative disco sound will be revamped for the clubs once more, and top the *Billboard* dance chart. So Yoko will get her first #1 after all.

9 DECEMBER

1966 ROTD: **The Who**'s second LP, *A Quick One* (UK #4), ends with a six-part 'mini-opera' described by Pete Townshend as an introduction to 'Tommy's parents', pre-empting the group's foray into long-form concept albums.

1968 NBC televises *TCB*, 'Taking Care of Business', a musical variety special starring **Diana Ross & The Supremes** and **The Temptations**, and produced by Motown in association with the makers of the comedy show *Laugh-In*. While showcasing many of their hits, the groups also cover showtunes ('The Impossible Dream', 'Somewhere') and other pop hits such as 'Respect' and 'Mrs Robinson'.

1972 **David Bowie** records 'Drive-In Saturday' (UK #3) in New York, on what is indeed a Saturday. One of his exercises in 'futuristic nostalgia' (i.e., recalling the past from the future), he had offered it to Mott the Hoople, who had accepted 'All the Young Dudes', but they had turned this one down.

10 DECEMBER

1949 Despite its title, 'Detroit City Blues' is recorded in New Orleans, as is 'The Fat Man', another song cited as a major influence on rock'n'roll. The artist, and co-writer of both songs, making his debut on record is Antoine Dominique Domino Jr – **Fats Domino**. The record will reach #2 on the US R&B chart in 1950.

1969 ROTD: 'Thank You (Falettinme Be Mice Elf Agin)', which will reach US #1 in February for **Sly & the Family Stone**. The lyrics express Sly Stone's frustrations that the messages in his songs are not being understood. Exactly 20 years later, its guitar part will inspire the groove on Janet Jackson's 'Rhythm Nation' (US #2, UK #23).

1973 Although Manhattan's Country, BlueGrass and Blues (**CBGB**) venue opens intending to cater for those genres, it will soon become closely associated with the punk and new wave movement, showcasing – amongst many others – Television, the Ramones, Patti Smith and Blondie.

11 DECEMBER

1965 Summit High School in New Jersey is the unlikely first venue for a **Velvet Underground** concert, especially when one of their three songs as opening act is 'Heroin'. Headlining are The Myddle Class, whose singer David Palmer will go on to front Steely Dan's songs 'Dirty Work' and 'Brooklyn' seven years later.

1970 ROTD: **John Lennon** and **Yoko Ono** both release new albums backed by *The Plastic Ono Band*, and the first material recorded after the couple attended primal therapy sessions with Arthur Janov. Yoko Ono's track 'AOS' features the Ornette Coleman Quartet, a live recording of that Albert Hall show collaboration we mentioned from Leap Day 1968. It all links up.

1984 ROTD: *Various Positions* is **Leonard Cohen**'s first LP for five years. 'After a long period of barrenness, it all just seemed to click,' he later says. His co-vocalist is **Jennifer Warnes**, and although it only really sells in Scandinavia, the LP has what will become two of his most popular songs: 'Dance Me to the End of Love' and 'Hallelujah'.

1988 Following a string of false allegations surrounding **Elton John**'s private life (during a period of particularly virulent homophobia in several British tabloid newspapers), and suggestions of cruelty to animals, the singer is paid £1 million in damages by the *Sun* newspaper.

12 DECEMBER

1970 On stage in New Orleans, Jim Morrison slurs and forgets his words, and resorts to telling jokes (which bomb with the audience). Though **The Doors** will record one last studio album, *LA Woman*, this is The End of their career as a live attraction.

1980 ROTD: 'It was doubly outrageous,' Joe Strummer will say of **The Clash**'s new sprawling triple LP, *Sandinista!* (UK #19, US #24). 'Actually, it was triply outrageous.'

1986 **The Smiths** play their final full set as a live band at an Artists Against Apartheid show at London's Brixton Academy. They end with a performance of their very first single: 1983's 'Hand in Glove'.

13 DECEMBER

1966 **Sonny and Cher** record 'The Beat Goes On' (US #6, UK #29) in Hollywood. In 1997, British dance act **The All Seeing I** cover it, shorn of topical references, and produce another cover of it for **Britney Spears'** first album.

2009 'Bad Romance' by **Lady Gaga**, musically in debt to German techno and lyrically about falling in love with the wrong people, reaches UK #1, having peaked at #2 in the US.

2019 ROTD: **Stormzy's** second album, *Heavy is the Head*, is one of pop's most effective reflections on the darker side of stardom. There are guest appearances from Burna Boy, Yebba, Aitch, Headie One, HER and even Ed Sheeran (he gets everywhere). There's also a sample of the theme to *Tracy Beaker*.

14 DECEMBER

1965 **Simon and Garfunkel** record 'Homeward Bound', penned by Paul Simon earlier in the year while he was resident in the UK. It may have been written at Widnes railway station. Or was it Wigan? Or Warrington? Anyway. In the same studio session, the duo re-record a track already released by Simon as a solo act, 'I Am a Rock'.

1969 With their debut Motown single 'I Want You Back' rising to US #19, **The Jackson 5** perform it on *The Ed Sullivan Show*. Sullivan's other guests are Jim Henson's Muppets, one of the attractions of the just-launched children's educational series *Sesame Street*.

1992 ROTD: *Insecticide*, a mopping-up of **Nirvana** demos, rarities and sessions, is issued by Geffen, and, as if to underline its stopgap status, the band originally suggested 'Cash Cow' as a title. In early versions of the liner notes, Kurt Cobain tells racists, misogynists and homophobes, 'Don't come to our shows and don't buy our records.'

15 DECEMBER

1956 In Shreveport, KWKH-TV's Saturday night variety series *Louisiana Hayride* welcomes back one of its former resident acts who has gone on to national stardom. After the end of his set, almost inaudible due to a packed, screaming audience, the show's host Horace Logan coins the phrase, '**Elvis** has left the building.'

1975 ROTD: George Clinton, a fan of *Star Trek*, brings us **Parliament** . . . in space! The outer space concept — Black astronauts, spacecraft shaped like Cadillacs, and alien lands — runs right through their fourth LP, *Mothership Connection* . . .

1992 ROTD: . . . And exactly 17 years later, the P-Funk of *Mothership Connection*'s title song is absorbed into the G-Funk of **Dr Dre**'s 'Let Me Ride', part of his solo debut *The Chronic*.

16 DECEMBER

1975 One seasonal revival few were expecting: **Laurel and Hardy**'s 1937 rendition of 'The Trail of the Lonesome Pine' (from their *Way Out West* film). After impromptu plays by John Peel on Radio 1, and its re-release, the record today moves up to UK #2, just behind 'Bohemian Rhapsody'.

1985 ROTD: **a-ha** follow up 'Take on Me' (UK #2, US #1) with 'The Sun Always Shines on TV', 'about the power of television and the way television presents life', according to its writer Pål Waaktaar. In the UK it will become the Norwegian trio's only #1 single.

1986 **The Housemartins'** acapella rendition of the Isley-Jasper-Isley soul record 'Caravan of Love' becomes their only UK #1.

17 DECEMBER

1971 ROTD: Almost nobody buys *Hunky Dory* at first – barely 5,000 copies in the first three months, according to one **David Bowie** biographer. The single 'Changes' will flop. Only after Bowie's transformation into Ziggy Stardust will interest flicker, before surging in summer 1973 (a peak of UK #3) after another track, 'Life on Mars?' (a 'parody' of 'My Way') is belatedly issued as a single.

1984 ROTD: Up until now, Billy Bragg's 'A New England', has had two verses, but he has specially written a third for **Kirsty MacColl**'s new version, which will hit UK #7 in the New Year.

1991 For **Biz Markie**'s track 'Alone Again', the rapper sampled **Gilbert O'Sullivan**'s 1972 million-seller 'Alone Again (Naturally)'. He asked for permission from O'Sullivan, but though the artist declined, Markie and his record company released the track anyway. That decision landed them in court.

Today, Judge Duffy finds Markie guilty of copyright infringement, and controversially refers the case to criminal court, as he believes the track is tantamount to theft. Although Markie is not charged with theft, several things happen as a consequence that will affect sampling practices in popular music. From now on, most recordings will be limited to just using one or two separate samples. Interpolation will become commonplace: different musicians will record the material that might have been sampled, with the songwriters of that material being paid appropriately.

Gilbert O'Sullivan is quite clear about why he refused permission for 'Alone Again (Naturally)' in this specific case, while granting permission in other cases. 'I do make sure that that particular song isn't used in an inappropriate context,' he will tell John Lewis in the *Financial Times* in 2007. 'I don't care about the credibility or the money. It's about integrity.'

18 DECEMBER

1962 Six weeks after completing its run at UK #1, **The Tornados'** 'Telstar' — about NASA's first communications satellite — becomes the first single by a UK group to reach #1 on the *Billboard* Hot 100. The group's rhythm guitarist George Bellamy will have a chart-topping son in the 2000s and 2010s: Matt Bellamy from **Muse**.

1970 ROTD: Somewhat buried in the pre-Christmas rush is folk singer **Vashti Bunyan**'s *Just Another Diamond Day*, recorded a year earlier. Thirty years later, during which time a cult following has been championing it, it is finally reissued on CD and leads Bunyan to return to music, making 2005's *Lookaftering*.

2000 Only a year after her last and perhaps best album, the Cuban-flavoured *Tropical Brainstorm*, 41-year-old **Kirsty MacColl** is killed instantly when she is struck by an unauthorised high-speed powerboat off the Yucatan coast of Mexico. Her family inaugurates a Justice for Kirsty campaign to push for a full investigation of the tragedy.

19 DECEMBER

1955 Two days after scribbling the words of a new song on a piece of scrap paper, country artist **Carl Perkins** records it in Memphis on his Les Paul guitar. While the opening of 'Blue Suede Shoes' is based on that of the nursery rhyme 'One for the Money', it is not quite so clear where the inspiration for the bulk of the song has come from. Perkins himself will claim that he played a dance a few weeks earlier and spotted one youth admonishing his female companion for scuffing one of his blue suede shoes. Alternatively, Johnny Cash will relate in his autobiography that he told Perkins about an airman he met in Germany who had similarly been keen to keep his footwear unscuffed.

On release in early 1956, 'Blue Suede Shoes' would be a local #1 in Memphis, before peaking at #2 on the national pop charts. Perkins' fame in pop music might have grown further had it not been for a road accident in March 1956 in Delaware (on the way to a TV appearance in New York) that would end in tragedy for Perkins' brother Jay (he would die in 1958), and result in Carl having an extended stay in hospital due to his extensive injuries.

Meanwhile, Elvis Presley – who will visit Carl Perkins in hospital – will have his own hit version of 'Blue Suede Shoes'. The flip side of Perkins' single, 'Honey Don't', will be covered in 1964 on *Beatles for Sale*, moving Paul McCartney to say, 'If there were no Carl Perkins, there would be no Beatles.'

1964 ROTD: Pete Townshend and Roger Daltrey would both later acknowledge how much their first single as **The Who** sounds rather like The Kinks. 'I Can't Explain', the result of a flurry of attempts by Townshend to write some original material rather than lean on cover versions, will reach UK #8.

1981 BBC1 broadcasts *The Police in Montserrat*, a documentary about the making of the trio's recent album, *Ghost in the Machine*. When guitarist Andy Summers decides to play a little bit of 'funk' during a break in recording, reporter **Jools Holland** cheekily decides to unplug the amp, saying 'I think that's best left to James Brown'. It is later said that this subversive act alone will get him shortlisted for the job of presenting Channel 4's forthcoming pop show *The Tube*.

1994 ROTD: **Oasis**'s fifth and final single of the year, 'Whatever', will later be co-credited to Neil Innes due to the similarity of its main melody to 'How Sweet to Be an Idiot'. On Christmas Day, it will enter the UK charts at #3, behind 'Stay Another Day' and Mariah Carey's 'All I Want for Christmas Is You'. One of the single's B-sides is 'Half the World Away', which in 1998 becomes the theme to the BBC sitcom *The Royle Family*.

20 DECEMBER

1972 ROTD: 'Vietnam was rumbling on, the rich were getting richer – so it was the perfect time to sing about social issues,' **The O'Jays'** Walter Williams will say of 'Love Train' (US #1, UK #9), a key track in the morphing of soul into disco music.

1981 Tom Eyen and Henry Krieger's *Dreamgirls* – a musical about a Chicago-based female R&B vocal trio called The Dreams – opens at the Imperial Theatre, Broadway. The star of the show will be **Jennifer Holliday**, whose performance of 'And I'm Telling You I'm Not Going' at the end of the first act will lead to Tony and Grammy Awards.

2009 In the late noughties, even when the Christmas #1 isn't someone off *The X Factor*, it's a reaction to someone off *The X Factor*. **Rage Against the Machine**'s 'Killing in the Name' was first a UK hit in 1993, prompting hapless Radio 1 DJ Bruno Brookes to make the mistake of playing the unexpurgated album version at teatime on the Sunday chart show.

21 DECEMBER

1967 Irish actor **Richard Harris**, who has just starred in the screen musical *Camelot*, records the Jimmy Webb song 'MacArthur Park' (US #2, UK #4) in California. Webb had written the complex, multi-part song for The Association (who had rejected it), inspired by the time he had spent in the Los Angeles park with his partner Susie Horton – before the two of them went through an amicable breakup.

1980 **The Police** perform in a huge marquee on Tooting Bec Common in south London with comedy magician Tommy Cooper sadly floundering as one of the warm-up acts.

1982 A future mainstay of seasonal airplay, 1981's 'Christmas Wrapping' by **The Waitresses** surprisingly never gets higher than today's UK #45. (The Spice Girls will cover the song in 1998, with self-reflexive new lyrics, on the flip side of 'Goodbye'.)

2005 On the day that civil partnerships become legal in England and Wales, **Elton John and David Furnish** register theirs in Windsor, Berkshire. Exactly nine years later, in **2014**, the couple marry, following the legalisation of same-sex marriage.

22 DECEMBER

1965 The ITV company TWW in Bristol begins a weekly pop music magazine series called *Now!*, with The Fortunes and Tom Jones in its first episode. Presenting the programme and also performing some sketch material is a young Oxford University graduate: **Michael Palin.** The series runs till July 1966.

1973 Peaking at US #5 is **Todd Rundgren**'s 'Hello It's Me', a complete remake of his 1968 single, a minor hit, with previous group Nazz.

2000 The Coen Brothers' comedy-drama *O Brother, Where Art Thou?* opens in US cinemas, with a Grammy Award-winning soundtrack of 1930s period folk music, realised by contemporary artists including Alison Krauss, Gillian Welch, The Stanley Brothers and Emmylou Harris.

2002 The winners of *Popstars: The Rivals*, **Girls Aloud**, reach UK #1 with debut single, 'Sound of the Underground'. Of their 23 chart singles over the next 10 years, 21 of them will reach the UK top 10.

23 DECEMBER

1966 In the early evening, ITV brings the curtain down on *Ready Steady Go!* after 175 editions, hosted by Cathy McGowan, and with guests The Who, Donovan, Spencer Davis Group and Chris Farlowe, Later on, Joe Boyd and John Hopkins' new countercultural nightclub opens on Tottenham Court Road. **UFO** has live music from Soft Machine and The Pink Floyd, plus offbeat films and slides, dancing and light shows.

1977 After 10 years of success under the name of **Cat Stevens** – he has just had his final hit single, '(Remember the Days of the) Old Schoolyard' – Steven Georgiou formally converts to the Muslim faith. In 1978, he changes his name to **Yusuf Islam**, but it will be the mid-1990s before he returns to releasing music.

1991 ROTD: The title cry of 'Everybody in the Place' by **The Prodigy** (UK #2) is sourced from a live recording of MC Duke and Merlin at the 1989 Hustlers Convention. The single might have reached #1 had its five-track CD single been eligible for the charts.

24 DECEMBER

1971 British pop group **Chicory Tip** record Giorgio Moroder and Pete Bellotte's song 'Son of My Father' at George Martin's Air Studios in London. Released three weeks later, it will become the first UK #1 single with prominent use of a synthesiser. Over in New York, **New York Dolls** play their first proper show, at a benefit concert for the homeless at the Endicott Hotel.

1984 After three weeks on sale, **Wham!** (at UK #2, behind the immovable Band Aid) reissue their single so that 'Everything She Wants' replaces 'Last Christmas' as the lead song.

1990 ROTD: With almost no new singles out this Monday morning, two heavy metal bands take advantage of a clear run at the charts. **Anthrax** cover Joe Jackson's 'Got the Time' (UK #16), while fans of **Iron Maiden** snap up a plethora of characteristically garish formats, like picture discs, for 'Bring Your Daughter ... to the Slaughter' – yep – which will knock Cliff Richard's 'Saviour's Day' off #1.

25 DECEMBER

1954 The sudden death of **Johnny Ace** on Christmas Night at the City Auditorium in Houston, Texas, is a shocking, tragic end to his flourishing career in the US. Ace, only 25 years old, suffers an accidental and self-inflicted gunshot wound while tinkering with the weapon during an interlude between live sets. Some 5,000 people will attend his funeral eight days later, while his recently recorded single 'Pledging My Love' will top the US R&B charts for 10 weeks – the first posthumous smash hit in pop music. Elvis Presley will record that same song in 1976, in his last studio session, while Ace's original will feature in several movies, such as *Mean Streets*, *Christine* and *Back to the Future*.

Nearly 30 years later, Paul Simon will write and record, with some affection, 'The Late Great Johnny Ace' for his *Hearts and Bones* album ('the first violent death I remember') while commemorating two other tragedies: the deaths of John F. Kennedy and John Lennon.

1977 The final concert played in the UK by the **Sex Pistols** during their original two-and-a-half-year career takes place at Ivanhoe's in Huddersfield, where the group play in aid of firefighters who are on strike. Exactly one year later, like a punk Morecambe and Wise special, Johnny Rotten, now John Lydon, is onstage again, this time for **Public Image Ltd**'s first London show. He would tell *Rolling Stone* of the gig: '"You're not allowed, really, to do anything on Christmas Day." Says who?'

2010 ROTD: Britain's high streets might be shut, but two bands take advantage of the internet's perennial accessibility. **The Klaxons**' website premieres an EP called *Landmarks of Lunacy*, which was 'too experimental' for their record company, while **Gorillaz** present an advance fan club release of their next album, *The Fall*.

2016 DOTD: **George Michael** dies at the age of exactly 53 and a half. In the days following his death, it is revealed that he privately donated £100,000 every year to Capital Radio's Help a London Child appeal;

anonymously donated £15,000 to fund IVF treatment for a contestant on TV's *Deal or No Deal*; volunteered regularly at shelters for the
homeless; paid off debts for numerous members of the public; and in
2006 – nearly a decade after the death of his mother – performed a
free concert for NHS nurses in north London.

26 DECEMBER

1967 Exactly four years after the US release of 'I Want to Hold Your
Hand' – the song that broke **The Beatles** there – BBC1 premieres their
abstract and eccentric *Magical Mystery Tour* film at 8.35 p.m. It is met
with plenty of bafflement and critical hostility, perhaps because it is not
what people who've just enjoyed *Brigadoon* and *This is Petula Clark*
either want or expect to watch on Boxing Night. The film is repeated
on BBC2's colour service on 5 January to a warmer reception.

1968 While **Led Zeppelin** embark on their first American tour in
Denver, D. A. Pennebaker's documentary film, *Monterey Pop* opens in
US cinemas.

1973 William Friedkin's *The Exorcist* opens in US cinemas, with a
section of **Mike Oldfield**'s *Tubular Bells* as the opening theme on its
soundtrack. Edited for single release, the excerpt will reach #7 on
Billboard's Hot 100 the following May.

27 DECEMBER

1963 In *The Times*, 'Our Music Critic' (later to be identified as William
Mann) nominates **John Lennon and Paul McCartney** as 'the outstanding English composers of 1963'. He goes on to say that although
British music has relied on the popular songs of the US in recent decades, 'the songs of Lennon and McCartney are distinctly indigenous in
character, the most imaginative and inventive examples of a style that
has been developing on Merseyside during the past few years'.

Mann also notes the 'pandiatonic clusters' of 'This Boy' and compares the end of The Beatles' 'Not a Second Time' to the chord progression at the close of Gustav Mahler's *Das Lied von der Erde* ('Song of the Earth'), pointing out that they have an aeolian cadence in common. John Lennon will later say, 'I still don't know what a fucking aeolian cadence is.'

In the same week as Mann's assessment, Richard Buckle, the music critic of the *Sunday Times*, describes John and Paul as 'the greatest composers since Beethoven'.

US reporter at 1964 press conference, JFK Airport, 7 February 1964: 'What do you think of Beethoven?'

Ringo Starr: 'Great, especially his poems.'

1967 ROTD: A year after his song 'Suzanne' is recorded by the folk singer-songwriter Judy Collins, **Leonard Cohen**'s own version begins his debut album, *Songs of Leonard Cohen*, which becomes a bigger initial success in the UK (#13) than in the US (#83).

1988 ROTD: 'She Drives Me Crazy' (UK #5, US #1), recorded at Prince's Paisley Park studios in Minneapolis, will make **Fine Young Cannibals** one of the hottest bands in the world in 1989.

1995 ROTD: 'Little Britain' by **Dreadzone** (UK #20) will become the biggest hit for the London dance act. It samples a line of dialogue from Lindsay Anderson's movie, *If. . .*: 'Britain today is a powerhouse of ideas, experiments, imagination.'

28 DECEMBER

1976 ROTD: 'Disco Inferno' (UK #11, US #16) by Philadelphia soul group **The Trammps** was composed after seeing a scene in the 1974 disaster flick *The Towering Inferno*, but will take off in mainstream pop only when the full 11-minute version is included a year later on the soundtrack of *Saturday Night Fever*.

1978 BOTD: John Roger Stephens is born in Springfield, Ohio. Two decades later, while still a student at the University of Pennsylvania, he lands his first major session, playing piano on 'Everything is Everything' by Lauryn Hill. In 2004, the Grammy-winning poet and songwriter J. Ivy tells him, 'You sound like one of the legends. That's what I'm going to call you from now on! I'm going to call you **John Legend**.'

1981 ROTD: None of the last three **Stranglers** singles has even reached the UK top 40, but 'Golden Brown', practically the three mellowest minutes of their career, will reach #2, helped by it becoming David Hamilton's Record of the Week on MOR station BBC Radio 2's afternoon show.

29 DECEMBER

1975 ROTD: Written by Bill Martin and Phil Coulter ('Congratulations', 'Back Home', 'Shang-A-Lang') 'Forever and Ever' will shortly become a UK #1 for the Glaswegian teen pop band **Slik**. Its lead singer James will have many more chart hits with The Rich Kids, Thin Lizzy, Visage and most famously Ultravox – as well as a solo artist – under the name **Midge Ure**.

1986 ROTD: After months on import, minimalist US house record 'Jack Your Body' by **Steve 'Silk' Hurley** is out in UK shops, and three weeks later knocks the 29-year-old 'Reet Petite' off #1.

1987 ROTD: 'I Should Be So Lucky', **Kylie Minogue's** second single is her first with Stock Aitken Waterman, and the first of her seven UK #1 singles between 1988 and 2003. Her previous single, an Australian-made version of 'The Loco-Motion', had topped her homeland's singles chart for seven weeks.

30 DECEMBER

1950 The Dominoes record 'Sixty Minute Man', a bawdy bridge between gospel and blues, and close to a novelty record, banned by many radio stations. It is a possible contender for the earliest mention on record of 'to rock' and 'to roll'. It tops the R&B chart for 14 weeks in 1951.

1987 'Don't buy *The Black Album*, I'm sorry,' is a blink-and-you'll-miss-it visible message in the video for **Prince's** 'Alphabet Street'. He records the song today, one month after withdrawing the album (he believed it to be 'evil'), which will become a popular bootleg as well as being briefly and legally released in 1994.

2010 DOTD: Exactly 94 years after the death of Grigori Rasputin, and coincidentally in the same city of St Petersburg, **Bobby Farrell** of the group **Boney M**, dies at the age of 61. The same Boney M who had a worldwide hit in 1978 with 'Rasputin'.

31 DECEMBER

1966 At 6.15 p.m., *The Monkees* debuts on Saturday night BBC1. By episode four, their cover of Neil Diamond's 'I'm a Believer' is UK #1.

1973 Following a spell as Sears, Schon, Errico, **Journey** play their first-ever show, at the Winterland Ballroom in San Francisco. Meanwhile, at Chequers Bar in Sydney, Malcolm and Angus Young's rock band **AC/DC** play their first public live show. Their sister Margaret has the bright idea that guitarist Angus should wear a new costume: a schoolboy in short trousers.

1974 The *Buckingham Nicks* album of 1973 has not sold (and will remain an obscurity), but Mick Fleetwood has been very taken with its closing track, 'Frozen Love', and so invites Lindsay Buckingham to join **Fleetwood Mac**. Buckingham accepts, on condition that his collaborator and girlfriend, Stevie Nicks, can join too.

1991 After nearly 60 years on air, **Radio Luxembourg** closes down as an analogue service. Its last record, which mentions the station as a tribute, is Van Morrison's 'In the Days Before Rock'n'Roll'. Luxembourg was a must for a generation of British listeners, especially in the 1950s and 1960s before pirate radio and Radio 1, and many familiar names began there, such as Kid Jensen and Steve Wright. (A satellite and short-wave service of Luxembourg continues for exactly one further year.)

ACKNOWLEDGEMENTS

Thank you, Simon Spanton for getting the ball rolling, and to everyone at Elliott & Thompson for their help, support and commitment, especially Robin Harvie, Amy Greaves, my editor Pippa Crane, my copy-editor Jonathan Asbury and my proofreader Jill Burrows.